CUBA UNDER SIEGE

Charles

Thank you for your
support!
at the Che Guevara
conference

3 Apr 2015

Also by the author

Voices From the Other Side: An Oral History of Terrorism Against Cuba

CUBA UNDER SIEGE

AMERICAN POLICY, THE REVOLUTION, AND ITS PEOPLE

Keith Bolender

First published in 2012 by
PALGRAVE MACMILLAN®
in the United States—a division of St. Martin's Press LLC,
175 Fifth Avenue, New York, NY 10010.

Where this book is distributed in the UK, Europe and the rest of the world,
this is by Palgrave Macmillan, a division of Macmillan Publishers Limited,
registered in England, company number 785998, of Houndmills,
Basingstoke, Hampshire RG21 6XS.

Palgrave Macmillan is the global academic imprint of the above companies
and has companies and representatives throughout the world.

Palgrave® and Macmillan® are registered trademarks in the United States,
the United Kingdom, Europe and other countries.

ISBN: 978–1–137–27557–8 (paperback)
ISBN: 978–1–137–27554–7 (hardcover)

Library of Congress Cataloging-in-Publication Data is available from the
Library of Congress.

A catalogue record of the book is available from the British Library.

Design by Newgen Imaging Systems (P) Ltd., Chennai, India.

First edition: December 2012

10 9 8 7 6 5 4 3 2 1

Transferred to Digital Printing in 2013

To Magalita for your support,
patience, and perspectives

CONTENTS

FOREWORD

Louis A. Pérez, Jr.

Keith Bolender joins the company of three generations of distinguished scholars who have pondered the Cuba-US phenomenon during the last 50 years, and especially the Cuban capacity to withstand unrelenting American hostility. The Cubans were not expected to survive the loss of the US sugar quota in the early 1960s, or the embargo during the 1970s, or the collapse of the Soviet Union in the 1990s, or even the punitive Torricelli (1992) and Helms-Burton (1996) sanctions that followed. And surely the Cubans would not survive the passing of Fidel Castro.

But survive they did.

Many factors have played a part in the endurance of the Cuban government. Certainly the oft-cited resort to repression is not without some basis in fact. The system has indeed relied on an extensive and efficient intelligence apparatus. It acts on authoritarian reflexes, and has been neither slow nor unwilling to apply repression as a means to maintain internal consensus.

But repression alone is not an adequate explanation for the endurance of a government that has survived under extraordinary circumstances, during years of enormously difficult internal adversities, compounded by decades of harassment by external adversaries, principally the United States. The Cuban government had its origins in an enormously popular revolutionary upheaval, a process in which the claim to power and the legitimacy to rule were initially never in question. No other aspiration so profoundly shaped the formation of Cuban national sensibility as much as the claim to national sovereignty and self-determination. The Cuban sense of collective selfhood had its origins in the nineteenth century, when Cubans arrived to the conviction that they too had a destiny to pursue, that they too had a claim to self-determination, that they too had a right to sovereign nationhood.

The Cuban leadership subsumed into the project of revolution a historic mission: the redemption of nation, which implied above all defense of national sovereignty—principally from the United States. The American response to the Cuban revolution was unambiguous. All through the early decades, the United States sought successively by way of sanctions, sabotage, and subversion to overthrow the Cuban government—policies, former deputy secretary of defense Roswell Gilpatric acknowledged years later, designed to "so undermine, so disrupt the Cuban system under Castro that it could not be effective." All in all, as Keith Bolender suggests, this involved acts that today would be understood as a policy of state-sponsored terrorism, including scores of assassination attempts against Cuban leaders, the infiltration of sabotage teams, and the disruption of Cuban agricultural and industrial production capacities.

With the loss of Soviet patronage in the early 1990s, Cuba found itself increasingly isolated and beleaguered, faced with dwindling aid, decreasing foreign exchange reserves, and diminishing resources: a good time, the Americans persuaded themselves, to expand the scope and increase the severity of economic sanctions as a way to hasten the "transition to democracy"; thereupon, the United States enacted another round of punitive sanctions in the form of Torricelli (1992) and Helms-Burton (1996).

There was a pathology at work here, of course, one profoundly inscribed in notions of North American self-righteous motive that has served to obscure the malevolence of the US intent. The Cuban people have borne the brunt of sanctions. This is not a matter of unintended consequences to well-intentioned purpose. On the contrary, US policy was designed purposefully with mischievous intent and malice of forethought, to make daily life in Cuba as difficult and desperate as possible, to inflict hardship and increase suffering, to deepen popular discontent with the intent to incite a people to rebellion. The North American purpose has been to politicize hunger as a means to foment popular disaffection in the hope that driven by want and motivated by despair Cubans would rise up against their government.

For more than 50 years the United States has unabashedly pursued a policy designed to destroy the Cuban government. It should not come as a surprise, hence, that internal security has developed into an obsession in Cuba. The American intent to provoke the Cuban people into rebellion was transparent and readily understood by Cuban leaders. They responded accordingly. Expressions of dissent were greeted harshly by authorities in Havana, ill-disposed to tolerate political opposition in the face of chronic adversities from within and an implacable adversary from without. Authorities moved swiftly and severely to contain political dissent. Terms of imprisonment, house arrests, and harassment are only some of the most common responses to the first signs of open political dissent.

The North American call for oppositional space within Cuba, in the form of an opposition party, for example, or for an opposition press, could not but arouse suspicion and raise the specter of subversion. That the United States acted to provide moral support and material assistance to dissidents groups served further to cast a pall over the legitimacy of critics of the government. The emergence of political opposition was denounced as divisive and subversive and characterized as a stalking "enemy within." This was the obvious purport of Raúl Castro's shrill warning in 1992: "Those who act as a fifth column of the enemy can expect nothing else but the crushing blow of the people, the weight of our power and our revolutionary justice."

It has been the height of cynicism for the United States to condemn Cuba for the absence of civil liberties and political freedoms, on one hand, and to have pursued policies variously employing assassination, sabotage, and subversion as means to topple the Cuban government, on the other. US policy contributed nothing to an environment in which civil liberties and political freedoms could flourish. So too with the failures of the Cuban economy. The embargo must be factored as a source of Cuban economic woes—indeed, that has been its overriding objective. The degree to which deteriorating economic conditions have been the result of internal factors, on one hand, and the consequences of external pressures, on the other, may never be knowable but neither is the relationship disputable.

US policy professing to promote a "transition to democracy" has had the opposite effect. The defense of the nation became indistinguishable from the defense of the revolution and, in fact, acted at once to accelerate the centralization of power and facilitate the curtailment of civil liberties—all in the name of national security.

The Americans pursue punitive purpose to punish Cubans into submission, to impose their will on Cuba and force Cubans to acquiesce to US demands—an approach that *New York Times* foreign affairs editor Thomas Friedman correctly characterized as "not really a policy. It's an *attitude*—a blind hunger for revenge against Mr. Castro." It is about power, of course, about a large country determined to bring a small country to heel. It recalls the purpose that President Ronald Reagan pursued with the Sandinistas in Nicaragua: to oblige them to say "Uncle."

The problem is that the Cubans have refused to say "Uncle." Americans appear incapable or unwilling to meet the one condition that the Cuban have insisted upon: to negotiate without conditions, on the basis of mutual respect, the very demeanor that American insistence on conditions negates.

Decades from now future generations of scholars will look back upon these years with a mixture of incomprehension and incredulity at the utter cynicism and the poverty of imagination with which 11 successive US presidential administrations have engaged Cuba. Scholars in the future will surely come to understand that US policy served to sustain the very conditions that it purported to remedy. Within the context of Cuban historic sensibilities, US policy has not only contributed to Cuban intransigence but, more important, has lent credibility to that intransigence. Rather than weakening Cuban resolve, sanctions have strengthened Cuban determination. US policy has served to bring out some of the most intransigent tendencies of Cuban leaders in the defense of some of the most exalted notions of Cuban nationality.

The woeful chronicle of Cuba-US relations that Keith Bolender documents serves to set in sharp relief under a prevailing truth: the United States has been less a source of a solution than a cause of the problem. It is difficult indeed to imagine a policy so exquisitely suited to the political needs of the Cuban leadership. Future scholars will also no doubt demonstrate what we today can only suspect, that the Americans lacked confidence in the ability of the Cuban people to resolve their own destiny. Or, perhaps, future scholars will reveal that the Americans really did recognize the Cuban capacity for agency, and that the prolongation of the status quo was far more preferable than a Cuban reaffirmation of national sovereignty and self-determination. And surely future scholars will arrive to an appreciation of the greatest irony of all: that in the end, the biggest obstacle to the "transition to democracy" in Cuba was the United States itself.

ACKNOWLEDGMENTS

I would like to acknowledge the following for their encouragement, which helped bring this project to fruition. Karen Lee Wald for her expertise and support. Noam Chomsky for his unfailing encouragement. Louis A. Pérez Jr. for his suggestions and invaluable contribution. Special recognition to John Kirk, Anthony Arnove, Frances Goldin, and many others for their personal encouragement Palgrave/Macmillan for their belief in the work, particularly Sara and Farideh. Everyone interviewed in Cuba and those who gave valuable suggestions, including the officials and staff at MINREX, Heriberto Nicolas, Rinaldo, Miguelito, and the others too numerous to mention. To my family and friends. Lastly, for all in Cuba who endure siege.

1

AN UNSEEN TRUTH

Liberties have a pretty hard time when people get...frightened.
—American Supreme Court Justice Hugo Black[1]

Ponderous Medieval mechanisms catapulting immense projectiles onto thick stone fortifications. Slowly, relentlessly, the strength of the wall weakens. Vast armies stand in wait while the helpless tremble inside. From the earliest days of civilized combat, siege has been an effective method to destroy the enemy.

Some of history's greatest events have centered on the technique. In the realm of the mythical the battle of Jericho told the story of a trumpet bringing down the barricades. Masada in 73 A.D. demonstrated the nobility of ultimate self-determination in the face of insurmountable odds. In the year 1453 Constantinople, the center of Eastern Christianity, fell to Turkish forces and for the next two centuries Muslim armies battered on Western walls until the failure at the siege of Vienna in 1683 ended the threat. The rout of the Ottomans yielded another result—the introduction of coffee to Europe, the beans of which were left by the Turks along with 10,000 dead and a huge quantity of supplies. The Alamo in 1836 was a never-to-be-forgotten defeat shortly reversed into independence for Texas and expansion of a nation, while Vicksburg in 1863 helped reforge that country. Some of the bloodiest conflicts in human history took place under siege, including the loss of close to a million at Stalingrad in 1942.

The most famous siege of all involved the acceptance of a large wooden gift that failed to arouse the suspicions of those inside the walls, much to the everlasting sorrow of the men, women, and children of Troy. Lessons of welcoming offerings from those who would do you harm and the potential rewards for thinking outside the box remain with us to this day.

In rare instances the citizens play a controversial role. Paris in 1870 when segments of the population, in this case communards, were in conflict against the military commanders as how best to resist siege. The discord gave indirect aid to the enemy and led to the short-lived Commune following the victory of the Prussians. The City of Lights represents a rare occasion, as nations typically demand utmost loyalty from its citizens in time of siege or threat to national security, in order to preserve strength of resistance through solidarity. Uniformity is classically expressed by instituting confining social/political policies that restrict civil right expressions of speech, free press, assembly, and dissidence to ensure conformity so as to deny the enemy the opportunity to exploit weaknesses in the resolve of the besieged. Citizens suffer equally under external aggression and internally imposed restrictions. All to ensure survival. Those seen challenging the methods the establishment uses to combat siege, or worse, who are in advocacy of the foe's intentions, are treated harshly, with authorities invoking the centuries old dictum of St. Ignatius Loyola: "In a besieged castle all dissent is treason." President George W. Bush commanded the modern interpretation when in front of Congress on September 20, 2011, he defiantly told America and the rest of the world, "Either you are with us, or you are with the terrorists."[2]

Siege is conventionally considered a structured affair with one side tormented within a stronghold, the other superior force encircles and attempts, patiently, to wear down and destroy resistance. The military component combines with efforts to break the resolve of the besieged through deprivation of food, water, economic activity, or assistance from allies. The results are typically unambiguous—either the attackers succeed and thus determine the fate of their captives; or the siege fails and the noose is released.

Dictionary.com offers: "The act or process of surrounding and attacking a fortified place in such a way as to isolate it from help and supplies, for the purpose of lessening the resistance of the defenders and thereby making capture possible."

It can, however, be multifaceted. Militarily, the strategy does not necessarily mean a complete encirclement of a target, as noted by history professor Paul K. Davis in his seminal work on the subject: "Many if not most sieges are of positions not completely cut off from outside contact. Thus, protracted warfare with steady pressure on a target position or city falls under the definition."[3]

Furthermore, the concept of siege in the modern period encompasses a wider application than strictly martial. In the era of the United Nations, economic blockade has been a familiar method to impose compliance on states deemed "rogue" by international consent, often defined by the most powerful members of the worldwide body. Recent examples include action against the apartheid South African regime in the mid-1980s, Zimbabwe in 2001, Serbia in the 1990s, and the deadly sanctions Iraq suffered from 1990 to just prior to the American invasion in 2003.[4]

There are, however, concepts of encirclement that supersede conventional purpose. Modern culture recognizes the theory can approach psychological characteristics; of a certain segment of life being unfairly threatened by outside, often alien forces, bringing with it a sense of fear and vulnerability. It may not have physical consequences, but the pressures accompanying the development of a siege mentality consistently have detrimental effects on the behavior of the individual and society. Governments can react with anger, irrationality, and defensiveness that warps decisions not normally taken under peacetime conditions.

In North America there are claims of an obstructed culture. The religious right asserts traditional customs are endangered by secular influences threatening the social fabric, such as gay marriages. Unchecked immigration, often illegal, lays siege to neighborhoods with unfamiliar practices, forcing communities to legislate against the potential implementation of foreign-based civic rules and regulations.[5] Once a year Christmas is beleaguered by extreme politically correct forces who object to public displays of Santa Claus, Christian imagery, and even the reindeer with the red nose, or so various high-profile pundits assert.[6]

An individual can experience the stress of enclosure by hostile forces, as does a professional sports coach of a losing team. Response can range from external anger against critics, or the internalization of all emotions as a coping mechanism. When a group of individuals feel threatened by outside forces, in sports or society, it is an easy task to be convinced of the need for solidarity, to work together in order to survive, or triumph, in the face of seemingly impossible outside forces.

* * *

Within the United States no single event of the past century has facilitated the radicalization of society and development of a sense of siege than a clear, crisp September day when more than the towers fell. That morning of terrorism occasioned a vast array of politicians with the backing of the mainstream media to purport that Western civilization was under assault culturally and militarily from radical Islamic forces. American society, the beacon of openness and tolerance, had proven itself to be unexpectedly brittle. Apprehensions of a radical religious minority not nearly as powerful as the public was asked to believe led to external and internal repercussions. Foreign policy manifested itself in the military adventures in Afghanistan, Iraq, and increasingly in Pakistan. Internally the consequence of excessive demands for drastic new security measures came most notably in the hurried bipartisan approval of the Patriot Act in October 2001. The legislation permitted the easing of restrictions regarding wiretaps, search warrants, and subpoenas in a direct assault on civil liberties.

Even the death of Osama bin Laden did little to ameliorate the sense of government intrusions into civil society far beyond any security requirements under the act. Two Democratic senators Ron Wyden and Mark Udall represented a rare display of opposition, publicly stating the act continues to be interpreted in excess of its intentions.[7] "There is a significant discrepancy between what most Americans—including many members of Congress—think the Patriot Act allows the government to do and how government officials interpret that same law. We believe that most members of the American public would be very surprised to learn how federal surveillance law is being interpreted in secret." The senators failed in their efforts to force the attorney general and director of national intelligence to reveal where civil rights violations had occurred. American citizens continue to be spied upon and have private information exposed with little efficient oversight.[8]

On the heels of the Patriot Act the public was introduced to the Homeland Security Act (HSA), designed to "organize a government that is fractured, divided and under-prepared to handle the all-important task of defending our great nation from terrorist attack."[9] The November 25, 2002, passage consolidated more than 20 existing federal agencies into a single Homeland Security Department.

The Patriot and HSA legislation have been considered the foundation leading to the construction of warrantless wiretapping on thousands of American citizens, the illegal war in Iraq, and the dubious detention of hundreds in Guantánamo Bay, in clear violation of all international human rights norms. At its most excessive the legal responses to 9/11 allowed for the rationalization of disproportionate measures against suspected terrorists, admitted to by President George W. Bush.[10] The practice of waterboarding, long established as an illegal form of torture under the Fifth and Eighth Amendments, was justified as long as the country felt itself under threat. "Torture is not always impermissible," Charles Krauthammer wrote.[11] Even though President Obama decried the use of the practice, he maintains the operation at the naval base in Cuba continuing the indefinite detentions, the military commission trials, and many of the policies created under Bush Jr. as a result of the events of 9/11.[12]

In 2006 the Military Commission Act contributed substantially to the assault on individual freedoms with the passage of rules to indefinitely detain US or foreign nationals deemed to be aiding terrorists, the allowance to torture, and the elimination of habeas corpus in certain circumstances. These actions were aimed in the main at internal issues relating to the war on terrorism and the justification for national security; the usual reaction from governments faced with external threats. A year later the Protect America Act allowed examination of emails and phone calls, all to track communications between potential terrorists, according to national news reports.[13] Modern technology was seen as a potential tool for those who would threaten American society and came under close scrutiny. The Communications Assistance for Law Enforcement Act of 1994 was enhanced after 9/11, increasing official powers of surveillance, wiretaps, and Internet oversight.

In a remarkable attack on civil liberties, Congress passed legislation giving the President the ability to send armed forces anywhere to imprison civilians without charges or trial. Including within the United States. Citizens would be rounded up on the suspicion of terrorist activity or of supporting organizations hostile to the United States, a wide sweeping categorization, provided no opportunity to defend themselves, sent to secret penal locations, and never heard from again. The effort was found in S. 1867 of the 2011 National Defense Authorization Act (NDAA) drafted by Democratic senator Carl Levin of Michigan and Arizona's Republican John McCain.[14] In support, Republican senator Lindsey Graham explained that the bill will "basically say in law for the first time that the homeland is part of the battlefield" and people can be imprisoned without charge or trial, "American citizen or not." In a surprise move, President Obama signed the modified version of the act despite "serious reservations" about those provisions. Civil rights experts warned that his statement applies only to how his administration would use the regulations and not affect how the law could be interpreted by future presidents.[15] The bill indicates the extent to which the political process has abandoned its principles of individual freedoms in the name of keeping society safe in a post-9/11 world.

Various American civil rights have eroded incrementally, with the development of state surveillance programs, the reduced restrictions on authorities to access private communication and personal records, NSA warrantless wiretapping procedures, the targeting of immigrants on just the suspicion of illegal activity, and even the introduction of invasive airport scanners that caused a minor uproar at the end of 2010. The Supreme Court took a slice off the civil liberties loaf in April 2012 when it ruled five–four that jail officials will be permitted to strip search anyone arrested once they are incarcerated, even if waiting a hearing or trial.[16]

The extent to which American citizens are under watch by their government was exposed by a *Washington Post* series that ran in late 2010.[17] Through a coordination of FBI, local police, and homeland security organizations, the state has been able to collect a database on thousands of "suspicious" citizens at the cost of billions of dollars in order to attempt to prevent potential domestic terrorism. High-tech surveillance equipment first used in Afghanistan and Iraq is now being turned on the average person to instantaneously, and in complete secrecy, check personal information. The majority of the population supports such intrusions as tolerable measures to keep the nation safe. Few, however, realize the US government is keeping a master watch list with more than 440,000 names. All it takes is one tip for someone to end up on the terrorist sheet, irrespective of whether that call came from a total stranger or jealous neighbor.[18] Keeping personal information on file became easier for the government after the Obama administration in 2012 extended the time the National Counterterrorism Center (NCTC) can hold records on US citizens and residents from 180 days to five years.[19] The last vestiges of privacy protection may be lost if the government has its way with CISPA—the Cyber Sharing and Protection Act. This legislation would give "unprecedented power to snoop through people's personal information. This includes accessing medical records, private emails and financial information without a warrant, proper oversight or limits."[20]

Public anxiety transformed intrusive surveillance procedures to generate a series of overreactions including the September 2010 FBI raid of homes of peace activists in Minneapolis and Chicago. The Quakers, Catholic Worker, and Greenpeace have all come under scrutiny.[21]

More seriously, the new programs set in motion rationalization for civil rights abuse cases such as Maher Arar,[22] apprehended in New York, sent for rendition to Syria where he was subject to more than a year of torture. Jose Padilla found himself jailed without charges for years, emerging as a

broken man.[23] Arrests were made on the flimsiest of reasons, often motivated more by unfounded community fear than by actual threat. Mohammed
Butt was a 55-year-old Pakistani arrested for suspicious behavior, based in
part on a complaint by a neighbor who reported, "They hang their laundry—even their underwear—on the fence. Who does that?" Butt died in a
Queen's NY jail of a heart attack despite requests for medical treatment.[24]
Arrests have come down on allegations for passing classified information
to journalists in another illustration of how the war on terror has restricted
civil liberties.[25] Shamai Leibowitz, a former FBI linguist was sentenced to
20 months under the Espionage Act for giving documents to a blogger,
along with NSA employee Thomas Drake indicted for passing information
regarding his agency's warrantless wiretapping program to the *Baltimore
Sun*.[26] The threat to curtail traditional protection for whistleblowers under
George Bush Jr. became a reality under the Obama administration.[27] Acts
of frustration, loss of proportion, demands for security, a sense of helpless-
ness, and misguided desires for reprisal persuade societies to accept repressive
behavior usually considered well outside the norm in less dangerous times.

The aspect of siege mentality as a defense to external threat was also evident after 9/11 in the irrational reaction to nonexistent social intrusions—
certain American communities passing legislation banning Sharia law. Most
jarring was the Tennessee state legislation, which considered making it illegal
for two or more Muslims to practice their religion, carrying a jail sentence of
up to 15 years.[28] Islamophobia reached into the highest levels of government
when, in an echo of McCarthyism, a small number of Republican senators
claimed extremists connected to the Muslim Brotherhood had infiltrated
various federal organizations.[29] The fight against radical Islam has been
framed as a battle to protect a way of life, a civilization. The implication prevails that suspicion, government infringement, civil rights violations can be
justified in order to protect society.[30]

Those who tried to challenge or moderate America's response to 9/11
were subject to another facet of siege mentality—intolerance to opposing
viewpoints. The media, *Fox News* in vanguard, would call into question the
loyalty and patriotism of those who objected to the invasion of Iraq, and
deride civil libertarians who warned of the loss of rights under the war against
terrorism. Media provided prowar supporters a disproportionate amount of
coverage, and such respected institutions as the *New York Times* became
little else than stenographers for government proclamations.[31]

Political representatives came under the same pressures to support the
country unquestioningly, regardless of professional feelings of ambivalence.
Very few spoke out.[32] When a nation is under threat the most open society
will move toward intolerance and malice as the closing of the ranks becomes
no longer optional. Violence against the threat is standard operating procedure, as Bill O'Reilly summed up much of the public sentiment right after
9/11. On his September 17 *FOX News* broadcast he demanded swift retribution on Afghanistan if Osama bin Laden was not handed over: "The U.S.
should bomb the Afghan infrastructure to rubble—the airport, the power

plants, their water facilities and the roads...Remember, the people of any country are ultimately responsible for the government they have. The Germans were responsible for Hitler. The Afghans are responsible for the Taliban. We should not target civilians. But if they don't rise up against this criminal government, they starve, period."[33]

The country's most sacred belief that no man is above the law or Constitution, not even the president, took a beating when John Woo of the US justice department argued that whatever the president said was legal, is legal. George Bush Jr. grasped full advantage of that judgment, which authorized the CIA to become his personal extrajudicial branch of operations. The result was torture, rendition, illegal kidnappings, and the arrest and detention of innocents for years without charge or trial, even if it was known the prisoners had no connection to Al Qaeda.[34]

A close second American principle, the right to protest and free speech, also experienced post-9/11 trauma. While the Iraq antiwar demonstrations brought either media silence or disapproval, it rarely elicited a violent reaction from the government. That was not the case during the nationwide Occupy movement, aimed at the establishment's financial order, when protestors were abused by both media and state. With city officials taking the tack the protests were being permitted by authorities instead of being an ingrained right, the local force overreacted by pepper spraying women peacefully sitting on the pavement and arresting others outside a bank wanting to withdraw their accounts.[35] The activists met similar fates elsewhere, with dozens of arrests in Denver and thousands incarcerated nationwide.

Occupy Wall Street faced harsh censure from certain corporate media and politicians who degraded and mocked participants as unemployed bums, troublemakers, unfocused youth doing drugs and sex. *Fox* host Bill O'Reilly quipped, "Do we have all kinds of crackheads down there?"[36] "Starbucks-sipping, Levi's-clad, iPhone-clutching protesters denounce corporate America even as they weep for Steve Jobs," *Washington Post* columnist Charles Krauthammer complained.[37] The coverage facilitated efforts to turn public sentiment away from the protests, a condition ameliorated when society become less tolerant to antiestablishment movements in times of uncertainty and fear—a post-9/11 stress outcome and the inured acceptance of civil rights restrictions in order to ensure national security. Reports surfaced of extensive surveillance conducted on the protestors by various state and federal agencies in conjunction with private companies.[38] The greater the threat society is living under, the easier it becomes to turn protestors into dissidents and government tolerance into state approbation and judicial action.

The press fared little better after several journalists were taken into custody during the police crackdown at Zuccotti Park in New York in what civil liberty groups called an attempt to silence the message and control information, a criticism usually leveled against totalitarian state authority.[39] *Progressive Magazine* editor Matt Rothschild was in the middle of an effort to stifle free speech after his arrest in the Wisconsin Assembly for taking photos of the detention of another citizen who had been taking photos of proceedings on the Assembly floor.[40]

The events after 9/11 represent the most recent, and in many ways, the most devastating instance of a threat to America's national security. It has also resulted, not unsurprisingly, in a strong reaction from the public as to what is needed to prevent another attack. America has closed ranks since the terrorist attacks, suspicion and mistrust have risen in an expression of siege mentality, a natural outcome in large measure not only from the acquiescence but the insistence of the public. John F. Freie, professor of Political Science at Le Moyne College, conducted a series of polls that indicated a majority of Americans believe that the current terrorist threat is real and perhaps even underestimated by the government. Upward to 75 percent agreed that detaining immigrants for visa violations and jailing US citizens as material witnesses without indicting them is justified. Almost 50 percent were willing to give up some of their liberties for this war. "With little public discussion about what restrictions of our liberties—if any—are needed to make us safe, many are willing to give up rights that others have fought to obtain. Many believe that the restrictions will affect others, not themselves," he wrote.[41]

*   *   *

The United States did not stand alone in its answer to 9/11. Countries expropriated the event to establish programs designed to suppress difficult minorities or target troublesome individuals. Expanded Russian action against the breakaway republic of Chechnya was proclaimed to be part of the war on terrorism; others such as China, Turkey, Israel, Malaysia, Algeria, and Pakistan were accused of violations by Human Rights Watch, the all-encompassing conflict to eradicate this international scourge used as validation.[42] New policies were instituted in non- or barely democratic nations and it seemed straightforward to determine they were implemented for short-term national political objectives. By May 2003 Amnesty International reported the war on terror, "far from making the world a safer place, has made it more dangerous by curtailing human rights, undermining the rule of international law and shielding governments from scrutiny."[43]

The majority of modern liberal states succumbed to the temptation of trading civil rights for promises of increased protection. The European Union implemented an "anti-terrorism action plan" (October 2001) followed by The Framework Decision on Combating Terrorism (June 2002), based on augmenting surveillance and coordination with various police and state agencies in handling private information, which drew complaints of infringement on civil rights despite assurances to the contrary.

In Italy, new regulations handed down imprisonment of up to 10 years for those convicted of participating in organizations aiming to commit violent actions with subversive purposes against the democratic order—all defined by the state. An Italian lawyer complained that the provision did not provide those definitions or delineate what level of participation is required to run afoul of this statute, indicating it harkened back to the Fascist code.[44] Throughout Europe, the new laws helped spread Islamophobia. A 2011 study showed 58 percent of Germans favor restricting religious freedom for Muslims. Between 34 and 37 percent of French, Dutch, Portuguese, and Danes expressed negative opinions of Muslims. Social intolerance became a mainstream condition of post-9/11 media examinations.[45]

Canadian legislation made it easier to identify and persecute those deemed to have potential terrorist tendencies. The Anti-Terrorist Act of 2001 provided authorities with wide sweeping powers on electronic bugging and harsher penalties for suspected terrorists. The public was exhorted to inform on other citizens conducting suspicious activities.[46]

The United Kingdom passed the Anti-Terrorism, Crime and Security Act 2001 in the wake of the 9/11 attacks. The act permitted indefinite detention if the home secretary issued a certificate stating there was reasonable belief that a person's presence in the United Kingdom was a risk to national security, or a suspicion that the person was a terrorist.[47] Part of the act empowered authorities to expand Britain's CCTV, a program that places 24-hour monitors at most every corner in many cities. The citizens of London are under constant public surveillance regardless of their activity, all subjected to the watchful eye of the national police.

When it comes to keeping the government and its citizens safe during threats to the state, politicians and media from even the most powerful nations often have little tolerance for those objecting to policies that compromise personal freedoms. In 1994 following the release of the British report on the CCTV system, then prime minister John Major defended its intrusive nature, "I have no doubt we will hear some protest about a threat to civil liberties. Well, I have no sympathy whatsoever for so-called liberties of that kind."[48] The majority of the public has expressed scant resistance to the legislation or increased scrutiny, deemed to be not as invasive as it is protective—even if it is more against petty crimes than threats of terrorism.[49]

Major's opinion was reiterated in American form seven years later by former US attorney general John Ashcroft who said after the 9/11 attacks: "To those who scare peace loving people with phantoms of lost liberty, my message is this: Your tactics only aid terrorists, for they erode our national unity and diminish our resolve. They give ammunition to America's enemies."[50] Ashcroft has been portrayed as the mastermind of the Patriot Act, as well as upholding such diminishing of freedom of speech, criminal defendant rights, and illegal detentions.[51] Media voices came out in accord with Ashcroft's demand. Bill O'Reilly on *Fox News* explained straightforward what was needed: "We want to be protected now. We're willing to give up a little civil rights, a little protection under the Constitution to protect our families from killers."[52] If the ruling elites can instill a sense of fear in the population, implementing agendas that restrict civil rights is considerably simpler. Often those measures come at the bequest of the population, "When citizens grow fearful, they demand that their leaders protect them, and public officials quickly respond," Constitutional lawyer Cass R. Sunstein recognized.[53]

The demand for increased security weighing against the loss of civil liberties has been a serious challenge for Western democracies since 9/11—countries supposedly bastions of individual freedoms founded on the concept of the separation of state and personal privacy rights. Time and again the majority of citizens have accepted the compromise between civil rights and the insistence for security in times of foreign threat, of feelings of perilous besiegement. While objections have been raised that these laws potentially blur the line between legitimate protest, civil disobedience, and true terrorism,[54] polls reflect that majorities of up to 90 percent favor giving governments the augmented powers of surveillance, regardless of any intrusions into civil liberties.[55] The trade-off to gain increased protection, perceived or real, has been shown to be more than palatable. When it is safeguarding society against an easily identified religious, political, or cultural threat—in current times extremist Islam—the approval levels increase.[56] The public perceptions are frequently reinforced by leaders who provide credence to irrationality. Former British prime minister Margaret Thatcher declared all Muslims were responsible for terrorism; current prime minister David Cameron announces multiculturalism a failure. Canadian leader Stephen Harper calls Islamic terrorism a threat to the country, and all contribute to the perception of the need for unity, the rejection of internal nonconformists and external foreign influences, and the relinquishing of social sensibility for safety measures as defined by the ruling powers.[57]

"It is not unreasonable to expect governments to react to national security threats by increased surveillance programs. This is one of the things governments would do. It's hard to generalize about how all nations respond to threats, but this type of reaction would not be unexpected," said David Lyon, professor of sociology at Queens University in Kingston, Ontario. Lyon is head of the Surveillance Studies Center, the only one of its kind in the world. Renowned for research into how governments utilize modern technology to develop monitoring, tracking, management, and control systems, Lyon has studied these concepts for more than 20 years, including America's reaction. "September 11 has been a major factor in government implementing increased surveillance programs, not just in the United States but all over the world. It's not unexpected when you have this terrorist event—surveillance is one of the first and foremost reactions. The United States government used 9/11 as a rationale to expand surveillance, and it is easy for the public to accept it, regardless of the consequences to civil liberties or human rights."[58]

More concisely, US justice Louis Brandeis recognized that "fear breeds repression,"[59] a condition authorities have often taken advantage of to advance civil controls and establish surveillance agendas far in excess of the danger.

America is an illuminating examination based on its historical precepts of freedom and liberty, and how those concepts have been compromised while under national security threats. Additionally, the United States has throughout its relatively short existence experienced both sides of the siege and civil rights equation, receiving and giving, derived from its geopolitical position. During the Revolutionary War England did its best to situate a naval blockade against the 13 colonies, and in an historic irony it was the siege at Yorktown that ended the conflict and gave birth to a new nation. Loyalists left in thousands in solidarity with England, losing property and commerce. Lord Fairfex, owner of four million acres in Virginia, was driven off his land without compensation.[60]

Those who remained but suspected of retaining sympathy for the Crown were subjected to close scrutiny. New York passed an Anti-Loyalist Act of 1780, to "forbid Loyalists to hold property, to be protected by law in any way, or to vote."[61] Confiscation of property without compensation was a common occurrence, as were lists of those forbidden to settle back to their homes.[62] Most who decided not to stay were categorized as disloyal exiles and not welcomed back.

In 1798, with only a few years under its belt, the conflict with former ally France led the United States to pass the Alien and Sedition Acts.[63] The radical legislation emerged as a direct result from a sense of vulnerability engendered by the far more powerful adversary. America at that time was a small, fragile nation and its leaders had little tolerance toward those dissidents perceived to be a threat to the new political system, or to those thought to be disposed to favor the European monarchies. The Sedition Act made it a crime to publish or utter disloyal statements against the government, Congress, or the President. Penalties ranged from long imprisonment to banishment and were usually imposed with great dispatch.[64] Decades later during the Civil War President Abraham Lincoln infamously suspended habeas corpus; less well known is the series of arrests against those publicly speaking out against the administration. Politician Clement Vallandigham was imprisoned and exiled for his criticism of the war, the Emancipation Proclamation, and the President.[65]

World War I saw those in opposition to the conflict facing the Espionage Act of 1917 and the Sedition Act of 1918. Hundreds of Americans were imprisoned. Those convicted often received terms of 10–20 years, including Eugene Debs, Socialist candidate for the presidency who was jailed for criticizing the war and conscription.[66] The Sedition Act, a set of amendments to the Espionage Act, forbade the use of "disloyal, profane, scurrilous, or abusive language" toward the US government.[67] "Civil liberties go into the discard when a nation is engaged in war," philosopher John Dewey remarked ruefully.[68]

World War II saw the internment of thousands of citizens of Japanese heritage, out of Fifth Column fears from a racial minority whose loyalties were being questioned. In 1940 the passage of the Smith Act targeted antigovernment activity from aliens but was applicable to residents alike. It spoke to "whoever, with intent to cause the overthrow or destruction of any such government, prints, publishes, edits, issues, circulates, sells, distributes, or publicly displays any written or printed matter advocating, advising, or teaching the duty, necessity, desirability, or propriety of overthrowing or destroying any government in the United States by force or violence, or attempts to do so...Shall be fined under this title or imprisoned not more than twenty years, or both..."[69]

The act was used to restrict antiwar expressions, freedom of assembly and the press, criticism of the government's preparation for war, or the government itself. President Roosevelt refused to veto the act, claiming the enforcement could hardly "constitute an improper encroachment on civil liberties in the light of present world conditions."[70] It remained in force until 1957.

In the 1950s Federal Loyalist Oaths and cultural witch hunts dominated the search for suspected communists. Hundreds were jailed and thousands lost jobs during the worst aspects of McCarthyism as society withdrew upon itself in order to preserve the perception of the American way of life. During the 1960s the CIA in direct violation of its charter illegally spied on hundreds of thousands of Americans involved in the peace movement or civil disobedience in surveillance programs without precedence, until the current policies to combat the threat of Islamic fundamentalism.[71]

A decade later the White House was under siege, or so felt President Richard Nixon. Lashing out at his critics following the 1970 decision to expand the Vietnam War into Cambodia, Nixon treated dissidence as treason. The upshot was the Huston Plan, a direct assault on civil liberties that authorized wiretapping, mail opening, and spying on Americans. Nixon withdrew approval of the plan, but elements were used to stifle domestic opposition, leading eventually to the Watergate scandal.[72]

Fortunately for American self-perceptions, the actual perils and apparent threats to national security subsided after a period of time. The judicial and legal systems under First and Fourth Amendment guidelines recovered after facing the various external dangers. American political institutions examined where civil liberty violations went too far and refocused on the country's democratic tradition, most importantly the return of those rights. This was done during peace times; a condition that would be next to impossible while under war footing. This long historiography enabled the ruling elite to bring a measure of balance after 9/11 when the calls for more intrusive programs such as Terrorist Information and Prevention System (TIPS) or Terrorists Information Awareness (TIA) were rejected.

"The history of the United States has been we have traditionally regained the civil rights lost after war, we have been able to see where we had excess," University of Chicago The Law School professor Geoffrey Stone commented. "We learned where we overreacted and used that for the future."[73]

Using 9/11 as the most dramatic example, Stone noted that when the government, "aggressively reacted to the event with torture, renditions, unlawful imprisonment, NSA surveillance, black hole sites, when these excesses have come to light the public and politicians have been able to discuss and see where it has been too much."[74] The Patriot Act was considered appropriate, he noted, "mostly because America expected future attacks. But this examination of where we went too far is America's history because we are a free and open society, it doesn't always work out the way we want, and we are still dealing with the excesses we live under after 9/11."[75]

Historically the American public did not overly object to the constraints to civil liberties, accepting the trade-off in return for the perception of increased internal security against a dangerous and elusive enemy.[76] Would this submission to civil rights violations be maintained and augmented if the danger continued unabated for years, for decades? Or in the case of the current war on terror, if there were other attacks on American soil resulting in additional deaths and material destruction?

Professor Stone, an expert on how democracy has been affected in times of national threat, suggested, "If there were a number of 9/11 type events then all bets are off. No doubt. It would be realistic to predict if more 9/11s occurred the government would institute much more serious measures for safety, and that would affect civil rights. The programs found excessive after 9/11 might not be considered that if there were more attacks. The attitude would change within the population and government; you would see various kinds of repression. The more severe the danger the more severe the measures to ensure safety...If these additional attacks were shown to be done by Muslims living inside the US then you could see something like their incarceration similar to what happened with the internment of the Japanese in World War II. There would have been various kinds of repression and measures taken to ensure safety. TIPS and TIA would most likely have been implemented, and much more. The public would be demanding it."[77]

Surveillance systems expert David Lyon concurred. "They would ramp up internal security and clamp down on civil liberties. The government used 9/11 as an exceptional circumstance, if they had more 9/11s they would continue and amplify that, human rights and civil liberties would suffer worse and be lessened if there were more attacks." Society would no doubt turn increasingly inward, Lyon predicted. Intolerance to opposition, to free assembly, constraints to the press would assuredly increase, he added, as would surveillance systems, if in George Bush Jr.'s reference, "the long war"[78] did turn out to be a protracted struggle to protect the homeland instead of simply externalizing aggression against a foreign enemy on a far distant turf.

Others hold the same opinion. Former CIA agent Valerie Plame, who infamously had her cover revealed by a Washington columnist,[79] spent much of her career working on counterterrorism and the prevention of loose nukes from falling into the hands of extremists. While promoting a documentary on nuclear proliferation,[80] she was unequivocal as to what would happen in a worst-case scenario. "Countdown to Zero makes the point that if a nuclear device were to be exploded in any democracy in the world, you can forget about any rights, it would go out the window. Not because the government is evil, but because the people would be clamoring, to make sure they are kept safe. And any sort of, you know, the Bill of Rights, what we consider democratic purposes, would be sidelined until, who knows, indefinitely."

American society as a whole has never completely recovered from the shock and devastation of 9/11. In terms of surrendering a portion of civil rights to the call for protection, it may never return to before that September day. It lives under a new mentality where tolerance is being eroded by a sense of siege where the call for security and conformity prevails over individual rights. Or as Jonathan Turley said, "It is rare in history to see ground lost in civil liberties be regained through concessions of power by the government. Our terrorism laws have transcended bin Laden and even 9/11. They have become the status quo. That is the greatest tragedy of bin Laden's legacy—not what he did to us, but what we have done to ourselves."[81]

For many, it is now the natural order of things.

*   *   *

In one particular case, it has been the way of life for more than half a century. No other existence is known. This small revolutionary government has faced nonstop hostility from the world's most powerful nation since the early months of 1959; terrorism alone amounting to dozens of real and symbolic 9/11s. The unrelenting aggression has played a substantial role in the implementation of extensive security strategies, censorship programs, and restrictive political practices evolving from a severe mentality of siege—policies that are sustained by a population who have suffered the social consequences yet still consider security of paramount import and in the majority back the government's measures to confront the enemy. At no time in its short history has the leadership been afforded a respite to examine excesses or readjust extremes. The government faces rigorous international criticism for these restrictions, while the besieger does its best to diminish or deny the very existence of its actions. The hostile external force has blamed all of the besieged nation's ills on its political/economic system. There is even a lucrative industry that is built upon the precept of refusing to acknowledge any impact the siege has played.

Cuba since the Triumph of the Revolution has withstood all elements of siege warfare without respite. America's encirclement has encompassed military, economic, propaganda, and psychological characteristics. The siege has also brought with it a deadly history of terrorism against the Cuban people, almost completely unknown to the international community. It is divisive, as American obstinacy has butted up against the will of the United Nations in the annual vote against the embargo, and now more so against the wishes of its own people, with surveys showing large majorities in favor of lifting the blockade and normalizing relations with Cuba.[82] Respected global organizations have consistently condemned the siege, the latest being Amnesty International's September 2010 report concluding sanctions imposed affect the health of millions of Cubans. Secretary General Irene Khan described the blockade as "immoral and a failed policy." Her organization called on President Barack Obama to lift the siege that "has had a devastating effect on the daily lives of the Cuban people."[83]

The contemporary justification for punishing Cuba is based on moral grounds, but evidence of duplicity is abundant when the United States does not impose similar measures against far worse abusers of human rights, or those lacking in democracy, (under American terminology) such as China or the Medieval monarchy of Saudi Arabia, able to outlaw protests and demonstrations with little criticism.[84] While validations for brutal regimes in support of America-style imperialism come with little difficulty, Cuba is subjected to the full hostility of the world's most powerful nation that has had little historical comparison. The island's transcendent crime goes back a half-century when its revolution evolved into a society where politics and economics are entirely state owned—deemed an abomination to American democratic precepts of a free-market economy based on the foundation of compliant political parties. At least that is the public rationalization; behind it is the inability to forgive loss of hegemony over the Caribbean nation for close to 60 years.

The siege against the island has never been an absolute encirclement, but conforms to the definition of Professor Davis. The revolutionary government has known no time where it was not subject to American antagonism regardless of its relations with the rest of the world. Since the fall of the Soviet Union in the early 1990s US pressure has amplified significantly.

In response to this aggression the Castro administration instituted rigorous programs to ensure the safety of its socialist system. Those actions have helped radicalize elements of fear, limitations to civil rights including of assembly, establishing parameters of free speech, reluctance to reorganize an ineffective command economy, a collective demand for unity, a state-controlled press, intolerance to a certain brand of organized dissidence in support of American goals, hypersensitivity to criticism, and the constant defense of the country's sovereignty. Anti-Castro observers claim no push was needed to instill such repressions; that the intrinsic nature of the regime is the root cause for the oppression. However, it is not improbable to examine Cuba's social restraints in context to the depth of the threat, the longevity of aggression, and the power relations of the small island under the constant bull's-eye of the northern colossus. Every action Cuba has taken to combat siege warfare—the civil rights restrictions, political conformity, intolerance to dissidence, anger, and defiance to the attackers—can be seen in the mirror of America's response to 9/11 and its historiography of the past 200 years when under threat or war. Degrees, incidents, and outcomes are considerably different, based on ideological social structures and relative positions of power, rather than on inherent classification of either system.

It has impelled the government, with the support of the people, into "building trenches rather than bridges, because it was the only way to combat American hostility. They had to build trenches in order to dig in; to prevent the United States from doing to Cuba as they did to Guatemala, Chile, to so many other countries in Latin America," Washington-based lawyer José Pertierra explained.

One consequence of this unrelenting antagonism has been the movement toward the development of a siege mentality, a not unexpected outcome, according to Cuban-born Pertierra. "How would any government react when at war, and it has been a war," says Pertierra, who represents the government of Venezuela in its request to extradite alleged Cuban terrorist Luis Posada Carriles and is a longtime critic of US policy toward his native land. "This war has had many different aspects, not just military, although there has been that. The one main aspect, regime change, is war. The Cubans are criticized for civil rights restrictions. Look at what happened after 9/11. There were 19 guys who crashed planes, it wasn't a military attack, and was orchestrated by one guy in a cave. Look at how the US responded to that; by severely curtailing the great traditions of civil liberties in this country. To arrest without charges, to intern people, to send them for renditions, to torture. So it is absolutely no surprise to see a small country in the Caribbean, with a different social and economic system from the US, to be so threatened by the world's most powerful nation—not to take serious measures to protect itself. Those measures have had a restriction on certain civil liberties and other negative costs to society. The United States did it, most countries in the world have done it while under threat. Cuba does it and gets criticized without taking into context why they do it."[85]

This small island nation of 11 million people, called the most beautiful land by its famous European discoverer Cristóbal Colón, has been beleaguered without reprieve by American antagonism. While the forms and ferocity of the strategy has changed dramatically in the past half-century, the basic aspiration has not—to extinguish Fidelismo, to force the population to wake up from their inexplicable state and return to the comfort of America's embrace. This is to be accomplished by impelling the Cuban citizenry to overthrown their leaders or have the government itself simply give up the struggle against the imperial power.

The siege has several distinctive elements. It is held by one nation, the most powerful on earth, while most of the rest of the world tries to circumvent it to best advantage. Thousands of those who have escaped the siege, landing in the country that enforces the siege, return back to the besieged with money and goods designed to lessen the negative impact of the siege. The besiegers have actually had a foothold in the encircled land, Guantánamo Bay, for more than 100 years. The siege has characteristics of most things Cuban since the revolution: complicated, complex, and difficult to fully comprehend, yet with even a cursory observation it is possible to bring credence to both sides of the issue—the effect American hostility has or has not on Cuban society.

Siege is an instructive metaphor for the convoluted relationship between these two countries that have had a close but contentious historical association. Their current differences are based on the definition and ownership of such concepts as nationhood, freedom, sovereignty, human rights, democracy, and respect. The confrontation between Cuban authenticity to define *patria* (homeland) against the façade of American moral certitude is at the ideological heart of this siege. The disparity revolves on the weaker side struggling against genuine external impositions, while the other wraps imperial self-interest in a blanket of righteous indignation and condescending exceptionalism.

America's aggression has been abundant. Besides the well-documented military attempt to overthrow the revolutionary system at the Bay of Pigs, there has been devastating economic sanctions that in the early years restricted the sale of food and medicine, an action taken as evidence the American side acknowledged itself to be at war against Cuba. That consideration has not changed, following President Obama's continuation of the authorities under the Trading With the Enemy Act (TWEA), legislation applied only in time of war or national emergency.[86] The national emergency aspect has been doubly covered since 1996 when President Clinton sent to Congress Proclamation 6867 declaring such a condition existed between the two countries, as an aftermath of the shoot down of two private planes by Cuba.[87] There is little doubt Cuba points to those legalities as proof of US intentions and justifications for its responses.

Add to those measures the historic attempts to isolate the island from the entire continent when international support for America's siege was at its height in the first decade of the revolution. Only Canada and Mexico refused to bow to the pressure President Kennedy exerted to segregate the socialist government; the administration's success a determining factor in Fidel Castro's decision to try and internationalize his revolution, and then leading his country into the security of the Soviet Union, which was then turned to justify ratcheting up hostility. The revolution's evolvement to a constricted society and its embracement of Soviet orthodoxy can be examined in part as the outcome to siege. National survival methods radicalized as American hostility increased, the one feeding off the other.

Additional weapons in the arsenal of siege include the exclusion to world banking institutions, the extraterritoriality of policies that go against all international norms, the unrelenting disruption of legitimate business exchanges, and some of the most sophisticated and effective propaganda designed to denigrate all revolutionary accomplishments, no matter how trivial. Secondary to this has been the economic strain resulting from the necessity to direct valuable resources for security and defense systems far in advance of the needs of a small third-world country—at the expense of social programs. Government officials claim the financial toll due to the siege reaches more than $900 billion.[88]

The overarching attempt of American policy is to permit the Cuban government no opportunity to let down its guard, no chance to take stock of excesses and to establish social advancements on its terms. To do so would provide legitimacy to the system and corruption to the authenticity of its totalitarian nature. "We've been held hostage, never had 24 hours to breathe," declared Fidel Castro.[89]

There has been the threat of complete annihilation. During the October crisis of 1962 when Cuba recklessly allowed Soviet nuclear missiles on their soil based on the belief of an immediate full military invasion (of which proof existed), the island came close to obliteration, with Castro threatening to take the United States with him. In the 1980s the continued defiance led Secretary of State Alexander Haig to the point where he sought to ask President Reagan for a simple green light: "You just give me the word and I'll turn that fucking island into a parking lot."[90]

While there are multiple layers of complexity to the encirclement of Cuba, the most violent facet rests with the hundreds of acts of terrorism inflicted against civilian targets.[91] This unknown history led the government to institute a series of restraining internal security policies. The terrorism started early, short months after the Triumph when the Eisenhower administration determined to overthrow the insubordinate Castro by the unleashing of covert operations.[92] More than 700 documented acts have resulted in 3,500 civilian deaths, thousands injured.[93] The unremitting wave of terrorism between 1959 and 1961 prior to the Bay of Pigs invasion became an important factor in the Cuban government's decision to institute the ubiquitous neighborhood security program known as Committee for the Defense of the Revolution (CDR),[94] the validation for the implementation of state control of the press, the continuance of one-party rule, and the foundation of the mistrust of those involved with organized antirevolutionary activities, which evolved into intolerance against anyone perceived to be in support of American policy goals. No other event facilitated these impositions more than the American-sponsored invasion at Playa Girón in April 1961. Fidel Castro irrevocably declared the revolution socialist during the attack. Externally, the country committed itself once and for all to the security the Soviets were offering.

The Bay of Pigs invasion was bookended by hundreds of terrorist attacks. Since then Cuba has proportionally suffered dozens of 9/11s. Besides the internal security measures, the only direct external option has been to send intelligence agents into Florida to penetrate antirevolutionary groups blamed for most of the activity during the past 30 years. In the mid-1990s agents did just that, sending important information to Havana indicating more terrorist acts were being planned. The revolutionary authorities invited FBI officials to examine the evidence, which they did, taking the documents back to America for study. Shortly afterward the agents, later named the Cuban Five, who had been under surveillance by authorities for years, were arrested and continue to serve long jail sentences.[95] American authorities made no movement against the anti-Castro organizations, and many of the alleged terrorists including Luis Posada, remain free in Miami. International pressure led by the Cuban side has done little to alter the agent's status.[96] Military action against the location where the terrorism has originated from remains utterly impossible.

Cuba's approach to its national security threat posed by terrorism and other acts of American aggression has been internal surveillance, social control mechanisms, suspicion on a national scale, and exclusion of targeted opposition and dissidence. American policymakers understood and in fact expected the Castro government to react in that fashion. Strategy was designed to force the leadership to accelerate the process of domestic radicalization, which the United States expected would result in substantial citizen discontent. A 1961 CIA report outlined American action was to "plan, implement and sustain a program of covert actions designed to exploit the economic, political and psychological vulnerabilities of the Castro regime. It is neither expected nor argued that the successful execution of this covert program will in itself result in the overthrow of the Castro regime," only to accelerate the "moral and physical disintegration of the Castro government."[97]

Once the policies that were anticipated by the Americans were enacted, those security measures were displayed by mainstream media as proof of the extremism and iniquity of the regime; making sure none of the activities that forced the reaction were revealed. Those hostile actions, however, were well recognized in the rest of Latin America, and so Cuba became an effective example to ensure no other country would dare follow. America's violent response was not lost on others.

Aggression since 1959 has consistently and overwhelmingly been aimed against the Cuban population, described in extreme terms by then foreign minister Felipe Pérez Roque at a 2004 United Nations assembly: "The U.S. government has unleashed a worldwide genocidal economic war against Cuba."[98] While the term has been challenged as excessive, there is ample evidence to suggest that America is enacting collective punishment on the people of Cuba with the intent of precipitating the overthrow of the socialist experiment and end the siege.

Revealingly, American officials have been forthright in recognizing their wrath has been aimed at the civilian population's resistance levels, giving fabrication to the assertion there is no widespread support for the revolution. The punishment is appropriate, according to Deputy Assistant Secretary of State for Inter-American Affairs Lester D. Mallory, who on April 6, 1960, wrote: "The majority of Cubans support Castro. The only foreseeable means of alienating internal support is through disenchantment and disaffection based on economic dissatisfaction and hardship."[99] It was but a few months later that the Eisenhower administration set in motion the institutionalization of siege; economic dislocation to promote starvation, acts of terrorism, isolation, propaganda, and the planning for a military invasion.

The Kennedy administration shortly after reaffirmed the sights were on the citizens. "The Cuban people (are) responsible for the regime," Undersecretary of State Douglas Dillon proclaimed, and the President agreed that it was Washington's duty to cause "rising discomfort among hungry Cubans."[100] That attitude remained entrenched into the lexicon of justifications. "We wanted to keep bread out of the stores so the people would go hungry," a CIA officer explained as the economic sabotage continued during the 1970s. "We wanted to keep rationing in effect and keep leather out, so people got only one pair of shoes every 18 months."[101]

The strategy of having the population end siege through the overthrow of their own government, based on the inability to further endure the deprivations caused by the besiegers, has long been considered legitimate by politicians and commentators on the outside. US Congressman Robert Torricelli admitted in 1992 that he wanted to "wreck havoc on the island" in response to his desired expectation following the passage of the embargo-tightening legislation that bears his name.[102]

Vice chair of the Westchester County Hispanic-American Republican Committee, Lorenzo Delgado was unashamed to acknowledge the affect the sanctions were having on Cuban society, during a 1995 televised debate. "Is there a limit on embargos? Until it works. In South Africa the embargo worked. It should do the same in Cuba. Make sure the embargo is tight. That nothing gets through. I have loved ones in Cuba. I know it hurts. It hurts me very close. I would venture to say a poll of Cuban people, a true poll of the Cuban people, would say 'strengthen the embargo so we can get rid of Fidel Castro.' We are not talking about the next meal for the Cuban people, we are looking at their future."[103]

There has been scarce indication the Cuban population has entertained the notion of overthrowing their own government, nor appreciation of outsiders promoting measures designed to make their lives worse. Even the majority of dissidents oppose the siege as policy to enforce change.[104]

Professor Paul K. Davis contends there is no historical model to support America's intentions. "There are no real examples I can think of where the citizens overthrow their own government because of the siege making things so terrible. Quite the opposite usually happens, the citizens rally around their leaders to ensure the siege is not successful. And the government as a matter of course demands support, they don't tolerate opposition or dissidents—they usually kill or expel them. So the concept of a country being besieged, like Cuba, I think it would be historically normal that the government would want its citizen's support, and that the people would support the government as long as they were under siege. American policy of making things so bad that the people would rise up, that just doesn't have any historical precedence."[105]

US expectations that the guards will open the gates voluntarily to let the enemy in has been the most unrealistic aspect of its siege strategy, unless examined from the perspective of encirclement being utilized simply for punishment, or the "bad example" premise to dissuade others from following the same path.

While the failure in breaking the people's will may be credited in equal amounts to the porous nature of the siege as to the continued support of the revolution, America's course of action has nevertheless been effective by encouraging some of the best and brightest to leave, thereby weakening society through attrition of precious human resource. In the first years thousands of professionals and businessmen left for political reasons, more recent immigration has been predicated on economic factors. Estimates range in excess of two million exiles since the revolution, an equal indictment to ideological incompatibility, the deficiencies of the system, and to the effectiveness of siege. The majority of the new wave represents those who have simply become tired of the life they have with few future prospects. There is no intention to overthrow the system, now so firmly entrenched, just to leave behind the struggles of daily existence for the more welcoming arms of friends and relatives in Miami or elsewhere.

Segments of the younger generation who stay are increasingly disconnected with the revolution, having grown up knowing little else but financial dislocation since the collapse of the Soviet Union in the early 1990s, an event that spiraled Cuba into its great depression known as the Special Period. That economic disaster was exacerbated with the tightening of the siege through such policies as the Cuban Democracy Act (Torricelli) and the Cuban Liberty and Democratic Solidarity Act (Helms-Burton). The result of this augmented pressure, besides a rise in immigration, has been the frustration of and disillusionment with the continued political goals and economic failures of the revolution, revealed in the rampant corruption at all levels of the economy as often the only means to survive. Many Cubans increasingly direct their irritation at a government that now seems incapable of meeting basic requirements. It is another intended realization of American policy; for the population to see failure only through an internal perspective, and no longer acknowledge or appreciate the siege's sustained corrosive effects.

Concurrent to the attempts to contain blame are the consistent efforts of certain US officials, academics, and many involved in the multimillion dollar siege industry to reduce the blockade into terms of a bilateral decision that has little impediment to the island's ability to conduct economic relations with other countries, ignoring the social, political, and cultural costs. In truth the blockade has tremendous extraterritorial application, both at multinational corporate levels down to the individual businessman outside of the United States contemplating a Cuban connection. On a higher level the siege has affected Cuban society—community interactions, family relations, the government's ability to distinguish internal friends from foes. It has had a significant impact, and to suggest the siege is strictly a bilateral affair that has only economic consequences is disingenuous in the extreme.

Denial of the affect of siege has been standard operating procedure for antirevolutionary elements, made more convincing as the encirclement of Cuba has never been all-encompassing. Since the mid-1960s Soviet patronage assured the island's economic survival and national security. There was relative prosperity during this time and the impact of America's hostility was diminished. After the collapse of the Soviet Union in the early 1990s Cuba reached out to the world promoting tourism and international joint commercial ventures as remedy to financial collapse. Most nations now trade with Cuba, a fact proembargo supporters use to show there is little harm done by encirclement, but still the objective of siege remains. America sustains a disproportionate amount of authority over vital international institutions, most notably financial, which Cuba cannot access. US-controlled medical patents often deny Cuban doctors and patients much needed medicines and various high technologies in communications and industry are unattainable. While the rest of world can choose whether to abide by the siege or not (unless subsidiaries affected by US laws, which constitute a substantial consideration), American strategy as world leader continues as a constant and influential dynamic in the retardation of Cuban society and its economy, which in turn impacts the daily life of its citizens. At the opposite end, siege has been used as an expedient excuse for Cuban government officials to deflect systemic internal problems instead of attempting to overcome them; thereby allowing detractors to call into suspect the affects of US hostility when it properly needs to be held responsible.

Regardless of how and to what extent siege has impacted Cuban society, it has remained the cornerstone of US strategy of regime change. Past administrations have utilized it to varying degrees, with certain presidents actively involved in tightening the screws—Eisenhower, Kennedy, Reagan, and Bush Jr. On the other side Jimmy Carter was singular in his desire to move toward rapprochement, while Johnson, Nixon, Ford, and Bush Sr. were more circumspect, vacillating between rapprochement and punishment. Cuban policy was often put on the backburners by the various administrations, most noticeably in the 1970s even while siege policy remained. Bill Clinton had a major role in approving legislation, the Helms-Burton Act, which continues to complicate relations, although he did so reluctantly. Obama came into office with high expectations for real change, although so far he has maintained and in some instances increased the pressure. But for the citizens of Cuba the siege has been placing obstacles in their daily lives constantly, it has shaped their relationship and perception of its government and leaders, and has been a major, if not consciously accepted, factor in thousands of individual decisions whether to stay or go. While the actual harm the siege continues to inflict is debatable, its cumulative significance is difficult to ignore.

Professor of political science at Purchase College, Peter Schwab addressed the negative integration encirclement has imposed on the island: "Although economic and social dislocations insofar as they do exist in Cuba can be judged, as they are by some, as failures of a domestic government and political party, over time it will have to be accepted that the rotten state of Cuba's economy is predominantly a result of the frightening, mean-spirited...war against Cuba conducted through the US embargo. To blame Castro for Cuba's economic demise, without fully taking into account US activity, is disingenuous and a travesty of analytic judgment."[106] Ecuadorian President Rafael Correa presented a clear indication of how long his or other South American countries would survive such a siege. "It is important to emphasize that it is impossible to analyze the Cuban reality without taking the blockade into account. Imagine if the US blockades us or Colombia or Peru, we would not even last three months, while Cuba has resisted for several decades," he said, describing the embargo as an attack against Inter American rights and the human rights of Cubans.[107]

America's rationale for its hostilities over the decades have been as flexible as a Cirque de Soleil performer, moving fluidly from neocolonial expectations, ideological expediency, historical acuity, to mean-spirited vengefulness. As the revolution began nationalization of agricultural holdings, it soon became clear the United States was going to lose much of its financial investments, industrial infrastructure, and political influence in a country perceived to be built by them. With the revolution no more than three months old President Eisenhower was informed it was time to replace Fidel with someone more amenable. While under hegemonic control from 1898 to 1959 it was expected that Cuban presidents and/or dictators would accept orders from Washington. When Fidel made it clear things were different, the United States responded by implementing the early stages of siege—cutting off Cuban sugar quotas, refusing to sell arms, enabling covert terrorist operations, and moving toward full blockade. The Castro government in step increased its program of agrarian reform, social justice programs, and nationalization concurrent with its increasingly severe security measures, which revolved into another validation for hostility.[108]

The dominant justification for siege endured three decades during Cuba's turn toward, and final acceptance of, orthodox Marxist communism Soviet style. That validation served extremely well until the Soviet Union collapse in 1989, leaving Cuba fiscally eviscerated and politically exposed. The Soviet defense was the most durable, even if it was recognized as dubious as all others. "It didn't make much difference whether Castro was a Communist or not. He was...bitterly hostile to the United States," Assistant Secretary of State R. Richard Rubottom Jr. admitted, indicating obedience was the dispute, not politics.[109]

Fidel was opposed not because he was a communist but because he rejected America's control mechanisms over Cuba; he challenged the counterindependent consequences of American actions on the citizenry of Latin America; and he offered an alternative economic model that might be seen as more attractive. His beliefs coincided with much of communist theory, which was the evil boogeyman for all Americans at that time. But whatever the revolution was to be labeled, the power to the north was determined to eliminate it—because at its heart the action represented a rejection of America's social/political imposition. That could not stand.

Castro soon recognized ideological terminology and its fearful implications would become an important weapon to justify hostility and ignore revolutionary accomplishment. "At any rate, you wish to write that this is a socialist revolution, right? And write it, then...Yes, not only did we destroy a tyrannical system. We also destroyed the philoimperialistic bourgeois state apparatus, the bureaucracy, the police, and a mercenary army. We abolished privileges, annihilated the great landowners, threw out foreign monopolies for good, nationalized almost every industry, and collectivized the land. We are fighting now to liquidate once and for all the exploitation of man over man, and to build a completely new society, with a new class contents. The Americans and the priests say that this is communism. We know very well that it is not. At any rate, the word does not frighten us. They can say whatever they wish."[110]

During the period between 1961 and the collapse of the Eastern bloc there were a series of subsanctifications—supporting rebels in Latin America, interfering in the internal affairs of African countries such as Ethiopia and Angola, and Cuba's undue influence on the world stage. Castro's reasoning for the small nation's foreign affairs overreach was to break the isolating aspects of siege and challenge hostile right-wing dictatorships in the region.[111]

When Cuba ended activities the United States claimed were an impediment for normalization—nothing changed. In 1982 Castro stopped shipments of arms to Latin America, publicly stating the move was made to demonstrate proof he was serious to talk to the United States; his overture met with silence.[112] Currently the Obama administration asserts political repression and a reluctance to move toward a market-based system hinder engagement, disregarding the release of almost all political prisoners and major economic reforms. Even the case of Alan Gross, an American jailed for bringing in illegal high-tech communication equipment under a controversial USAID program, is used as grounds to remain intractable. One long-standing rationale for siege, one of the most contentious, is the assertion Cuba is a state sponsor of terrorism. It is particularly galling to Cuban officials who point out their citizens have been victims of counterrevolutionary terrorist acts originating from South Florida for 50 years.[113] Inclusion on the list of state sponsors of terrorism provides yet another motive for siege, bringing with it real consequences. US laws place serious financial restrictions on those countries and provides for the ban on arms-related export and sales.

America's ever-evolving reasons for siege serve the purpose of maintaining the possibility of ending the socialist government instead of reforming it, normalization would accomplish little except instill final legitimacy. Promises of improved relations have forever been dangled just out of Cuba's reach, with the leadership deciding long ago to no longer play this political game, the rules and conditions of which constantly change.

"The goalposts have always been moved by the United States—they say to do this and we'll lift embargo; the Cubans have done it, and nothing has happened. In so many cases, Africa, Soviet Union, all the conditions have been met and the US has done nothing to move towards normalization," according to Washington lawyer José Pertierra. "The Cubans have learned to take what the US says with a grain of salt, they can't get over-enthusiastic about a new presidency, because they've seen it all before."

In the opinion of Robert A. Pastor, professor at the American University and former national security adviser under the James Carter administration, the shifting standards continue along under Obama. "There has not been, and in fact, there isn't any real US political willingness nowadays to normalize links with Cuba on an equal footing. There has always been a demand for Cuba to do something first."[114] It is another manifestation of how Cuba has been treated within an ideological framework different than any other country, communist or not. The historical relationship, loss of control, and the effrontery of rejection constitute the basis for America's obsession to punish this small island, although political/economic differences persist in being portrayed as the continued raison d'être for implementing such a destructive encirclement of the Cuban people. The idea that the revolution was made by Cubans for Cubans, and the imperial power standing in its way was the United States, has been conveniently tossed down the historic memory hole. Rafael Hernández, editor of the influential Havana-based *Temas* magazine, stated the Americans "don't want movement towards reconciliation, nor real Cuban independence. Cubans are well educated, even those not supporting the socialist model. But even these Cubans criticize the policy of siege and reject US intervention in Cuban affairs. We have a government of national independence, this is not only about socialism, this is about Cuban nationalism."[115]

After the fall of the Soviet Union the American side recognized the need for a new stick to beat Cuba with. It didn't take long. Reemphasizing the cause of human rights, Cubans had to change its system to allow for increased political pluralism, civil rights restrictions must end, along with the freeing of dissidents and a move toward a more market-driven economy before the United States would consider normalization. Since the summer of 2010 the government under Raúl Castro has freed those arrested seven years earlier for having accepted material and financial aid from the American Interest Section in Havana. The 75 dissidents were accused of violating Cuban laws prohibiting organized support of American policies that compose the construction of siege.[116] The release coincided with a series of economic reforms based on an island-wide conversation on the country's economic and socialist future. The government itself created new space for diversity through comments Raúl Castro made on Cuba's shortcomings and for the need for a recommitment to the work ethic and an immediate effort to increase productivity.[117] He has at the same time reached out to America in the hope of easing the siege; expressing a willingness to discuss any matter as long as it didn't compromise national sovereignty.[118] Shortly after taking power in 2006 Raúl clarified his position by opposing 50 years of American hubris: "They should be very clear that it is not possible to achieve anything in Cuba with impositions and threats. On the contrary, we have always been disposed to normalize relations on an equal plane. What we do not accept is the arrogant and interventionist policy frequently assumed by the current administration of that country."[119]

Raúl, showing a more pragmatic managerial style as opposed to his older brother's ideologically driven methodology, is furthermore making an attempt to move away from the strictures of blaming the embargo for all of Cuba's ills. At the April 2011 Communist Party Congress he recognized the country's systemic economic shortcomings had to be overcome by new initiatives based on internal responses. It was not acquiescence to American demands, but a realization that improvements were obligatory for the survival of the revolution. The damage being done by the siege was still in place, but flexibility within the socialist context was a key to the future, the new President noted.

These deep economic changes were initiated through a set of announcements in the fall of 2010, designed to lessen the grip of the command economy and to attempt to contain rampant bureaucratic corruption and widespread black market activities.[120] Thousands are currently involved in private enterprises under government regulations, helping to streamline the economy into a mixture of state and free-market components.

In a well-reported comment at the National Assembly (Cuba's legislative body) in 2010 Raúl faced the siege head on when he admonished the political leadership to ensure they did not lay all the country's shortcomings on America's doorstep. "After the U.S. war of aggression against Vietnam, the heroic and undefeated Vietnamese people asked us to teach them how to grow coffee, and there we went, and we taught and transferred our experience. Today Vietnam is the second-largest exporter of coffee in the world. And a Vietnamese official said to a Cuban colleague: "How is it possible that you taught us to grow coffee just the other day, and now you are buying coffee from us?" I don't know how the Cuban responded. Surely he said to him: 'El bloqueo.'"[121]

His exhortations to overcome the counterproductive position of blaming all on "the blockade" come as the island works to emerge from an economic crisis that threatens its socialist nature. Internationally the reforms have been met with encouragement and Cuba's standing in Latin America is considered stronger than at any moment in its revolutionary history.[122] Internally the changes have engendered positive response on a conceptual level, although with considerable hesitation among those who have seen similar promises come to nothing in the past, and frustration over the shortages of a new system pledged but as of yet unprepared to meet growing material demands. There is a growing sense this is the government's last chance to get it right.

The siege, however, carries on. Other than allowing Cuban-Americans to visit their homeland without restrictions and permitting newly licensed travel for cultural, educational, and religious groups,[123] President Obama has offered little encouragement to the major political and economic restructuring taking place inside Cuba. He has instead relinquished opportunity to engage for short-sighted hesitancy.

"We haven't seen those changes in a realistic way yet," the President remarked in an interview with a Miami television station. "The economic system there is still far too constrained. And so my hope is that Cuba starts moving into the 21st century. If you think about it, Castro came into power before I was born—he's still there and he basically has the same system when the rest of the world has recognized that the system doesn't work. Obviously everything we do as an administration is going to be focused on how do we deliver more prosperity and more liberty for the Cuban people."[124]

Obama came into office with expectations for a shift toward rationalization if not normalization. His preelection website described Cuban policy "a failure" and called for a new approach. It soon became apparent prepresidential pragmatism gave way to the narrow political considerations for the all important swing state of Florida, where so much hard-right exile inflexibility toward Cuba is rooted. Obama has become the latest in a long line of presidents to bypass reason for expediency, to use terminology and definitions based on narrow American interpretations of "liberty" and "prosperity" that have consistently been construed by the Castro government as reimposition of hegemony.

Wayne Smith, former head of the US Interest Section in Havana and now director of the Cuba Project at Washington's Center for International Policy, agreed the actions out of the White House have been a disappointment. "We'd hoped for a new approach. We haven't got it. Obama lifted restrictions on Cuban-American travel and remittances and has allowed a few more Cuban officials and cultural figures to come to the United States, but that is about it. The same attitudes that drove the Bush administration regarding Cuba seem to be present in Obama."[125] Officials claim the administration is in fact intensifying the siege aimed at restricting Cuba's international financial transactions.[126]

The island has always had a peculiar effect on American presidents, betraying foreign relations principles in favor of dysfunctional or misplaced national self-interest considerations. In March 1953 President Eisenhower spoke idealistically of "any nation's right to form a government and an economic system of its own choosing is inalienable" and "any nation's attempt to dictate to other nations their form of government is indefensible."[127] A mere six years later he reflected on how those attitudes had no application for the Caribbean island, "The sentiment of self-determination for Cuba was abandoned in favor of siege, destruction and overthrow of Castro. It's one thing to describe an ideal, it's quite another when geo-political reality gets in the way."[128]

Proximity brought threat to America's security and its interest; as though a small nation of 11 million could legitimately challenge the most powerful country on earth. Deconstructing "security" and "interests" usually reveals objections to Cuba's attempted interference in America's imperial influences particularly in Latin America. America's safety has never been truly menaced by the island. The reverse has been much closer to the mark.

While the intensity of siege and its explanations have ebbed and flowed during the past five decades, the revolution's response has remained consistent. In accordance with historical standards, the institutional counter to external hostilities impossible to overcome is the development of internal control policies that often leads to the cultivation and reinforcement of a siege mentality. The government of Cuba responded to unrelenting foreign aggression by establishing security practices deemed vital for survival, and in the process tried to advocate a level of legitimacy for its actions. The outcome of those measures has been the creation of distinct perceptions of the revolution among its supporters and detractors. One side sees unity and sacrifice in face of an enormous enemy; the other sees a despotic regime denying individual freedoms cloaked under injudicious jingoism and misdirection of true responsibility.

US strategy has played a substantive role in developing the paradigms for that duality. The call for political solidarity in order to survive has been a constant reply to besiegement; officials oft times propagandizing siege to justify maintenance of revolutionary dedication. Conflated with the strong sense of Cuban nationalism at the heart of the revolution, its leaders have promoted *Patria o Muetre* (homeland or death) as the defiant *grito* (shout) to overcome the reestablishment of hegemonic ambitions. The tactic has come at the expense of a more pluralistic civil society, the low tolerance of opposition for fear of weakening solidarity, and has been an impediment to the establishment of expected advancements. It is the basis for the vehement criticisms from hard-right Cuban-American exiles and their political and media sponsors, as well as American public's negative perceptions of the revolution. US aggression and Cuban retrenchment can, however, be interpreted as symbiotic. The delay in revolutionary aspirations and the implementation of social conformity controls has been defended as indispensable to effectively combat US hostility. Cuba has often exploited America's determination for regime change to validate legislation designed to thwart those efforts, laws that often have a detrimental effect on human and civil rights. Evoking American hostility is often the reliable position of the government when addressing constraints—justified in Havana, inexcusable in Washington.

Despite the internal restrictions and controls, US officials, reluctantly, unofficially, acknowledge continued levels of support for the revolution, "during most of his time as President, Fidel could almost certainly have won an election," in any multiparty race.[129] Implicit in that is the population's rejection of extreme corporate capitalism and corrupt political practices, which was the historical experience for more than 60 years prior to Fidel Castro. There is also substantial rebuff of the twenty-first-century version of US plutocracy where lobbying finances rule politics, equating the system with the worldwide economic meltdown of 2008. What the citizens have indicated through a nationwide survey conducted by Raúl Castro's government in 2007 is the lessening of the command economy, further economic and political freedoms, and the reestablishment of original social goals.

Those and other indications of change have done nothing to soften American hostility. Since the fall of the Soviet Union and the collapse of the Cuban economy, US efforts at siege have increased. Legislation in the 1990s gave legitimacy to the violation of Cuban laws if in conformity toward encouraging a transitional government, leading to direct interference by a number of American government agencies into the island's internal affairs.[130] In specific response the Castro government passed what detractors have called the draconian Law 88, the Reaffirmation of Cuban Dignity and Sovereignty, passed in 1999. The legislation calls for jail terms for those convicted of crimes such as "soliciting, receiving, accepting, facilitating the distribution of, or benefiting in any way from, financial, material or other resources received from the United States Government or channeled by it through its representatives or by any other means, in connection with the Helms-Burton Act." Seventy-five dissidents fell afoul of this law in 2003 after evidence showed they had accepted money, aid, and instruction from the United States Interest Section in Havana.[131]

Law 88 is connected to but separate from the Cuban Penal Code, much of which deals with state security issues. One of the most controversial aspects of the code is Article 91, declaring: "Whoever, in the interest of a foreign state, commits an act with the aim of undermining the independence of the Cuban state or the integrity of its territory, shall be punished by imprisonment of ten to twenty years, or death." It has been used against those claiming to be independent journalists, but whom the Cubans assert accepted money and aid from the American government to write exclusively negative articles.[132] The most severely criticized section permits action against "anyone who has a dangerous manner that may have intent to commit a crime against the state" (72–90). Opponents complain it gives carte blanche for government repression. All carry jail terms of up to 15 years.[133] Adversaries call it the litany of civil rights abuses under the revolutionary government, utilized to crack down on opposition organizations and individuals who don't conform to revolutionary orthodoxy. The government describes it as legitimate legislation needed to ensure solidarity, combat American aggression and to keep its law-abiding citizens safe during this time of national security threat. Every country has similar legislation, with varying degrees of severity, revealed openly after 9/11. How it is implemented, and to what extent, is often based on perceptions of threat. How it is manipulated, or abused, is also nation-dependent. The Cuban revolutionary administration has rarely, if ever, been given the luxury of having their most controversial sections of the Penal Code put into context by media or politicians inside the United States. Neither have they had the ability to examine those laws under a reality that does not include siege.

Peter Roman, professor at CUNY Graduate Center and a Cuban watcher for the past 30 years, assured the legislation is nothing unique, "American laws address security issues, and after 9/11 more so, laws that have civil rights implications. Critics say Cuban laws are extreme, but that's up to each nation to decide based on how they perceive the threat. Every country in the world has comparable laws."[134]

Similar American legislation can be found under the US Penal Code, chapter 115 entitled "Treason, Sedition, and Subversion," Section 2381 stipulating any US citizen that "adheres to their [US] enemies, giving them aid and comfort within the United States or elsewhere, is guilty of treason and shall suffer death, or shall be imprisoned not less than five years and fined under this title but not less than $10,000; and shall be incapable of holding any office under the United States."[135] Americans seen to be accepting aid, instruction, or material goods from the enemy, currently in context to terrorist organizations such as Al Qaeda, would be subject to these laws.

The Cuban government has never had to look far to defend the rules aimed against its few citizens who openly support the US declaration of regime change and its desire to destroy the revolution. America continues to amply provide ammunition; a major propaganda coup for the Castro side occurred in 2004 when the Bush Jr. administration released the Commission for Assistance to a Free Cuba.[136] Coming from one of the most strident antirevolutionary administrations, the Castro government indignantly proclaimed America's plan for a postsiege Cuba was contained in the document. The commission outlined in unambiguous detail exactly what the island's economic and social structure would look like, going so far as to determining who could and could not be included in a leadership role, specifically demanding the exclusion of any Castro regardless of the population's wishes. "The programs outlined by the Commission are still in place, and the financial recommendations are being used, the millions of dollars allocated to subvert the Cuban government. Alan Gross was part of it. It is still there and while Obama hasn't made any official comments on it, a Republican administration could bring it back to the front," José Pertierra speculated.[137]

The commission remains the road map for Cuba's reintegration into the American sphere of interest. It has been capitalized by island officials to strengthen the resolve of those inside the walls, demonstrating there is now written proof of the cultural, social, and administrative raping and pillaging that will take place following capitulation.

Besides the counterproductive recommendations in such documents, another aspect that complicates the move toward normalization is based on ethnicity. The group principally determined to ensure the continuance of siege is made up of the same nationality as those being besieged. Particularly since the 1980s the vanguard of American policy has traveled through the hard-right Cuban-American political and civil leaders in Florida, who battle for the continuation of siege based on a combination of prerevolution romantic idealism with the determination to uphold political power as one of the most influential lobbies in Washington. Many have long envisioned themselves as the government in waiting.

This small segment of hyphenated Americans is the face of the siege, although it is the official strategy of the United States that remains the foundation of intransigence. Policy is retained through the millions of dollars in taxpayers' money that passes to exile organizations in order to ensure bipartisan support for anti-Castro legislation. Cuban-American congressmen, some who have never been to their homeland,[138] generally are allowed to frame and direct the overwhelmingly negative perceptions of Cuba and the justifications for the continuance of siege. Besides the money, vast amounts of political capital have been expended to ensure the status quo, often despite the wishes of Congress.[139]

On the other side of the historic line that has separated the winners and losers of the revolution, the retort has been vitriolic in opposition to leading exiles who sustain the siege, using invectives such as "*gusanos*" (worms) to describe the few who would enable so much injury against their former citizens, regardless of perceived injustices or harms. The tone from the Cuban side has softened in the past decade, as has the inflexibility of the Miami community, and there is now substantial interaction between those who left and those who have remained, with the government welcoming an estimated one billion dollars in annual remittances sent by family members in

Florida.[140] While in the past the first-generation émigré community was a major obstacle to a move toward normalization, driven by memories of lost homes, business, and claims of brutal treatment, the demographics of the younger Cuban-Americans could in the not so distant future represent the impetus to release the stresses of siege.

An additional vehicle for engagement would be the elimination of travel restrictions for average Americans to visit Cuba. It remains a vital element of siege, key to controlling the message of the assumed ills of life on the socialist island.

Temas magazine editor Hernández, whose publication is known for its often critical examination of Cuban society, is convinced that "if we had a million US citizens come to Cuba, all those negative perceptions they normally have will be questioned. But that is what scares the Cuban-American right wing, if the travel restrictions were lifted they would lose their message; this is the weakest link of the embargo. The way they want to deal with Cuba is to deny Americans to travel here, to deny freedom of trade, to deny these freedoms they say they are so supportive of in Cuba, but they deny those freedoms to their own citizens. There is a perverse logic to it, and their rationale is ridiculous. Are they afraid that the Americas would become Fidelistas or Communists if they visited Cuba? They believe this political system is awful, so let them come and see for themselves. They will find that what the American press says about Cuba is not true, the US press controls the message about Cuba, based on the right wing agenda. If Americans came here they would see for themselves, and see that message is false."[141]

Or as Tony Martínez of the antiembargo US Cuba Now Political Action Committee (PAC) observed, "If you say you are American in some parts of the world, you could get attacked, spat on, even kidnapped. In Havana if you say you're American they'll talk to you, tell you about their relatives who live in the US, ask about baseball, culture, computer games. Compared to other places in the world, Havana is a relatively safe destination for an American to visit. Our travel restrictions are absurd and as Americans we should be free to visit Cuba and see for ourselves."[142]

The probability that tourists from the 50 states will flock to Cuba in the near future continue to face obstacles from Cuban-American congressmen, and anti-Castro critics such as the director of the Center for a Free Cuba Frank Calzón, who said now is not the time to consider any change in policy: "Ending the embargo now not only ignores the atrocities perpetrated by the Castro regime, it also hands the Cuban government a huge financial boost at the exact moment they need and want it most. Friendship and an economic relationship with our nation must be earned, and Cubans deserve the freedom, democracy and human rights they lack. Until Cuba has demonstrated meaningful progress, unilateral changes in American policy would undeniably reward horrific behavior."[143]

Justifying siege has been a public relations achievement for the antirevolutionary industry. What is often intentionally overlooked or misunderstood is the consideration that the shortcomings in Cuban society can be considered

equally to be a defensible evolutionary reaction to America's strategy of destabilization as it is to the radicalization and limitations of institutional Cuban
socialism. The excesses of government command of all aspects of social, commercial, and political life is well documented. What has rarely been examined is how those policies—that are not as severe as portrayed in the United
States—can be influenced not only by ideological extremes, but in defense
of tangible external hostility. When that aggression is unrelenting, when it
comes from the world's most powerful nation on earth, and when the bel-
ligerence represents concrete tactics to destroy the existing social/economic
system, the consequences usually manifest when national programs to secure
the homeland become excessive. Fear, anger, defiance, stubbornness, and the
lashing out at those perceived to be perpetrators or their kindred spirits easily induces irrationality, intolerance, churlishness, and radicalism. Siege has
worked those conditions well in Cuba. The response has been shown to be
historically consistent within other countries regardless of political makeup,
mitigated only by perception of the threat and longevity of hostility. Cuba
has suffered both in the extreme. In the case of American bellicosity against
the island the radicalization can be demonstrated as an element of effect that
continues to shape and influence government actions. To what extent the
siege plays a part in reaction is the subject at question.

The citizens of Cuba are led to believe the actuality of America's objective to destroy the revolution and reestablish hegemony, based by merely
revealing the United States own public proclamations to that end. With
those intentions clear, the Castro government validates a go slow approach
to transformation, and the continued necessity of institutional surveillance
and control systems. Add to that the element of the threat to Cuban nationalism so inherent in revolutionary fundamentalism, it is an effortless matter to elicit support for and implementation of restrictive civil measures the
majority of the public perceive as necessary for national self-determination
while under siege. Those internal policies, however, have come in part at
the expense of social stagnation, government paranoia, financial errors,
economic dislocation, and extreme sensitivity to criticism from both friend
and foe. Revolutionary dogma maintaining the common good outweighing
individual rights adds to the intolerance of diversity and to the justification
of programs sustaining security for the whole over concerns for individual
constraints. It is a dichotomy as much enforced upon the government as it
has been developed as a socialist evolution.

Revolutionary society was meant to be open, challenging, welcoming to
critical thought and ideals of how to construct a new reality. Che spoke of
the necessity to criticize in order to improve, that a stagnant, closed culture
was not conducive to building what the revolution wanted to achieve. He
did not hesitate to react harshly to the political system he helped bring about
in Cuba: "Socialism is young and has made errors. Many times revolutionaries lack the knowledge and intellectual courage needed to meet the task
of developing the new man with methods different from the conventional

ones—and the conventional methods suffer from the influences of the society, which created them."[144]

The revolution, however, had little opportunity to implement Che's advice, seeing internal criticism as a luxury it could not afford while under threat of destruction. Instead it devolved into a state of martial laws ostensibly designed to protect itself through the implementation of restrictions, boundaries, controls, and denials. All in the name of security. The result is a garrison society where discipline, loyalty, and blind trust in leadership became not a requirement, but an act of supplication. It led to such abuses as Ariel Hidalgo sent to seven years in prison, according to Amnesty International, on the charge of "hostile propaganda," for writing a pamphlet in 1984 criticizing the "prerogatives" enjoyed by managers but "denied to nearly the whole rank-and-file working population."[145] Zero tolerance for criticism of almost any kind while under siege made easy fodder for critics who condemn the revolution for these faults and constraints, ensuring no examination of what if any portion American policy commands.

Fidel Castro recognized the social harm the siege was enacting, telling *New York Times* reporter Dick Eder in 1964 that easing tensions would enable him to release political prisoners and relax some of the harsher internal measures made necessary by the life-and-death struggle with the United States.[146] At the 2005 Ibero-American summit in Spain, Cuban foreign minister Felipe Pérez Roque put it bluntly: "The blockade is the central obstacle to our economic and social development."[147] Hindering advancement is the obvious consequence to the pressures created by hostile external forces, but the internalization of besiegement by those born after the revolution additionally has a determining effect on the perception of government inadequacy, the siege "sometimes disappears into the background and becomes just one more aspect of the country's reality, devoid of a clear explanation," Cuban author Andrés Zaldívar observed.[148] Little then is needed for society to close on itself, to lapse into lethargy; its ability to articulate deficiencies lost in the unrecognized acceptance of the debilitating condition.

* * *

The United States has become a more fractious culture as a result of the attacks of 9/11. New immigrants have often borne the brunt of the new state of affairs, particularly if they are of Muslim heritage. More disturbing, the public responds supportively to torture, prisoner mistreatment, indefinite detention, presidential abuse of power, intrusive surveillance systems, and extensive intelligence programs that all result in civil rights restrictions, to try and prevent another 9/11. Throughout history American society condemned and incarcerated nonconformists, individuals and groups, seen not to be sufficiently in line with the establishment in times of war or national security threat. It had, however, the ability to take a breath and step back from excesses once the immediate threat subsided.

Cuban revolutionary society never had the chance to be anything but restrictive, unable to fight the terrorism and siege "over there" as Bush promised to do after 9/11, so they had to fight it from within. The conflict manifested in some of the worst aspects of political constricts and economic failures of the Castro administration.

The current government under Raúl Castro has made efforts to rise above those constraints. During discussions regarding the emergent self-employment opportunities under the new economic reforms, he addressed the bias many of the older party leaders have toward market-influenced economic reforms, "It is fundamental that we modify the existing negative attitude that quite a few of us have towards this form of private employment."[149] He was commenting on a half-century of well entrenched ideological preconceptions that have provided easy cover for bureaucrats to choose inactivity over innovation. Raúl has articulated there is no value in constantly blaming outside hostility. The President's message was that while American aggression cannot be denied as a negative social and economic force, revolutionary Cubans have to work harder to overcome it, to improve their living conditions despite the siege, not to surrender to it through lack of resolve, nor use it to defend inefficiency, shortcomings, or failure.

What remains opaque is to determine the balance between the extent the Cuban government does call on siege as a method to deflect systemic internal shortcomings, and to the legitimacy of its ability to negatively impact Cuban society. To what degree has the government artificially created fear and hatred of an enemy, using the threat to national security to justify control of the population and restrictions? Or are American actions a real and constant danger, the aggression and hostility a contributing factor in a warping affect on Cuban society since the early years of the Revolution.

Revolutionary shortcomings have elicited explanations usually framed under defense and survival of the nation—from both internal and external aggressions. It is an outcome of social extremism, either inherent in the system or helped develop by the siege. Governments of all political bent are susceptible to enacting policies of internal controls well beyond the norm if perceived to be under threat to national security. While American excesses in response to 9/11 are most often vindicated by the magnitude of the event, or rationalized as the actions of officials who went too far, Cuba's response to 50 years of terrorism, propaganda, economic warfare, and all other aspects of siege have been utilized by detractors to call for regime change and the substantiation of the supposed innate ill worth of the revolution.

Unquestionably there are significant inadequacies within Cuban society, and many of its economic structures have not entirely been influenced by siege; the government's decision to commit to a strict centralized economy is but one example. The elusive if not impossible search for equality has led to economic rationing and a compromise with quality in products. The top heavy bureaucracy has often created decision-making paralysis at national levels, resulting in inefficiencies in production and distribution, particularly in the agricultural sector. Cultural mistakes in the first few decades such as the Grey Years where political orthodoxy trumped artistic expression, or the internment of gays and nonconformists in the harsh UMAP rehabilitation camps continue to put a stain on the government. Little of those failings are the direct fault of American aggression.

So while US policy cannot be used as the reflex to exculpate responsibility for institutionalization of social restrictions, dogmatic approaches, and political limitations under orthodox Marxism, the siege can be examined as an influential factor in driving the revolution into Soviet arms, in justifying the construction of invasive surveillance systems and societal restrictions, of demanding conformity and seeing most critical opinion as potentially counterrevolutionary, of the rationale for rejection of the worst predatory aspects of Western liberal economic practices. Fidel Castro's revolution from the beginning articulated communal justice programs and populous agendas that America labeled communist—a pejorative term particularly terrifying during the height of the Cold War. And when the revolution was aimed primarily at American hegemony, it was a logical assumption that the resultant hostility would be answered by Cuba's closer accommodation to the other side— the Soviet model for economic surety and military safety—within a decidedly Cuban-influenced authenticity. However, America's consistently clear and articulated obsession to destroy the revolution is based not predominately on Castro's embrace of communism, but on a much more complicated historic relationship; its genesis founded on the island's aspiration to achieve sovereignty under its terms, no longer accepting imperial definitions of independence, freedom, liberty, and prosperity. Castro could have declared the revolution Nihilist, Anarchist, or Maurrassisme, America's response would have differed not one bit. It was the political times of the Cold War that had the determination on the revolution's movement to confining classification.

Recognizing the Cuban government has often overplayed its hand on blaming siege, it must then be acknowledged the other side repeatedly refuses to recognize the impact its hostilities has had on a small country's desire to advance socially, culturally, and economically under a system that has been decreed illegitimate by the most powerful force on earth. A keystone of US strategy has been to deny the influence, sometimes even the existence, of the siege. This has been done in an effort to downplay America's role in Cuba's difficulties, thereby permitting no other answer than that of the incompetence of the revolution. America has long ago won the propaganda war in its attempts to shine a powerful light on Cuba's excesses while keeping its own aggressions deep in the shadows.

Whether the siege has influence on the behavior of the revolutionary government, or is of no import on its supposedly inherent totalitarian nature is an issue that remains current. As Cuban-born University of Denver professor Arturo López-Levy said, "The Cuban government and others have argued for years that Cuba is living under siege, as the victim of an illegal U.S. policy aimed at overthrowing the government...Studies have shown that the deterioration of social and economic indicators in Cuba, the number of political prisoners, and the implementation of emergency laws that limit liberties have all increased in parallel to the strengthening of the embargo . . . Although the threat of U.S. intervention is not valid to justify the violation of Cuban's civil rights, it is an accepted view in human rights norms that governments can suspend some rights during emergencies."[150]

Consideration of when and if the emergencies have ever ended is the consistent yardstick for the revolutionary government, as is the rationalization for the continued vigilance within US society more than a decade after 9/11.

The idea that the embargo is of little consequence and is simply a convenient excuse dominates anti-Castro discourse. One of the most famous critics of the government is Yoani Sánchez, who writes an internationally recognized blog from her Havana residence. Her comments are translated into 18 languages and Generation Y receives millions of hits a month. "In any case I think the embargo has been the perfect argument for the Cuban government. I don't think it (American hostility) has contributed to it (Cuban government action) but it has become the main argument for claiming that we live in a besieged fortress and that all dissent is treason. I think in reality that the Cuban government fears the disappearance of this conflict. The Cuban government wants the economic sanctions to continue."[151]

The alledged lack of cooperation in America's war on terror became the latest contention the Cuban side would prefer the siege to continue, that it does not want to remove the excuse for the revolution's deficiencies; and so the Castro leadership continually finds way to subvert any American approach. A close study of the historical record indicates more often the opposite.[152]

Secretary of State Hillary Clinton reinforced the position that Cuba's economic problems are their own fault and siege is the simple convenience to blame: "The Castro brothers do not want to see an end to the embargo and do not want to see normalization with the United States because then they would lose all the excuses for what hasn't happened in Cuba in the last 50 years."[153] The bluff was called by National Assembly President Ricardo Alarcón, "If she really thinks that the blockade benefits the Cuban government—which she wants to undermine—the solution is very simple: that they lift it even for a year to see whether it is in our interest or theirs."[154]

Ending the strategy of siege is a problematical prospect for America. If the policy was lifted and Cuba advanced, it would provide proof that the embargo was a root cause of the country's many ills and give slander to the statement that the siege is in place to help the people. The fact the Cuban leadership is allowed to continue using besiegement as an excuse could offer some insight into America's concern.

The idea that Cuba wants to maintain the embargo, said José Pertierra, "is without merit. Cuba is not afraid of having Americans come, they'd welcome them. They want the embargo lifted, it would have a great economic benefit. It is another lie that the government is afraid that it would destroy the socialist system, the government would react and respond and continue. Cuba has suffered tremendously under the embargo, for anyone to say American policy hasn't had a detrimental effect is not telling the truth."[155]

Officials inside the island have consistently maintained the embargo should be lifted, the siege ended, so they can get on with fixing their own problems. America, however, has so far refused that consideration until specific conditions, ever changing, are met. "They are afraid to end the embargo, for fear of what we could achieve without it. Give us the chance, let us improve things here without the blockade, let us see what we can do," said *Temas* editor Hernández.[156] He speculated America is hesitant to give up its greatest bargaining chip in the desire to regain the lost island. The siege remains a key element in the prospect for inducing regime change, all in order to bring America's description of freedom and liberty to the Cuban people.

The actions against Cuba illustrate the contradictions inherent in America's foreign policy—the objective to impose its designation of democracy through imperial means. By definition the systems are anathema to one another, yet America has tried its best to compel this contortion on those unfriendly nations deemed that should have to swallow it—Cuba being the longest standing recipient. Key is to control the message where deeds are promoted in pursuit of such noble goals as freedom and liberty, and where destructive excesses (if ever discovered) are blamed on conditions beyond anyone's control and not on overall intent. The island residents have experienced the strategy of siege in its purest and most effective form. They are the recipients of the punishment and yet their protests are given no serious or legitimate voice outside of Cuba. America's exceptionalism for the citizens of the revolution is often seen as an attempt to reestablish domination through the use of democratic phraseology in the guise of imperial animus. The government of Cuba reacts by instituting social parameters meant to establish security yet culminate in restraints to public diversity.

For those who see American policy as hostile and counterproductive, projections of virtue are misplaced. "It shows the limits of American justice, how America has treated Cuba while we say we are a moral country. The Cubans have seen that, if we haven't here, and they see we are not moral or righteous when we treat Cuba the way we do, and it undercuts America's position that what we are doing is for the good of Cuba. It undermines the image of the United States as a moral power," Wayne Smith observed. "America tries to diminish or deny our policies, for one example the history of terrorism is very well know to everyone in Cuba, but outside the country very few know of it, and for Americans to recognize what we have done, it is a very difficult concept. But it's there, you can't get around it, we have conducted acts of terrorism for years, polices of hostility, and that has an effect."[157]

Castro recognized the vulnerabilities posed by an external threat, real or created, embody a powerful tool for government to utilize in demand of solidarity against internal opposition and acceptance of personal restrictions for the sake of national security. Cuba's defensive tactics came from the genuine hostility of its northern neighbor, and permitted the extraction of a level of certainty from its citizens, particularly from the mid-1960s onward. In return the government would fulfill its side of the social contract; education, housing food, health, and most importantly—safety. The government additionally promised and delivered stability compared to the upheaval, political murders, civil wars, and material destruction taking place throughout Latin America in the 1970s and 1980s, much directed covertly by the hand of American foreign policy. The revolutionary accord has evolved into a social radicalization where everything, no matter how trivial, has been politicized. That is not been a function of siege, but a utility used to great affect by leadership.

How much the government took the arrangement to signify a guarantee of security, but also to deflect systemic political and economic shortcomings, apply civil rights confinements beyond what was necessary, to react with anger and to impose institutional pettiness on opponents with a pro-America agenda as well on those who were sincerely trying to achieve critical discourse without threatening the socialist existence, is the dividing line between pro- and antirevolutionaries. The debate has extended itself with the new parameters of the changing social contract under Raúl Castro's expressions of rising above the limitations imposed by siege. The current Cuban leadership is entering into a new arrangement with its citizens, where both sides understand government can no longer provide for everything. And that it no longer should be in the "business of making shoes" as Raúl recognized.[158]

The average Cuban looks anxiously to this changing relationship, as well as how their powerful northern neighbor will react. It is the individual citizen that siege has consistently been aimed against, using all its overwhelming political and economic might to destabilize society and promote civil unrest among the population. This has been done with the compliance, cooperation, and direction of a small group who lost the most from the revolution— the bourgeois class of Cubans now calling America their home, and have for clear reasons a self interested perspective to direct their anger and frustration at their former fellow countrymen who have decided to remain and work with, not against, the socialist government. Many of the exiles still carry that resentment, maintaining the decades old pretense that Castro has everyone "hostage" and it is only the breaking down of the walls that will provide freedom.

As in all military-related conflicts, the innocent suffers. This siege is no different, yet unique in its length, scope, and complexities that go far beyond armies surrounding castles. The encirclement requires examination of its historical development, impact, and affect on both sides of the Florida Straits. To reveal the limitations, justifications, and culpabilities of this half century of encirclement. To determine if it is reality or vapor. To disclose if there is an "unseen truth" to Cuban society and its citizens—and where the future may lie.

And to discover why the walls still stand.

2

LAYING THE SIEGE

> There is something absurd and inherently false about one country trying to impose its system of government or its economic institutions on another. Such an enterprise amounts to a dictionary definition of imperialism.
>
> —Chalmers Johnson, Dismantling the Empire[1]

From 1898 to 1959 America impressed a distorted type of absurdity upon the Pearl of the Antilles. The 60 years of US hegemony was a fundamental element in the culmination of the Cuban Revolution, and continues to this day to shape and define the relationship between these two "closest of enemies."[2]

The termination of the imperialist imposition preordained the laying of siege.

America's possession of Cuba ended in the actuality, if not in the desire, with the January 1959 triumph of the revolutionaries. The event set in motion a series of collisions between the giant to the north and its island neighbor. As Cuba moved to eradicate the stigma of neocolonialism and assert authentic national sovereignty, the United States reacted with animosity, indignity, and incredulity, manifesting itself in the construction of a Cuban social fortress. America's answer was based deep within the historical relationship of these neighbors and the incompatible differences it eventually impressed upon each other—an essential facet to understand the separate yet parallel experiences.

Prior to this period Cuba was the jewel in Spain's colonial crown. For centuries it held firm the gateway between the new and old worlds: Havana, the vital stop for thousands of vessels loaded with plunder heading home to royalty in Madrid. While the rest of Latin America threw off Spanish colonialism to forge self-determination in the early nineteenth century, Cuba remained tightly under foot until 1868 when the First War of Independence was declared under the leadership of Carlos Manuel de Céspedes. Ten years later the conflict ended with the mother country still in command. The island's dominant economic influence had shifted, however, to the emerging American power. By 1877, the United States accounted for 83 percent of Cuba's total exports, the preponderance resulting in the management of investment, industry, and the country's monoeconomy—king sugar.[3]

With American economic influence now enveloping Cuba, long simmering political interests began to reawaken. As far back as 1804 US officials had expressed their desire to control, and in 1832 Secretary of State John Quincy Adams famously commented, "There are laws of political as well as of physical gravitation; and if an apple, severed by the tempest from its native tree, cannot choose but fall to the ground, Cuba, forcibly disjoined from its own unnatural connection with Spain, and incapable of self-support, can gravitate only towards the North American Union."[4]

Various efforts were made by the American side toward outright purchase, but all were rejected. When direct financing failed, intentions were legislated through the Ostend Manifesto in 1854 indicating war with the disagreeable Spaniards might be warranted in order to seize Cuba. Failing that, if the island was released by Spain to the locals, America would be justified in ensuring it remained a slave state and in preventing the encroachment of any other European power. Ostend became the first in a line of legislation that sought to determine Cuba's fate under the more worthy American authority, based on the political dynamic that framed Cuban rebels as incompetent, lazy, and unworthy of self-government, thereby denying them the capacity for true sovereignty. America as savior was the only alternative. Thus began the historical conceptualization of benign necessity to establish the process of independence under US patronage. The modern contrivance maintains the Cuban revolutionary government is unfit, undeserving, ineffective, and dictatorial; only under US parentage will the country regain prosperity.

As American commercial weight and political interest dramatically increased in the latter parts of the nineteenth century, the nationalists recovered and in 1895 launched another rebellion that ended with defeat being snatched from the jaws of victory. Cuba's Second War of Independence, known in the United States as the Spanish-American War, provided the opportunity for the northern empire to realize its geopolitical aspirations. Conflict broke out with the *Grito de Baire*[5] and after three years of destruction the rebels were within grasp of the prize. Cuba was led by national hero José Marti, who fell in battle shortly after hostilities began. At the moment the insurgents were most confident of Spanish withdrawal and acceptance of terms for independence, America stepped in. With demands of revenge for the sinking of the *USS Maine* providing the popular rallying cry, yellow journalism the emotionalism and political expediency the occasion, the United States landed troops in the southern part of the island in June 1898. Teddy Roosevelt's ride up San Juan Hill and the defeat of the Spanish at one of the few set piece battles in Santiago ended the conflict a mere six weeks following America's entrance. The short and bloody action convinced the Spanish there was no hope of resisting the insurgent tactics and traditional American force. The North American colonists had experienced a similar set of circumstances during the 1776 Revolution. The revolutionary forces required France's superior navy and the part it played at the siege of Yorktown to ensure the final defeat of the British. America would have had a more difficult, if not impossible, rebellion if money, arms, and soldiers from

France were not available.[6] Once defeated, the French left the nation's new leaders to their own devices and gratitude, neither proposing nor imposing an absolute monarchal system. The Americans fought for its revolution, accomplished with the help of an imperial power, as did the Cuban rebels. In 1898, however, the Yankees insisted on staying and taking best advantage of the aftermath. The rightful victors were left standing out in the warm, humid tropic air.

Cuban forces were refused permission to enter Santiago following its surrender. Little if any credit was afforded the rebels efforts of the previous three years.[7] The worst insult came through political legerdemain, which justified prohibiting Cuban representation at the Paris peace treaty—America having refused to designate those fighting for their freedom as legal combatants, then invoking that unofficial status as reason for exclusion. It was apparent there would be no contemplation to permit the rebels to control their own homeland, or share in the glory.

Cuban sentiment of American purpose in the second war of liberation was ambivalent. Many rebel leaders had lived for years in the United States and sought financial and military assistance as the only way to ensure victory. A portion desired outright annexation. Others were wary of allowing their powerful neighbor an avenue into the island's national affairs, fearing the potential of exchanging one colonial master for another. National icon José Marti warned against "any attempt to sell his *patria* as if it were some negotiable merchandise, and of course, without taking into account the wishes of people, was completely unacceptable—particularly when the prospective purchaser was the United States."[8] Both Marti's hope and life fell in the battle for Cuban independence. He understood there was a strong sense within the American populace that the Cubans desperately wanted aid to free them from Spain, that US might was essential to accomplish that goal. Marti was also convinced the majority of his countrymen sought true autonomy. The will of the people on both sides was soon usurped by imperial expediency.

Real politics soon combined with economic expansionism to maintain Cuba's colonial status, this time with a new master. If most Cubans expressed uncertainty over its entrance into the rebellion, there was near unanimity for the removal of US forces once victory was assured. That stance seemed to be previously declared by American legislation under the Teller Amendment enacted April 1898, which "hereby disclaims any disposition of intention to exercise sovereignty, jurisdiction, or control over said island except for pacification thereof, and asserts its determination, when that is accomplished, to leave the government and control of the island to its people."[9]

Unfortunately, legal assurances were of little consequence. Instead of handing over sovereignty to those who fought so long and hard, America's long-stated objective was implemented—to allow these unworthy combatants run of their own country would be immoral, unnatural, and intolerable in accordance to the blood and treasure expended. What was demanded was the United States' steady hand and cordial goodwill over the ungrateful

Cubans who were not mature or intelligent enough to handle independence. Complaints against that charge simply provided proof of its validity.

It was America's efforts alone that brought freedom to the island, went the historiography, so to hand over administration to the insurgents was unthinkable. The only right thing was to provide uplifting guidance and tutelage in the proper ways of government, as a parent would tender suitable expertise to an ignorant child. "Our new subjects, foolish, impulsive, headstrong, unreasonable...We are old in this learning and they must obey as those who are in tutelage. They are children and we are men in these deep matters of government and justice," Woodrow Wilson commented on his impression of the Cuban condition.[10]

The parental benevolence came by way of a three-year military occupation, beginning January 1, 1899. During this time investors and commercial interests flocked to Cuba in order to purchase lands at low prices, made easier as the occupational government refused to provide loans to locals. Within a few weeks American officials were handing out franchises, railway grants, street line concessions, electric light monopolies, and similar privileges to foreign syndicates and individual capitalists—predominantly to their fellow countrymen. One of the first interested in acquiring large tracts of territory was the United Fruit Company. By the time of the 1959 Revolution the company owned an estimated 250,000 acres of prime agricultural land and dozens of sugar mills and banana plantations.[11]

A legislative attempt to halt and make illegal the favorable concessions provided to American interests was introduced by Ohio senator J.B. Foraker. His Amendment of February 1899 was one more example of good legal intentions made irrelevant by political convenience and economic advantages. The amendment was designed to prevent the military administration from handing out license rights to US commercial interests. But presiding governor Leonard Wood circumvented those objectives by granting revocable licenses allowing US industry to build the railroad under the newly formed, influence-peddling Cuba Company.[12] Public works were released to northern operations, with Wood appointing sympathetic nationals in positions of authority to help solidify the relationship between American capital and Cuban compliance. So began the development of an important class of bourgeois strongly in support of American political and economic purposes. They formed part of the rank and file who fled the revolution to Miami and have maintained such virulent anti-Castro sentiments and support for the siege.[13]

Any further doubt as to Cuba's fate ended in 1901 with the introduction of a rider appended to the Army Appropriations Act. Known as the Platt Amendment, the policy was the price the newly created Cuban Republic had to pay for the foreign army to leave. It was vociferously opposed by the *independentistas* who ultimately bowed to the inevitable when it was narrowly passed three years later. For the next six decades under the Republic, to rule Cuba meant to obey the demands of the foreign-dominated social/economic matrix.

The Platt Amendment set up conditions for America to direct Cuban foreign policy and to intervene in the country's internal affairs, arranged political and economic systems for American benefit primarily, prohibited the transfer of land to any power other than the United States, mandated that Cuba would contract no foreign debt without guarantees that the interest could be served from ordinary revenues, encouraged American investment at favorable conditions, and promoted the colonization of Cuban land.[14] Direct American interests controlled 80 percent of all sugar mills, the banks, electric and telephone company, and all oil refineries.[15] US speculators bought up hundreds of thousands of prime acreage, leading to approximately 75 percent of all arable land under foreign command by 1958, predominately American. What was left for the nationals was civil service and local government participation, often leading to corruption and manipulation as the only means to advance politically and socially.[16]

Finally, Platt demanded the sale or lease of "lands necessary for coaling or naval stations at certain specified points to be agreed upon." The Americans wanted two large bases, one on the north and another on the southeast end—they settled for Guantánamo Bay. To this day the agreement persists, despite Cuban protests.

The Platt Amendment obliged the republic to protect foreign property as a stipulation for continued autonomy. Every major strike in the first few decades after Platt faced American opposition and the government that wanted to remain in power had to react accordingly—to repress the strikers and unions. If they didn't, a change in management would be threatened, as transpired when the sugar workers were forbidden to strike on US orders during World War I.[17] The amendment created circumstances where labor became subservient to foreign property interests in Cuba and when labor expressed its objections, those interests shut them down.

Under Platt not even the smallest policy could be formalized if it ran afoul of imperial authority. The 1915 Cuban Congress thought to liberalize divorce laws and reform religious marriage; the US State Department opposed both and the matter never went further. In typical fashion American leaders spoke of not wanting to interfere in Cuban affairs, but had no hesitancy in expressing resistance when proposed measures went counter to their political, economic, or moral sensibilities.[18] In the 1920s the national government moved to pass minimum wage laws and to establish levels of Cuban employees in all foreign-owned businesses. The American overseers prohibited both proposals.[19]

Rudimentary functions of state apparatus—agencies of law, courts, army, had all become under US control.[20] Governor Leonard Wood knew exactly what the United States had accomplished. "There is, of course, little or no independence left in Cuba under the Platt Amendment. It is quite apparent that she is absolutely in our hands."[21] He also had no doubt as to when that situation would change: "The US must always control the destines of Cuba."[22]

Defenders of Platt claim while the amendment was recognition, if not appreciation, of what American efforts to free Cuba had accomplished and was justly due, "we are entitled to exercise a protectorate. We should have conceded to us the right to intervene in order that no harm comes to her and that a stable government may be maintained. All these things Cuba ought to be more than willing to grant...In view of the cost of Cuba's freedom to this country in treasure and in blood, gratitude should impel her to lean upon America as her best friend and protector," so proclaimed New York congressman Townsend Scudder in support of the Platt Amendment.[23]

Others maintained the amendment was treatment properly administered. "In general, it might be said, the Platt Amendment was not an uncalled-for infringement of Cuban sovereignty, for the islanders badly needed tutelage and preparation for self-government. It certainly was not a heavy burden on Cuban life, even if Latin patriots sought to describe it as such," historian Robert Ferrell explained.[24] The ability to diminish or deny the impact American legislation has imposed on Cuba continues in modern terms. Frank Calzon, executive director of the Center for a Free Cuba, a staunchly anti-Castro organization, stated during an interview in 2011: "I think American policy has been at least, after the Bay of Pigs, very very minimal in its response...I don't think American policy is aggressive at all."[25]

Neocolonial interference arrived in a series of military interventions to quell internal political unrest in 1906, 1909, and 1912. It was in no greater evidence than during the unsuccessful revolution of 1933. Under the violent dictatorship of Gerardo Machado, a series of nationwide strikes and protests forced the United States to withdraw support, turning instead to Carlos Miguel De Céspedes who had the backing of American ambassador Sumner Welles. Machado, under threat of an American military invasion, resigned. The Cuba public saw this as replacing one foreign lackey with another, and in a matter of weeks following a series of strikes and a major debt crises De Céspedes was gone (thanks as well to the Sergeants Revolt led by a then unknown young opportunist by the name of Fulgencio Batista) and a new government with Ramón Grau at the head and Antonio Guiteras as Vice President was installed. That administration lasted 100 days but in that time it repudiated Platt, nationalized US properties, lowered utility and interest rates, introduced agrarian reforms as well as a series of social justice programs and progressive labor laws including wage and minimum hours. Grau proclaimed a radical policy of proto-nationalism, anti-imperialism and socialism (not Marxism), highly popular among the locals, not so much to the Americans. Refusing to recognize the administration, which was considered as effective a form of destabilization as direct intervention, US inveigling of the ambitious Batista resulted in Grau's removal in 1934. It was the start of Colonel Batista's rise as Cuba's political powerbroker from 1934 to 1940, President from 1940 to 1944, and finally dictator in 1952.

Grau's failure was rooted in the inability to establish radical reforms into a revolutionary movement to overcome the foreign master and its economic backers, which were able to reject the new restrictions and laws favoring labor over capital. Reactionary elements sustained in power those foreign influences that controlled investment, finances, and the national political process.

America's institutional opposition to reforms proved to be the stronger force over widespread populist support.

Although Grau's social restructurings were denied, the United States did permit the abrogation of Platt Amendment, as by then American domination had been completely integrated into all aspects of Cuban life. From 1934 to the end of the Batista dictatorship in 1959 Cuba was operating smoothly under American direction.

Economically Platt set in motion the opportunity for American capital to exercise near complete authority of the island, the center of power situated in the capital Havana, a city that still holds romantic appeal for those who visit, and thanks to the siege, those who cannot. The city ranked fourth most expensive in North America in 1956,[26] which made it enjoyable for rich foreigners, but a struggle for the residents who earned a wage on average one-third of their American counterparts. In all social aspects Havana was a major step superior from the other Cuba and the differences played a contributing role in generating sufficient support for revolution.

Comparisons between prerevolutionary Havana and the rest of the country[27]: Sixty percent of physicians, 62 percent of dentists, and 80 percent of all hospital beds were located in Havana in 1956–57. There was only one hospital in rural Cuba. Four out of five workers in the countryside received medical attention only if they paid for it; as a result most had no access to health care. Infant mortality averaged 60 per 1,000, reduced by more than half in Havana. In 1958 there were approximately 6,000 doctors in Cuba for a population of seven million. An estimated 70 percent of non-sugar industrial production was located within a radius of 70 kilometers around Havana. Industry in the rest of the country was overwhelmingly sugarcane. Within the same area 85 percent of the country's electricity was produced. Between 80 and 90 percent of all shipping was handled in the port of Havana. The strength of the city's head was in stark contrast to the rural body's frailty. This dichotomy was well understood by the prerevolution ruling class; "Havana is Cuba, all the rest is landscape," said a Cuban minister of education.[28]

Those living in the countryside suffered from a daily deficit of 1,000 calories and were 16 percent under average height and weight. Average life expectancy was five years less in rural Cuba. Before the revolution 23.6 percent of the Cuban population was illiterate. In rural areas over half the population could not read or write and 61 percent of the children did not go to school. To address this problem Castro asked young students in the cities to travel to the countryside and teach the people to read and write. Known as the Literacy Campaign, the 12-month program starting in early 1960 involved hundreds of thousands of volunteers. By its end Cuba had a literacy rate comparable to any first world nation.

Employment during the nine months when there was no sugar to harvest, known as the dead time, was 20 percent, underemployment averaged 13.8 percent annually. Government statistics showed that 30 percent of the lowest income population earned only four percent of Cuba's total income. Social security covered just 53 percent of the population. Although Cuba ranked ahead of most other countries in Latin America purely in average GDP, thanks to the skewing of the economics in Havana, a third of the population lived in poverty. In 1957 most Cubans in the countryside had no running water (85 percent), toilet (54 percent), electricity (93 percent), or a refrigerator (96 percent). Urban residents with electricity was at 87 percent, a refrigerator 40 percent, running water 82 percent, and toilet 93 percent. Disparities in cultural and social facilities were extensive. Havana had 60 theaters in 1958, there were only 125 in all the rest of Cuba. While Havana was the first place in Latin America to have a television broadcast, more than 90 percent of the rural population had never seen a television before 1960. Life expectancy in 1959 was 59 years; in 2006 it was 75. Literacy rates today average 99 percent of the whole country; education is accessible to 100 percent of the population, up to and including university. Access to water, electricity, proper housing is averaging 80 percent, including the most remote regions of the country. In all of Cuba, the number of hospitals has risen from 57 before the revolution to 170 today, plus 250 polyclinics (health centers), previously unknown; beds available in hospitals and clinics have doubled, from 21,000 to 42,000, from 3.3 per 1,000 inhabitants to 5.4. By 2006 there were 70,000 doctors for a population of 11 million, almost all with one or two specialties. In 2010 infant mortality had fallen to six per 1,000, on par with American statistics. Of the 19 Latin American countries only Argentina and Uruguay surpass the present Cuban figure.[29]

Economically those who lived in the countryside before the revolution faced practices dating back to medieval times. Many of the major sugar mills, including the vast United Fruit Company operation in Boca De Samá, worked on the truck system, where the laborers would be paid in script that could only be used to purchase food and goods at the company store. Prices, usually much higher than elsewhere, were set by the company. The system permitted the *campensinos* to gain credits during the months they were not working the cane, in order to survive. It also allowed the company to keep the workers constantly in debt and poverty.[30] Wages have been put forward by the anti-Castro adherents as proof Cubans were actually well off before the revolutionaries arrived. Statistically the island appeared to be in fine company in 1958 when comparing income levels to advanced nations, coming in eighth in the world for industrial workers, and seventh for agricultural laborers—ahead of most European countries and behind only the United States, Canada, Sweden, Switzerland, New Zealand, and Norway. The predominance of Havana's economy and status as an expensive city helped produce averages that misrepresented overall conditions.[31] Both sides of the revolutionary divide have been able to call upon facts and figures to promote the viewpoint of either a prosperous nation benefitting from American affluence or a neocolony suffering from the economic inequalities imposed by a foreign power. The price of independence under revolutionary value continues to be measured through those perspectives.

Cuban intellectual Manuel Yepe described what life was like prior to the revolution. "The truth is that the background for the crimes of the tyranny, and the insurrectional armed struggle against it, was very different from the idyllic image that, 50 years after the fact, some people try to paint for the Cuba of the 50's. In reality, hundreds of children sought sustenance through begging, cleaning car windshields and shining shoes or selling newspapers in the streets and city squares or in the country where poverty was extreme. Many of the elderly and handicapped lived on charity. Long lines of men waited for work. And there was the widespread anguish of thousands of women looking for employment as domestics or prostitutes in brothels or working the streets."[32]

Although no friend of revolution, a 1957 report by the Catholic University Association revealed the extreme disparages that existed between the have and have nots: "Havana is living in extraordinary prosperity while rural areas, especially wage workers, are living in unbelievable stagnant, miserable, and desperate conditions... It is time our country cease being the private fiefdom of a few powerful interests. We firmly hope that, in a few years, Cuba will not be the property of a few, but the true homeland of all Cubans."[33] The church's optimism for the future materialized two years later, but not the way it either envisioned or supported.

The economic inequality and social unrest was brought to a head under the brutal Batista dictatorship, supported by American arms, money, and authority.[34] An estimated 20,000 were killed opposing the government from 1955 to his overthrow, with even President John F. Kennedy using this figure in a rare expression of sympathy for revolutionary goals.[35] Kennedy also came closest to recognizing America could not claim ignorance of the harm its neocolonial control was inflicting on the inhabitants. He understood that Batista was the final expression for but not the cause of revolution when he spoke to an unofficial envoy, French journalist Jean Daniel, who was going to Cuba in late 1963 to meet with Castro: "I believe that there is no country in the world, including all the African regions, including any and all the countries under colonial domination, where economic colonization, humiliation and exploitation were worse than in Cuba, in part owing to my country's policies during the Batista regime... I approved the proclamation which Fidel Castro made in the Sierra Maestra, when he justifiably called for justice and especially yearned to rid Cuba of corruption. I will go even further: to some extent it is as though Batista was the incarnation of a number of sins on the part of the United States. Now we shall have to pay for those sins."[36]

What Kennedy and all other American presidents since could not countenance was Castro changing all rules of the relationship. It was one thing to admit to imperial animus, quite another to have it completely tossed aside. The rarity of Kennedy's insight gave way to the unwavering inability to make intellectual sense of the revolution, allowing base emotionalism to frame the response to the perceived insults and damages levied against America.

Despite the political manipulation and corruption, extrajudicial murders organized by such secret police forces as BRAC and SIM, domination of Cuba's economy and social institutions, rampant racism, a mafia-controlled Havana, a rural population underemployed, illiterate, and with scarce medical or education facilities, and a growing population demanding true self-determination by whatever means, the US reaction was one of disbelief when Fidel made it clear his revolution would not be compromised or rehabilitated as happened in 1933. America's aspirations of rebuilding the system whereby Batista was removed but the pillars of dominion still stood were quickly dashed. It was not long before the United States recognized Castro could neither be controlled nor replaced, and what was gained in 1898 was soon to be lost.

By 1959 the balance had shifted irrevocably, reform was discarded for revolution. Castro successfully propagandized the revolution as truly nationalistic, which by default evolved into a crystallized anti-Americanism, and then focused on the marginalization and removal of the internal opposition he knew the United States would mount. Transformation came swiftly, completely, and often framed in direct conflict with American immoderations. Popular support for radicalization was possible only by aiming it at the social inequalities associated with foreign domination, of which the greater part of the Cuban population, particularly in the rural areas, had tired of finally. The backing of the countryside permitted Castro to act ruthlessly to ensure his revolution would not suffer the same fate as Grau's. Concurrently, America's hostile reaction worked in harmony, if not intentionally, with Castro's political ambitions. He comprehended the turmoil and incongruities of American-dominated prerevolution society had to end. Fidel's strength of personality and force of certainty imposed singularity of purpose to the new structure. It was beyond mere leadership, he became the embodiment of aspirations for the majority. It was his stand of defiance against American hegemony in support of true sovereignty that resonated at the innermost level within much of the population. Fidel has remained the lightning rod for pro- and antirevolutionary fervor ever since.

Castro never wavered in his conviction as he dismantled the old order. He proclaimed history would not repeat itself, and began the process of establishing a Cuban narrative of the past century. "Spain's power had wasted away in our country. Spain had neither the men nor money left to continue the war in Cuba. Spain was routed. The Cubans who had fought for our independence, those Cubans who at that time were laying down their lives, trusted completely the Joint Resolution of the United States Congress. That illusion ended in a cruel disappointment."[37] Clarifying his position, Fidel stated, "The *mambises* (liberators) initiated the war for independence that we have completed on January 1, 1959."[38]

And to the Americans who could not comprehend, "I must think in terms of what is good for Cuba, not for the United States" was his simple explanation to Illinois representative Barratt O'Hara.[39]

Cuban nationalism through triumphant rebellion did not happen in a vacuum but as the culmination from 60 years of foreign domination, abuse, and denial of aspirations. Batista was a means to an end; he was utilized as the final example of American ignominy and made the rallying cry of true revolution easier for the various forces opposed to his methods. Fidel understood reform was insufficient; in the aftermath the hegemonic elements that were rejected were replaced in favor of the other extreme—complete state domination of the political/economic structure. Cuban embrace of that position was expedited by American hostility and siege, which assisted in proving imperial capitalism was anathema to revolutionary socialist ideals.

In less than three months Castro swept aside much of what had been known. New laws cut rents by up to 50 percent, evictions were made illegal, property owned by Batista and his ministers confiscated, the telephone company nationalized and the rates reduced by 50 percent, and racial segregation of public facilities abolished. The morally conservative Castro eliminated the casinos, nightclubs, strip joints, and sex clubs. Free education and health care were evidence of the commitment to the radically changing egalitarian structure of the revolution, and while these programs currently suffer greatly from insufficient resources and material, they remain the foundation blocks of popular support.

On the political front diplomatic relations were established with the United States on January 7, 1959. Initial civility lasted but a few weeks before conflict ensued, the spark ignited by the judiciary investigations against the worst elements of the Batista regime still in country. Many of the trials and executions were televised as a demonstration of the permanency of the new social order, eliciting strong criticism from American politicians and the media, although the vast majority of the Cubans supported the prosecutions, seeing them not only as legitimate but also as a method to end the unrestricted retributions being meted out in the streets. The actions continue to be used as evidence of the ruthlessness of the revolution. Disputes linger as to numbers, with government and outside observers suggesting less than 500; while anti-Castroites claim 20,000 or more. At least one US official realized the necessity to impose such harsh measures, when CIA head Allen Dulles, while opposing what was happening, admitted, "When you have a revolution, you kill your enemies. There were many instances of cruelty and oppression by the Cuban army, and they certainly have the goods on some of these people. Now there probably will be a lot of injustice. It will probably go too far, but they have to go through this."[40] Cubans to this day concur with the assessment. Carlos Manuel Tejera fought against Batista as part of the Havana underground. The young student who later became an important figure in Cuba's opening of the tourist industry after the fall of the Soviet Union was caught by police at the end of the dictator's rule in November 1958 and was severely tortured. "They whipped me, pulled out my nails, kicked me in the kidneys while I was on the floor and I don't hear from the left ear because of the hits they gave me," the 77-year-old resident of AltaHavana, who still bears the scars on his back, recalled. He survived by luck following a mix-up by the authorities with the identity of his brother, who was not wanted. After the arrests of Batista's cohorts began, Tejera was able to identify the man in charge of his abuse, "Captain Mata of the police station, he wasn't the one who hit me, it was Colonel Conrado Carratala, but Mata was the one who ordered the beatings and I was on his list of people to be killed. They executed Mata two weeks after I accused him. Some cases were necessary, so many of Batista's police were killing anyone they could get their hands on. There were lots deserving. But others didn't need to be executed; I remember a prosecutor asking for 20 years for one person, and the judge said the sentence would be the firing squad. It happened like that, it happens in every revolution. Sometimes it went too far."[41] Those executed, Cuban officials insisted, were Batista murderers who kept photographic records of their torture and killings.

Although the trials were effective antirevolutionary propaganda, it was Castro's preliminary policy implementation that convinced the Americans to start plotting a strategy of siege. The new government, as promised, began the process of nationalization of foreign holdings, including the Cuban Telephone Company, a subsidiary of ITT, in March 1959. Next to be targeted was land reform, legalized with the passage of the Agrarian Reform Act two months later. The act established a new society was being created with no turning back. It persuaded internal opposition of Castro's radical intentions, many leaving the country to work against the revolution. Last, the Americans were convinced the new regime could no longer be tolerated. "With the signature of the Agrarian Reform Law, it seems clear that our original hope was a vain one; Castro's Government is not the kind worth saving," so noted a high-ranking official.[42] The Cubans shrugged and as the minister of state Raúl Roa pointed out, "Transforming the system of land-holding... is the indispensible prerequisite in every underdeveloped country for its industrial, political, social and cultural progress."[43]

American officials on the ground recognized the measure was over-whelmingly popular and even necessary. They simply objected to how it was being applied to their property, an estimated 500,000 acres worth. Cuban land, including that of Castro's parents, was also affected. Aimed at break-ing up the large tracks of prime agricultural property and redistributing it to the peasants, farm sizes were limited to 3,333 acres and real estate to 1,000. Holdings exceeding those limits were passed on to farmers in 67-acre lots or developed into state-run cooperatives. An excess of 200,000 farm workers benefited from the reorganization.[44]

Regardless of the depth of the act's implementation, the impact in America was visceral. Political opposition was instantaneous and intense, centered on Cuba's inability to offer immediate and just compensation under US terms. Rejected outright was the revolutionary government's proposed reparation plan based on 20-year fixed-term bonds at interest rates of 4.5 percent, more than one point higher than what was available in the United States at that time. Calculation for compensation was based on the October 1958 assess-ments, unadjusted for 30 years due to landowner pressure not to increase taxes. America demanded payment on the value they put on the land, regard-less of what was reported on the tax rolls.[45] When Cuba refused to submit, the repudiation was used as justification for increased hostility. The lead-ership pleaded with all foreign companies and governments to understand the financial difficulties it was facing—claiming an estimated $500 million was stolen from the treasury when Batista and his followers fled, an assertion backed by US media.[46] While instant payments were nearly impossible, the administration was willing to make good its obligations under accepted international practices, going so far as to offer to set up a committee to resolve the differences and arrange payment schedules—which the United States refused.

Once it was clear no negotiations were possible, the revolutionary administration started nationalizing private business, hotels, storage facilities, and their contents, with no regard to reparation. Cuba soon represented the most uncompensated amount of American claims in history. Eisenhower administration officials told businessmen not even to bother to ask for compensation as it would only complicate the upcoming response, which was articulated by assistant secretary of state for inter-American affairs R. Richard Rubottom Jr.; "We should plan to throw the economic book at the Cubans."[47] Thus was initiated the historical perception that siege was levied as a consequence to property confiscation, a conflation that continues to be heard after two Washington lawyers in early 2012 demanded Cuba start paying back $7 billion in claims.[48] The reform laws were perceived as an act of self-defense required to return Cuban resources to its people, vital for the development of the country. "The nationalizations carried out by the revolutionary government became the Cuban peoples heritage through a process of nationalization undertaken via a forced expropriation procedure which responded to public utility needs, under a constitutional mandate," according to Olga Miranda Bravo, Cuban expert on international rights.[49] At the end of the process the Cubans refuted America's price to pay, reasoning that the only legal mechanism to determine value was on the assessments duly recorded, if those appraisals were artificially manipulated in order not to pay the proper taxes then it was either willful fraud or unintentional deceit. It was also an impressive denial of memory, ignoring the thousands of Spaniards who lost business and property to the Americans after their intervention in Cuba in 1898, compensation neither offered nor discussed.[50]

Cuba's legal framework to initiate the nationalization of land and industry was predicated on UN resolutions, including General Assembly 626 (VII) of December 21, 1952, "The right of people freely to use and exploit their natural wealth and resources is inherent in their sovereignty and is in accordance with the Purposes and Principals of the Charter of the United Nations," ratified by General Assembly Resolution 1803 in December 1962 and charter of Economic Rights and Duties of States approved by Resolution 3281 December 1974.[51]

In the years following the implementation of the Agrarian Reform Act, Cuba settled property ownership disputes with Britain, Canada, France, Italy, Mexico, Spain, and Sweden. The US government refused to accept reparations and the matter remains an enduring propaganda tool. In 1992 State Department spokesman Joe Snyder told the *LA Times*: "The Cuban government, in violation of international law, expropriated billions of dollars worth of private property belonging to U.S. individuals and has refused to make reasonable restitution. The U.S. embargo—and I point out it's not a blockade—is therefore a legitimate response to the unreasonable and illegal behavior of the Cuban government."[52] In November 2001 the United States refused a Cuban offer to negotiate compensation of American properties, holding to its position that the expropriations were illegal.[53] Siege has its role in the matter, with Cuba declaring compensation cannot be fully resolved until the embargo is lifted; the Americans retort the embargo won't be released until their claims are satisfied.

The conflict over compensation solidified America's aggression against the Castro government. Two days after the Agrarian Reform Act went into effect on June 3, 1959, Democratic senator George Smathers from Florida called for the reduction of the Cuban sugar quota.[54] Altering the quota would cause substantial economic damage to the nascent government and signal an irreparable rift in the benevolence of the northern power. It would represent the first attack on Cuba's new society.

American businessmen knew well this Achilles' heel. In June 1959 Robert Klieberg, owner of valuable cattle land in Camaguey, met with US secretary of state Christian Herter to talk about the agrarian legislation that was threatening his holdings. Klieberg said the "communist inspired" law should be opposed and the way to "achieve the necessary results was by economic pressure" aimed at eliminating the sugar quota, "causing widespread further unemployment. The large number of people thus forced out of work would begin to go hungry." Disillusionment, starvation, discontent, and the overthrow of the revolution was the expected outcome, concurrently proving the incapacity of the government. "They would then readily perceive the catastrophic nature of Castro's program, and that would mean the end of Castro politically,"[55] he concluded, articulating the strategy of change through the denial of food and medicine that would be a dependable tool in the arsenal of siege over the next decades.

Fidel Castro understood the tactic of starvation was in large measure a consequence of land reform. In a speech on October 21, 1959, he acknowledged, "We are practically being told that if the Agrarian Reform is carried through, we will strangle you economically. In other words, that on top of having 600,000 unemployed, on top of having a production per capita of 300 pesos, on top of having one fifth of the hospitals we need, of the schools we need and of the most basic things we need, on top of all that, if we do something to get rid of all that, they threaten to starve us."[56]

Intimidation did nothing to alter the program. In January 1960 Cuba expropriated 70,000 acres of property owned by US sugar companies, including 35,000 acres from the United Fruit Company, a move that antagonized the powerful entity known for its involvement in the overthrow of the Arbenz government in Guatemala six years earlier for similar acts.[57] The same month President Eisenhower moved to end all Cuban sugar quotas, which Congress passed in July.

The initial policies of land reform and nationalization of public services became the lightning rod for America's determination to destroy the regime, resulting in a series of initiatives that included the move to deny further loans to Cuba, pressure on other countries to end trade relations and stop selling arms, to accelerate the ending of the sugar quota and begin planning for sabotage and terrorist actions, "for the purposes of hitting Castro on the head," so promised Al Powell of the Office of Foreign Trade.[58] The other function was to ensure the isolation of the Cuban virus, according to a State Department report in 1964, "The primary danger we face in Castro is...in the impact the very existence of his regime has upon the leftist movement in many Latin American countries."[59]

By the early months of 1960 the two dialogues of Cuban history under American protectorate became entrenched, framing the next 50 years of hostility, misunderstanding, and intransigence.

Senator Karl Mundt expressed the prevailing northern perspective, "We who in living memory rescued the island from medieval bondage, we who have given order, vitality, technical wisdom and wealth are now being dammed for our civilizing and cooperative virtues." Fidel Castro presented the revolutionary rejoinder. "We no longer believe in your philosophy of exploitation and privilege. We no longer believe in your philosophy of gold, the gold you rob from the work of other peoples. We no longer are willing to submit to the orders of your ambassadors. We no longer are disposed to follow in tow your reactionary policy, which is the enemy of human progress."[60]

With scant prospects left for negotiation or compromise, what remained was external hostility and internal defenses, policies to encourage financial discomfort and social discontent to the level where the population would overthrow the revolution; against measures designed to prohibit that through a communal contract providing welcomed social programs in return for accepting strict political and economic conformity as the only means to ensure the survival of *patria*.

The development of a siege mentality was accelerated from early 1960 to the Bay of Pigs invasion in April 1961 with the introduction of one of the most violent aspects of American policy—terrorism. Committed by counter-revolutionaries with the backing of the American government both directly and indirectly, the acts included bombings of sugarcane fields, sabotage against commercial and industrial sites, as well as the strafing of Havana residential targets. One such raid in October 1959 resulted in the death of several civilians, followed by other light aircrafts dropping incendiary bombs and antigovernment leaflets, so beginning the long mistrust and intolerance of unauthorized violation of Havana airspace, a situation that externalized in the tragedy of the shoot down of two Brothers to the Rescue planes in 1994.[61]

The sabotage of munitions ship *La Coubre* killed close to 100 after exploding in Havana harbor in March 1960, and later that year the developing social justice programs designed to eliminate illiteracy and bring cultural activities to the countryside were targeted. During the Literacy Campaign more than a dozen teenaged teachers and their adult students were kidnapped, tortured, and killed.[62] A massive psychological terror program in the early

1960s culminated in thousands of Cuban children being sent out of country by their parents based on the lie that the government was going to take over parental authority. The scheme, known as Operation Peter Pan, was coordinated by church officials in Havana and Miami, eventually administered by the State Department. Hundreds of children were sent to orphanages or institutions where many suffered physical and mental abuse.[63]

The vast majority of the early acts were conducted by anti-Castro elements still inside Cuba; by the late 1960s it had shifted to terrorist organizations in South Florida made up of the extreme right-wing opposition that had left the island. In between were the murders, bombings, and sabotage of the terrorist program Operation Mongoose. A series of incidents of biological terrorism affected plants and animals in the 1980s, the worst when Dengue 2 was introduced in 1981 causing the death of 101 children and forcing the government to sustain an expensive annual spraying regimen. The next decade brought a bombing campaign against tourist facilities in Havana and the beach resort of Varadero, killing Italian Fabio Di Celmo and injuring dozens. The single most horrific incident struck in 1976 with the destruction of Cubana Airlines Flight 455 as it was taking off from Barbados, killing all 73 on board. It remains the second worst act of air terrorism in the Americas after 9/11. One of the internationally recognized masterminds of the act, Cuban-born Luis Posada Carriles, continues to live unfettered in Miami.[64]

The terrorism played a major role in the government's need to establish intensive internal security systems as the most effective way to thwart future acts and to assist in determining who supported the revolution and who did not. A mentality of assuming guilt before innocence of suspected antirevolutionaries was being established within revolutionary law, based in part on the nation's Spanish legal heritage.[65] The population was told these intrusive surveillance measures and restrictions to civil rights were required if the new social order was to survive, and to ensure personal safety.[66] American officials understood the acts of terror during the early years were specifically designed to disrupt, destabilize, and force the Cuban government to divert precious resources, as well as induce intrusive civil measures. A CIA report of May 1961 acknowledged that in response to the terrorism the government would be "stepping up internal controls and defense mechanisms" directly leading to civil rights restrictions that could be propagandized by the US government as evidence of the totalitarian nature of the revolution. The intent was to force the government to build the siege walls higher. With little other option, Fortress Cuba strengthened itself through unconditional commonality.

Politicians had no hesitation in supporting the violence. South Carolina representative Mendel Rivers invoked historical perceptions while threatening in 1960, "That bearded pipsqueak of the Antilles, who seized American property in a country that was conceived by America ..." will soon regret his actions. "When ingratitude on the part of a nation reaches the point that it has in Cuba, it is time for American wrath to display itself in no uncertain terms."[67]

American and counterrevolutionary aggression persuaded Castro to increase internal surveillance systems, which placed limitations on various civil rights, and additionally provided the leader with the rationalization to move against more moderate elements within the government who were continuing to preach accommodation with the United States, such as President Manuel Urrutia and popular revolutionary Huber Matos.[68] The early indications of a siege mentality—increased intolerance to differing viewpoints in order to maintain security—was demonstrating itself by late 1960. It would only worsen as American hostility traveled in step with Cuban inflexibility throughout the following decades. The extremes of each brought aggression, fanaticism, and a restrictive society to the people of Cuba.

By the end of 1960 the overthrow of Castro was official government policy. Millions of dollars were going through the CIA and the State Department to that end, by any means possible. A major component became the development of a more traditional military response, President Eisenhower approving the CIA document drafted by J.C. King, officer in charge of Latin America in the Western Hemisphere Division. The proposal was one part of the all-encompassing strategy being laid under the April 1960 State Department punishment guidelines: "Every possible means should be undertaken promptly to weaken the economic life of Cuba....a line of action which, while as adroit and inconspicuous as possible, makes the greatest inroads in denying money and supplies to Cuba, to decrease monetary and real wages, to bring about hunger, desperation and overthrow of the government."[69]

Conditions in Cuba facilitated American intentions. Three months prior to the State Department's April declaration, Cuba had signed a trade agreement with the Soviet Union, which included the purchase of Soviet petroleum. When the oil reached the island in June, American-owned ESSO and Texaco and the British-Dutch company Shell refused to refine it. Castro calmly responded that if they wanted to continue to do business in Cuba, they would have no choice. Company heads declined, the refineries were nationalized. In retaliation the United States canceled all sugar imports from Cuba. Castro responded with Law 851[70] on August 6 by nationalizing American businesses, industries, and farms. By mid-September, Castro took over the US-owned banks, declaring in terms that heightened jangled American nerves, "It is not possible for a considerable portion of national banking to remain in the hands of imperialistic interests that inspired the reduction of our sugar quota by an act of cowardly and criminal economic aggression."[71] The radicalization provided additional proof that El Comandante was unstable, and worse, a communist. On September 18, 1960, Castro addressed the UN General Assembly and protested what he called US aggression. A month later the Urban Reform Law was put into effect, nationalizing all commercial real estate and transferring residential renters into buyers. Weeks after more US properties, including the Readers Digest printing plant and Pan Am's airport equipment, fell under the drive to nationalize. The Eisenhower administration responded to Cuba's moves by a partial embargo on commercial goods, including prohibitions on certain food and medicine.[72]

In retaliation, the rest of US property was taken. Embassy staffs were reduced by both sides on charges of spying, providing cover for the United States to close its office in January 1961. The President made good on his threat to suspend sugar purchases by the end of the year, the economic pain alleviated by the Soviet Union and socialist bloc countries purchasing all excesses based on five-year agreements taking 20 percent of Cuban sugar at fair market prices, twice what they were getting under US quota. The arrangement set off a three-decade-long rationale for siege—Cuba being nothing more than an economic and political servant to Soviet will. American officials had themselves exposed the duplicity of the charge months before, making it clear that any movement by Cuba to leave the American sphere would have been considered just as damaging to US security. Neutrality was not an option. "Witness our shock when it was recently reported that the revolutionary government of Cuba planned to be neutral," a member of the House subcommittee detailed after Castro publicly stated in late 1959 his desire to strike a balance between the Cold War participants, shown in the criticism at the United Nations of the United States for Guatemala, China for Tibet, and the Soviet Union for Hungary.[73]

Cuba's embrace into the Soviet arms has overwhelmingly been portrayed as purely ideologically driven, with far less examination of the substantial economic and security components rooted in scarce options to maneuver elsewhere under unwavering hostility and isolation. In the Cold War realities of the time it was not a hard decision which side to pick when one had a knife in its hand, the other a dollar bill. The policies started under President Eisenhower had a considerable role in the decision to move into the protection of the Russian umbrella, a matter equally of pragmatism than creed.[74] Conversely, Cuba's welcome of the Soviets was more complicated, hesitant, and problematic than has usually been portrayed in official revolutionary history. Che made his preference toward the militant China model known openly, and Fidel and much of the leadership were often derisive of the Soviets personally. Cuba's first trade deal with a socialist country occurred in October 1960 not with the Russians, but with China.[75] Anibal Escalante, a hard-line prerevolutionary communist and a leading figure in the old Cuban party, was pushed out of the reformation of the political form for being too cozy with the Soviets. Fidel consistently criticized the international communist parties having to take marching orders from Moscow. But economics, siege, and pragmatism finally convinced the Soviet bear was better to hug than to keep at arm's length.[76] The triumph of 1959 was born without Soviet assistance, and while the Moscow connect was vital for its continued survival, the revolution never lost its Caribbean flavor or its Cuban obstinacy.

From the early 1960s to the end of the socialist block 35 years later, the Cuban Revolution fought siege within the embrace of orthodox communism to a benefit of billions of dollars in preferential trade arraignments, political conformity, and national security. Fidel might have been an ideological neophyte in the early days, "In January 1959 I didn't know a single Soviet, or the leaders,"[77] but he soon appreciated who had the carrot and who had the stick. "Here you took our planes, the Soviets give us planes" was his reaction to American authorities confiscating his aircraft while he was at the United Nations speaking for the first time in 1960. Before leaving, Khrushchev lent him one to get back home.[78] Months later the Soviets gave Cuba more than planes; buying the excess sugar quote, sending technical assistance, arranging multimillion-dollar loans and grants. And considerable military assistance.

The Soviets provided the only viable alternative within the Cold War context, recognizing the small country's desired attempts to establish a third option through the Non-Aligned Movement. Motivated by US hostility demonstrating itself incapable of serious negotiation other than demands for dismantling the regime, Castro pragmatically moved toward the Eastern empire that was portrayed to be tightly aligned to the revolution's social and political aspirations. Embracing Soviet welcome and security was consequence as much as design. The arrangement immediately provided a military bulwark against the threat of American interference. "We are defended by one of the most powerful military forces in history," Che Guevara commented in response to Khrushchev's backing up of his Latin comrade, "Soviet artillery can support the Cuban people with their rocket fire if the aggressive forces in the Pentagon dare to launch an intervention against Cuba."[79]

Fidel's announcement of the socialist nature of his revolution at the Bay of Pigs provided the stage to claim he had been a closet communist all along. Dispute still lingers if his comment was honest or opportunistic, a matter of little concern as the revolution wholeheartedly welcomed the Soviet system and its Eastern Block allies. In spite of letting these foreigners inside the castle, the Cuban Revolution retained its unique Latin socialist flavor that often saw it go its own way in foreign relations, much to the consternation of the benefactors.[80]

American measures that encouraged Cuba's move into the Soviet fold fit perfectly into siege strategy, providing the most plausible and appropriate pretext from the 1960s to the 1990s as to motivation why polices of opprobrium, aggression, and blockade had to be implemented. Prerevolution the Americans would have been able simply to shut down the trade association, as they had done with England in 1904. With Fidel in charge, policy had to be more extensive than just pressuring other countries not to do business with Cuba, however an effective option that remained. America was successful in persuading the Brits not to follow through on a jet fighter order, and was applying considerable diplomatic weight on others to end all relations. As countries from the "free world" refused to sell arms or anything else to Cuba, CIA director Allan Dulles expected that the Soviets would offer to step in, which they did, accomplishing two US policy goals. The first would provide propaganda to show the Cuban Revolution willingly giving themselves over to Soviet influence, ignoring America's real efforts to deny any other option. The United States now had the pretense to take care of the communist menace so close to home, unhindered by any level of violence or policy extremes that would have met public resistance if applied to anyone but Fidel Castro. Media and political elite were invaluable in framing the debate—it was one thing to lose Cuba, quite another to lose it to the official enemy. Cuba became the most imperative hotspot in the proxy war against the Soviets. This one was considered far too close to home, giving officials the perfect warning flag to wave while ignoring the more historically relevant motivations for the revolution. At the time Dulles relayed to the British ambassador, "he hoped that any refusal by us to supply arms would directly lead to a Soviet bloc offer to supply. Then he might be able to do something."[81]

The second policy aim, once the Soviets started selling arms to Castro, was to reveal Cuba as a military threat working under the proxy of the enemy with intent to endanger American interests in Latin American.[82] Dulles's circular logic was not entirely based on an unfounded accusation, as the revolutionaries were trying their best to spread their word to similar movements around the globe struggling against right-wing dictatorships, although often without the compliance, and in many cases the direct disagreement, of Soviet geopolitical objectives. Cuba's support of resistance movements, principally the Latin American types, was based as much on ideological compatibility as well as a method to break America's isolation attempts, which in turn provided enough ammunition to tighten siege; "They internationalized the blockade. We internationalized guerrilla warfare," Castro observed.[83] More modern, nonmilitary efforts to break the seclusion have been developed through organizing comradeship groups throughout the world, overseen by the Cuban Institute of Friendship Between People (ICAP).

Besides the extraterritoriality arm-twisting to induce other nations not to engage, with the resultant Soviet-relationship consequences for Cuba, the United States also became disposed to conduct more direct action against Castro. The increasing hostility against Cuba, including a proposed military response, was intended to achieve a multiplicity of outcomes, according to the State Dept memo, "to bring about the replacement of the Castro Regime with one more devoted to the true intentions of the Cuban people and more acceptable to the US in such a manner as to avoid any appearance of US intervention."[84] Castro wasn't fooled by America's attempts at misdirection. The final straw for Havana came on November 1, 1960, when the US ambassador to the United Nations, James Wadsworth, called Cuba's charges of a planned attack "monstrous distortions and downright falsehoods." The Cubans responded they had irrefutable proof of the invasion, information that had become common knowledge in Miami.

The United States decided it could no longer tolerate the insult and ingratitude of the Castro government—nor its accurate reading of purpose— severing diplomatic ties three months prior to the single act that solidified the revolutionary government and convinced America of no other response than siege. Planning for the Bay of Pigs incursion, code named Operation Pluto, had begun under the Eisenhower administration in early 1960, and a little more than a year later the ill-fated mission was given the green light by President Kennedy. An estimated 1,500 antirevolutionary exiles landed on the southern coast swamps of the Zapata Peninsula on April 17, soon finding themselves overwhelmed by the defending forces led by Castro himself. Most were captured, eventually returned to the United States for millions of dollars of medical and food supplies. The return of the prisoners was seen by the Cuban side as indemnity, Americans as ransom.

Cuba had turned Thucydides's theory[85] upside down at Playa Girón, and it could not be tolerated. The disaster that had befallen America's international reputation elicited intense expressions of revenge from those such as Under-secretary of State Chester Bowles who was determined "to punish Castro for the humiliation that he has brought to our door."[86] The punishment, as usual, came down disproportionately on the citizens.

The failure of the Bay of Pigs exposed America's indisputable objective toward the Castro government, and established decades of rancor, misunderstanding, and mistrust. Antirevolutionaries were more convinced than ever that the Cuban people were looking for any chance to rise up; top Castro officials were equally determined not to let that happen through foreign manipulation and so constructed a closed society as the only alternative to protect what it was trying to build, and to secure what was accomplished. It left the inhabitants with a stark choice—those who supported the new order stayed; those who did not were marginalized or left. It was the physical establishment of Castro's June 1961 call to combat siege: "Inside the revolution everything, outside the revolution nothing."[87] His declaration plunged Cuban society into 20 plus years of stratification that restricted cultural, economic, and political expressions of a revolution in great part developed on the necessity of self-criticism. That luxury was eliminated in favor of conformity; the condition not to alter in any serious form until the last half-decade under the openings of Raúl Castro and the need to examine new alternatives in the face of a crumbling bureaucracy and international economic meltdown. The current reforms are confronting the obvious deficiencies of a severe command economy based on administrative overload; attempting to strike a rational compromise among market incentives, rudimentary entrepreneurship, and the preservation of the *logros sociales* (social success) programs the revolution was built upon.

Following the Bay of Pigs debacle the American policymakers helped deflect the failure by developing the premise the invasion was justified because Castro had betrayed his own revolution, yet another attempt to validate increasing siege for the population's sake thereby sanctioning future attempts at overthrowing the regime. "The Cuban leaders had betrayed the authentic and autonomous revolution to achieve freedom, democracy and social justice," declared the official white paper on Cuban policy.[88]

The disaster of Bahia de Cochinos has been blamed historically on poor preparation and the refusal of the White House to engage the air force. As important was the repudiation of the local population to bow to US expectations and rejection of the endeavor to reinsert foreign authority. Castro turned the invasion into a stunning propaganda victory—gaining the acceptance from the majority to his declared commitment to socialism, which shortly evolved into Soviet-style Marxism. An equally significant outcome in 1961 was the irreconcilable demand for solidarity in order for the revolution to endure siege. Historically Cuba had been socially and politically fractured while under US rule, lived through a revolution in 1933 that was ended by American fiat, and then found itself in a dangerous split between those who desired the maintenance of a form of US overlordship and the greater populous who supported the revolution's promise, if not all the methods. To unify the various anti-Batista forces, to ensure the establishment of the new social order, and to survive both American and internal anti-revolutionary aggression, Fidel Castro moved down the path of "*Patria o Muere*"—homeland or death. In order to achieve the social configuration required to instill this wall of national unity, Castro and the top echelon incorporated the leadership skills of the old Cuban Communist Party (PSP), an organization that until the last minute before the triumph had been opposed to Castro's violent methods. The need for the PSP expertise, and the undeniable influence of the sympathetic views of Raúl Castro and Che Guevara, helped convince Fidel to bring in some of the top officials of the party such as Armando Hart, Blas Roca, and Anibal Escalante, the latter two eventually falling into disfavor.[89] Moving the revolution administratively toward the communist formula and abandoning the practice if not the expressions of walking the middle ground of nonalignment were made easier by unequivocal Soviet assistance and unrelenting American aggression.

Resistance to the direction in which the revolution was heading was soon being equated with dissidence, one small step away from treason in a besieged castle, particularly when factions within the opposition then as now have been proven to be aligned with the enemy's objectives. The answer to counterrevolutionary activity came early on with the establishment of the Committee for Defense of the Revolution (CDR). Created in late 1960, the primary purpose of the CDR was to neutralize the extensive net of American spies and anti-Castro cadres operating inside the island. The CDR, based partially on an American antecedent,[90] worked as a pre-electronic social network where neighborhoods would be on guard for those expressing pro-US, or antigovernment, sympathies. Thousands were rounded up and jailed before the invasion at the Bay of Pigs, many on nothing more than idle gossip, attempts to settle personal scores, or acts of petty jealousies. The CDR has evolved into a deeply integrated community-based program not only to keep vigilance against antirevolutionary sentiment, with all the irrational rumor elements still in play, but also in its current appearance as a method to maintain neighborhood safety and social connectivity, as well as to report on infrastructure repairs.

David Lyon, at the Queens University Surveillance Studies Center, commented that the CDR is not unique. "It has reflected influence of the US style of intelligence; the CIA works dependent upon informants to gain information. In Cuba their surveillance efforts are very much based on that same thing, the use of informants. The CDR was set up in the early years as a way to determine anti-revolutionary activity. It's curious that the Cubans are using the same techniques against the Americans, to help withstand the pressures that the Americans are applying."[91]

Shortly following the establishment of CDR the government configured its mass participation organizations in the form of the Young Communist League (UJC), the Federation of Cuban Women (FMC), Trade Union Federation of Cuba (CTC), National Association of Small Farmers (ANAP), Federation of University Students (FEU), José Marti Children's Organization, and Association of Combatants of the Cuban Revolution (ACRC). One of the earliest associations to help combat antirevolutionaries in the country was the National Revolutionary Militia (MNR) set up in early 1960. This construction of populous assemblies constituted a major development in the government's stipulation for solidarity through participation, as well as a technique to combat siege through a sense of patriotic comradeship.

Life in the early 1960s after the Bay of Pigs was being structured on the posts of mass organizations in order to create the sense of community responsibility and personal investment in the radical new society—vital elements for the survival of the revolutionary order. The other purpose aimed to implement social conformity standards. It was an easy matter to determine the few who were not involved in these groups, and to establish why. The government used the threat of identification to instill political solidarity and spotlight those who did not obey the rules. Taking advantage of the real but abnormal conditions of siege this ability was manipulated to create fear and mistrust among neighbors, to marginalize the nonconformists, to jail those who stepped too far outside the norm, and to help push out potential opponents. The massive base of the collective pyramid came to a sharp summit at the head, figuratively and literally, of Fidel Castro. His strength of personality, confidence, oratory skills, and the accomplishment of promising true Cuban sovereignty for the first time in its history gave him impetus to challenge and defeat US hegemony and to implement a set of strict rules that had to be abided if the citizens wanted to participate in the benefits of the social justice programs—free education, health, housing, and enough food to eat in return for accepting the government rules for security, including one-party rule, civil rights boundaries, control of the economy, and prejudice against those who didn't conform. The more extreme elements of those rules have been partially predicated on the construct of defense against American hostility. The accord between government and citizen holds to this day, although not as secure as it once was, and continues to be intentionally denied or disingenuously ignored by the American side.

The consequences of the Bay of Pigs were well understood by the Canadian ambassador of the time, commenting that the Cuban government's installation of internal policies to combat US siege "substantiated the government's warnings against imperialist aggression from the United States; the ardent patriotism which it elicited enabled the Cuban regime to suppress all internal opposition, to step up the pace of its 'socialist' revolution and to sanctify as sacrifices the exigencies of the economic crisis which Cuba is experiencing."[92] Finally, the ill-advised invasion at the Zapata Swamp accelerated a momentum toward "the building of a surveillance state that Fidel Castro had once considered avoidable."[93] It removed the last major inhibition holding Castro back from a domestic crackdown to ensure the revolution would not be destroyed by America's siege.

The year 1961 marked the turning point for US planners who realized after the *Giron* fiasco there would be no simple or quick military success. Instead, strategy turned irrevocably to the forces of encirclement. In the 18 months from the defeat at the Bay of Pigs to the Cuban Missile Crisis of October 1962 the execution of besiegement was augmented, refined, and immutable. America responded as they desired to, Cuba as they had to.

Legislatively American policy included the presidential authorization of a total embargo of trade under the Foreign Aid Act and Cuban Import Regulations; confirming the Cuban sugar quota at zero and prohibiting the sale of medicine and food unless under strict, almost impossible to obtain, license requirements. State Department officials strong-armed NATO allies to end Cuban trade in military and strategic goods, Britain particularly susceptible despite denying cancellation of a shipment of arms as a result of pressure. A loan of $100 million by Western European banks was suddenly withdrawn following US complaints.[94] Postal service ended between the two antagonists. Extraterritorial aspects surfaced as the Foreign Assistance Act of 1962 warned American largess would be terminated to those countries that provide aid to Cuba. In conjunction, ships involved in trade with Cuba were to be included on a "black list" prohibited from calling on US ports. American officials insisted European and Latin American countries draw up measures to support the embargo.[95] Propaganda efforts were ratcheted up through the establishment of Radio Swan, a clandestine station set up near Honduras, broadcasting nonstop reports of the failure of revolutionary economic measures and social difficulties, encouraging the citizens to rise up and toss out the regime.[96] During this period a series of academic institutions such as the University of Pittsburgh, Harvard, and University of Miami, in support with think tanks Rand Corporation, Heritage Foundation, and American Enterprise Institute, developed Cuban study programs, most in conformity to US policy perspectives based on the transition back to prerevolutionary social and economic conditions.[97]

Cuba's economy suffered immediately from the early stages of the trade embargo. By 1962 replacement parts for many factories were impossible to obtain, nearly one-quarter of all buses inoperable, and 50 percent of passenger rail cars out of service. Supplies or raw materials for agricultural machinery and food requirements became unobtainable.[98] Almost 100 percent of machinery and infrastructure was American made, and the process of switching over to Soviet technology was slow, painful, and expensive.

Politically the United States clarified its position when President Kennedy authorized the application of the 1917 Trading With the Enemy Act (TWEA) in early March 1962.[99] The act, originally passed upon America's entry into World War I, had been utilized exclusively in times of war or national emergency, prohibiting trade or any assistance to the "enemy in time of war." It sanctioned the total embargo on trade between the two countries, legislating the economic component of siege.[100]

At the same time US officials were expanding the legal assemblage of besiegement by solidifying the blockade, intensifying propaganda, encouraging an internal opposition controlled externally, and escalating efforts to isolate Cuba from any and all potential trading partners, the terrorism expanded to target government and leadership figures. Bombs exploded in Cubana airlines offices in New York, Montreal, and elsewhere, Cuban diplomat Felix Garcia was assassinated outside the United Nations in 1980. The one person they couldn't get, despite hundreds of attempts, was the main man.[101] Historical records released in the past decade demonstrate the lengths the CIA and counterrevolutionary elements went to eliminate *El Comandante*. In the 1960s efforts ranged from poisoning his milk shake, an exploding cigar, a contaminated skin diving suit, and a potion that would make his beard fall off, apparently hoping it would cause him to die of embarrassment. Besides the well-documented connection with the US government and mafia figures to take out Castro, the CIA apparently made contact with high-level Cuban officials including Major Rolando Cubela who was involved in a plan to eliminate his boss with a poison pen. The scheme was revealed in 1966 and Cubela received 25 years in prison.[102]

Those who wanted Castro eliminated were convinced once the head was chopped off the serpent would die. American experts concluded he was holding the entire Cuban population under a cult of personality, assisted by the most insidious internal security controls in history. Justifying the removal was partially based on his lack of fitness to rule due to his mental instability. President Eisenhower described him as early as 1960 as, "a madman—a man mentally unbalanced."[103] The theme was reanimated by George Bush Jr. who dismissed Castro as beneath worth to consider as a rational person. "What's the point in talking to Castro?" The President added, "One day, the good lord will take Fidel Castro away,"[104] assuming then the population would wake up, overthrow the regime, and open the castle doors, letting the Yankees walk in and again rescue the undeserving nation and its ungrateful people, as in 1898.

Plans to kill Castro worked in concurrence with other plots to force the government to overreact. Acceptable proposals came under The Cuba Project, instituted in 1959 shortly after the Agrarian Reform Act, as the overarching clandestine agenda against the revolution. The most infamous offshoot of the Project was Operation Mongoose, running from just after the Bay of Pigs April 1961 to the end of the Missile Crisis October 1962, and employing more than 400 full-time agents. Headed by Air Force general Edward Lansdale, the operation coordinated hundreds of acts of terrorism, sabotage against Cuban industrial targets, increased propaganda efforts, and the tightening of the economic blockade.[105] One of the many objectives was spelt out in Task 21, asking for recommendations "for inducing failures in food crops." Less than a decade later Cuba was experiencing major problems with a variety of previously unknown plagues including swine fever, avian flu, sugarcane rust, tobacco fungus, cereal rot, rice pest—evidence pointing to the intentional introduction of the germs.[106] Tasks 16–20 was aimed at refusing Cuban ships entry into American ports, while Task 23 specifically cited Japan as a country to apply pressure to in order to convince them to end trade with Havana, which was substantially decreased over the following months.[107] Operation Mongoose has been described as one of the twentieth century's worst examples of state-sponsored terrorism.[108] Lansdale imagined a wide range of objectives, including sabotaging shipping in Cuban waters, transportation and communication systems, equipment to refine petroleum, power plants, industry good supplies, military and police installations. The stated goal "to help the people of Cuba to overthrow the Communist regime from within Cuba"[109] has been the longest-standing objective to the successful completion of punishment through siege. Knowledge of American strategy and the desired response from the Cuban side were recognized at the highest levels within government circles, not excluding the application of acts of terrorism. Robert Kennedy was assigned the task of synchronizing all efforts to bring down the Cuban government, declaring it was "the top priority of the United States government—all else is secondary—no time, money, effort or manpower is to be spared."[110] Violent methods formed an important component of the priority, as the Kennedy brothers sought to bring the "terrors of the earth" to Cuba, according to JKF advisor and historian Arthur Schlesinger.[111]

Operatives were able to identify weaknesses in the Cuban government and opportunities to exploit them, knowing it would induce the revolutionaries to enhance internal security measures, having no other method to oppose US strategy. CIA officials understood the deployment of Operation Mongoose would have an important contributing factor in the development of a siege mentality. In fact, they were counting on it, made clear in the 1961 report expecting the development of even more reactionary social measures through increasing internal security and defense systems[112] with the possible result, "to bring about the revolt of the Cuban people."[113] The intent was to oblige the government into ever more radical steps to ensure its safety and the safety of its citizens, ramifications well expected, as revealed in a frank CIA report: "The policies of aggression are pushing more Cubans into the Castro side, making it easier for him to control the population."[114]

Cuban society was beginning to close to those outside the revolution as narrowly defined by the state. Institutional pettiness against anyone who might share revolutionary goals but promote different means was becoming commonplace. Good citizens lost jobs, social standing, and the desire to remain simply for expressing concern for the hardening bureaucracy. Jorge Vilas was a university-level professor in 1961, a loyal revolutionary who objected to the government imposing strict conditions of what was acceptable course material. "Revolutionary thought was suppose to be critical, always thinking of what could be improved. Che often said that. The regime didn't want to hear that then, they told us how to teach, that everything was fine, that the Revolution would overcome American imperialism and that any teacher that said differently was counter-revolutionary. I was in support of the regime, but it became impossible to accept what they were doing. I was afraid to tell my students things I knew were true, problems we were having with the economy, with society, but the government said were not."[115] Vilas left at the first opportunity, turning his support for Castro into active, nonviolent opposition.

The government found itself increasingly as the small nail under the colossal American hammer, inducing it to proceed against all forms of what it considered to be antirevolutionary expressions. Nonconformity, a revolutionary value previously, was now a comfort that could not be afforded. Under American weight the breath of the great social transformation was being restricted, and in panic came the demand for internal singularity of purpose. The revolution established true Cuban sovereignty concordant to the fulfillment of the process started in 1898, this nationalism soon evolving into a society antithetical to the 1959 ideals of inclusiveness. Externally it imposed the progression into the security of an ultraorthodox policy ally; the embrace of Soviet-style communism validated by the inability to ascertain a diversity of international economic and political relations.

The dilemma was in the majority predicated upon American effectiveness in the creation of siege. It came at a cost, not just to Cuba. In strict financial terms the United States spent an estimated $40 million in the course of the Cuba Project, just the start of the hundreds of millions allocated in the past halfcentury to destroy the revolution. Institutions such as United States Agency for International Development (USAID) continue to allocate large budgets to the function, and millions more are paid to politicians on both sides of the aisle to manipulate support of siege.[116]

The fiscal equation for Cuba continues to be tallied in the amount of precious financial and material resources diverted for protection. Officials claim the siege has damaged the economy to the tune of hundreds of billions of dollars.[117] The social price became easier to observe. As American external hostility increased in the early 1960s, Cuban internal tolerance decreased. In equilibrium to America's antagonism from the period April 1961 to October 1962, the government abandoned all hesitancy in its nationalization program, cracked down on domestic opposition and antirevolutionary activity, constrained public assembly and freedom of expression, and installed expensive and demeaning procedures for citizens wishing to travel. The final vestiges of privately owned businesses were eliminated, including the last of American-supported media. Reciprocity to siege was put firmly in place. And then it allowed the fear of a second assault and the insecurity brought on by the economic blockade to play a determining factor in the events of October 1962.[118]

The Cuban Missile Crisis was balanced equally on American action and Cuban reaction. Revolutionary leaders firmly believed, with considerable validation, that the United States was planning another attempt at a military solution to the Castro problem.[119] It led to the reckless acceptance of the

Soviet offer to install nuclear missiles, resulting in their premature detection and near nuclear catastrophe. The resolution provided a major propaganda coup for the young President Kennedy, and a severe rupture in the emerging Soviet-Cuban relations that took years to patch up.[120] The Americans reluctantly promised not to attempt another assault, although the Cuban side did not fully trust the guarantee. With reason. Documentary evidence has shown the Kennedy administration set December 1, 1963, for a second invasion using the full force of the military. Run under the control of Robert Kennedy, the undertaking also involved assassinating Castro and replacing him with then head of the Cuban army Juan Almeida.[121] With JFK's murder a week before, everything was cancelled and history changed. The Cuban government believed the conspiracy claims against Almeida were a CIA destabilization plot, and no movement was made against the general, who died in 2009 with full state honors and a day of mourning across the island.

There was one additional effect of the October Crisis—the completion of siege. While resolution brought America's pledge to relinquish any future military solution to the revolution, it also shifted policy irrevocably to a solution based on economic deprivation, propaganda, isolation, and unremitting hostility against the support population. Efforts at preventing others from helping to alleviate the encirclement were highly successful. In late 1962 Cuba was expelled from the Organization of American States (OAS).[122] American diplomatic persuasion played an important part in the final tally, as was a timely $2.8 million bribe to the Haitian government from USAID to build a new runway at Port Au Prince.[123] Multilateral sanctions were imposed by the OAS on July 26, 1964, kept in place for the next decade. It took until 2009 before the island's membership suspension was lifted, and to date Cuba has declined the offer to reintegrate itself into the organization.

"Limiting the flow of hard currency into the country as much as possible by making Cuba's commercial dealings with other nations as difficult as possible, through the use of blackmail and pressures against foreign counterparts and by preventing Cuba from making use of the hard currency obtained" was a key component in siege policy, according to Dr. Andrés Zaldívar Diéguez, an expert on American subversive activities.[124]

With efforts to cut Cuba from much of the rest of the world heightening, the next stage was codifying the economic blockade components, settled by the establishment of the July 1963 Cuban Assets Control Regulations (CACR) under section 5(b) of the Trading With the Enemy Act. The stated goal of the sanctions aimed to "isolate the Cuban government economically and deprive it of U.S. dollars."[125] The act has encompassed all essential aspects of the blockade in effect since then, including the freezing of Cuban capital in the United States and mandating the Treasury Department to regulate the prohibition of all economic, financial, and trade transactions related to the revolutionary government. Travel restrictions were put in place, prohibiting Americans from spending money in Cuba unless under government guidelines, thereby effectively making it impossible for the average person to see for themselves what the revolution was all about. The CACR has been modified over the last four decades; travel restrictions were eased under the presidency of Jimmy Carter and then tightened under Reagan. Currently President Obama has permitted Cuban-Americans to visit their homeland unrestricted, and eased back on some of the people-to-people licensed program limits, but tourists are still not legally entitled to go. Furthermore, the CACR prohibited the direct or indirect export of US products, services, and technology to Cuba. The Treasury's Department Office of Foreign Assets Control (OFAC) remains in charge of interpreting and implementing the CACR provisions through a set of regulations, providing criminal penalties for violation of the rules, ranging up to 10 years in prison and corporate fines of $1 million. Tourists can also be faced with a $55,000 penalty, though rarely imposed. Most are offered negotiated settlements of $1,000 or less. For years no judges were assigned to the cases for fear of constitutional challenges, and those caught were often able to circumvent the demands for a payment by asking for a hearing; the matter then dropped. George W. Bush appointed two adjudicators to handle the backload, to little effect.[126] A sore point with antiembargo critics surfaced when it was reported the amount of staff allocated to OFAC was considerably higher to catch violators of Cuban travel than those assigned to track down terrorist money after 9/11. According to a 2004 letter sent by OFAC officials to Congress, the Treasury Department had four full-time employees to investigate Osama bin Laden and Saddam Hussein, and over two dozen for embargo violations.[127] An estimated 60 percent of all cases between 2000 and 2006 involved Cuba.[128] The upshot has been charges laid against unsuspecting little old ladies who went on unlicensed cultural trips, to the detriment of efforts to crack down on funds used for international terrorism.[129]

The new CACR restrictions prohibited Americans from conducting financial dealings with the Castro side, making it almost impossible to settle nationalization claims. Products containing Cuban raw materials or parts were barred from sale in the United States by companies outside of the island, and funds were cut off to countries that did not adopt measures "to prevent ships or aircraft under its registration from transporting articles of economic assistance, weapons or equipment, materials or merchandise to Cuba."[130]

Cuba's access to the capitalist markets had been effectively blocked by the end of 1963. America's threatening "black list" of ships was doing its work. Only 59 vessels docked in Cuban harbors, compared to 352 during the same period the year before. The island experienced a 60 percent drop in the number of transports from capitalist countries, from 932 in 1962 to 359 in 1963. The National Security Council affirmed Cuba was "substantially isolated from the Free World."[131]

With little other option available, the government through ideological alliance and economic pragmatism moved rapidly into the Soviet sphere. The increasing intolerance leading to the implementation of harsh internal policies to counteract siege would in all probability have been less radical if the opportunity remained to engage in normal trade and diplomatic relations with more than just the socialist block. Any moderating influence the "free world" might have had on Cuban domestic strategies and international relations were negated by American action. The siege hastened Castro's journey to orthodox Marxism of the Soviet kind, accommodating those critics who believed him to be a fellow traveler all along. With other social/historic elements and personal relationships additionally playing an influential role, it was the siege that became the motor driving the social radicalization of one side and the hostile narrow-mindedness of the other.

And America had no intention of letting up.

Fabian Escalante, one of the foremost authorities on US covert operations against Cuba explained, "The economic, information, cultural and political blockade would be stepped up. To this end, in the first months of 1963 the Treasury Department created a special police force, the 'global detectives' whose mission was to visit the capitals of all countries that traded with Cuba, to pressure governments, business people and even, to inform CIA operates of Cuba-bound loads warehoused in ports, so that they could be sabotaged."[132]

Diplomatically the Cuban Asset Control Regulation was utilized to convince other nations to end relations with the revolutionary government. Only Mexico and Canada resisted American persuasion. Aid to England, France, Spain, and other allies was drastically scaled back for their hesitancy to abide by the no-trade demands. State Department representative Richard Phillips announced in July 1963 that the US government wanted Britain, Canada, Mexico, and Spain to shut down commercial air flights to Cuba. The reaction was mixed.[133] The economic pressure persisted in lockstep with the more direct aggressive action. Programs under Operation Mongoose ended, but the violence maximized over the next years through the exploits of such Miami-based counterrevolutionary organizations as Omega 7 and Alpha 66, with the indirect assistance and financial aid of the government.

The next serious addition to siege came with the Cuban Adjustment Act, 1966—designed to encourage those inside the walls to escape to the safe confines of those imposing the encirclement. Cubans were given immigration advantages that no others were offered, such as permanent residence status after only one year in the United States.[134] Additionally they were reclassified as political refugees regardless of the reason for leaving Cuba, provided with a package of social service benefits including welfare, unemployment payments, job training, child care, English classes, and free medical care. Assistance is provided even if they lived in a third country, or if they have family in the United States that will care for them.[135]

Passed under the Johnson administration, the privileges were what Ricardo Alarcón, President of the National Assembly, has called, "one of the oldest weapons the United States has used against the Revolution. It gives incentives to people to leave illegally and to do so under often dangerous conditions."[136] Thousands of Cubans have fled the country on flimsy rafts, dangerous boats, and have died on the waters trying to reach the Florida shores. Advocates claim it proves how desperately people want to leave the communist country but can't due to the regime's restrictions on free travel; the counter argument establishes the American-imposed blockade makes things so terrible for Cubans, then gives them an easy out, which is constantly used for propaganda purposes. Recent changes to the act now impose the provision known as Wet Foot, Dry Foot, requiring Cubans to physically touch American soil. Those picked up on the seas are returned, the changes increasing the controversy for both sides of the dispute. The act is "definitely a pull factor" in the lucrative business of smuggling Cubans to the United States, admitted Vicki Huddleston, former chief of mission of the US Interests Section in Havana.[137]

"Proportionally there are more Haitians, more Mexicans, more from the Dominican Republic illegally coming to the US. They are all turned back when caught. Cubans though, are welcomed, given benefits and are used by media and anti-revolutionary groups as propaganda against the government. There are no political refugees leaving Cuba now, practically none, people are leaving for economic reasons. And one of the reasons the economy is bad is due to US policy," University of New Mexico professor Nelson Valdés noted.[138]

The Cuban Adjustment Act remains in force despite the legal arrangements that now allows for 20,000 visas a year for Cubans who want to leave through proper channels. Initially the United States rarely granted the full amount, permitting only 2,000 in 1993, the problem compounded by the decision to count those dry feet Cubans who arrive in the United States as part of the total.[139] The immigration issue has consistently been commandeered as a propaganda tool by both sides and personal cases of manipulation are not uncommon.

A Cuban individual related his personal experience of how immigration has become a weapon of siege warfare: "My first hand knowledge came because I had a cousin who wanted to leave Cuba for strictly economic reasons; it had nothing to do with politics. Although his father—my uncle—a long time legal US resident, asked the US to grant his son a visa, it was denied repeatedly. After being frustrated for a long time, what did he do? Since he knew full well that if he landed on US shores he would get immediate immigrant status with all the perks, he stole a boat. What happened? He was caught by the Cuban coast guard and sent to prison for a few months. Guess what the INS did thru the US Interest Section in Havana? After it had repeatedly denied him a visa to migrate legally to the US, it was now willing to offer him a visa. There was one catch. INS would be willing to give him a visa if he signed a statement declaring himself a political prisoner!! My cousin who at least had some degree of integrity never signed it. By the way what does this little incident tell you about political prisoners? But that is another story to be told."[140]

By the end of the 1960s the siege mentality was firmly establishing itself within the Cuban psyche, as the population began the process of internalizing American aggression and accepting it as another part of the difficult day-to-day life. It has affected, "Everyone, constantly, everywhere. So much that we may not even realize the impact on a personal level," explained Ricardo Alarcón, President of the National Assembly.[141]

During the 1970s and 1980s American policy saw substantial swings in siege based on the shifts in White House attitudes. Under the Carter administration prospects for a weakening of the walls appeared close on a number of occasions. The Democratic President rescinded travel restrictions, allowing American tourists to travel to the forbidden land. Serious overtures were made to take steps toward ending the embargo and normalizing relations. An agreement was reached to open interest sections in Havana and Washington. American subsidiaries could again trade with Cuba, penalties on other countries were eliminated, and the OAS voted to end sanctions. The government spoke favorably to these overtures, but actions proved decisive as it all came crashing to an end when Cuba's continued involvement in the war in Angola, its solidarity with revolutionary movements in Latin America, and the optics of such internal overreactions as the fiasco at the Peruvian embassy leading to the 1980 Mariel boatlift[142] provided hard-liners in the Carter administration with abundant new grounds to keep the island besieged. President Carter's reluctant movement to the obdurate side proved too late to repair the damage done to his reputation as soft on his opponents, and Republican candidate Ronald Reagan handily won the 1980 election.

The relative easing of siege in the mid-1970s created a reciprocal reaction in the civil rights conditions on the island, a situation that did not go unnoticed. Amnesty International recognized the link between American hostility and Cuba's response in its 1975–76 report, arguing that the "persistence of fear, real or imagined, of counterrevolutionary conspiracies (was) primarily responsible for the early excesses in the treatment of political prisoners. By the same token, the removal of that fear has been largely responsible for the improvement in conditions."[143] No comment was made as to what would happen if the siege ended.

Not that there was any possibility of that occurring. Following Carter's defeat, the newly installed Reagan administration took a tougher approach against the revolution by immediately reinstating the travel restrictions, thanks to some legal sleight of hand from the Supreme Court.[144] Remittances were eliminated, rhetoric was increased, and the temporary thaw under Carter was frozen. While Cuba indicated the desire to maintain engagement, the Republican White House preferred an uncompromising line, including duplicity as in the case of El Salvador during its civil war; when Castro ended arms shipments at the request of the Americans, Reagan announced they were increasing weapons delivery.[145] Within the administration were a group of inexperienced Cuban hands, led by Secretary of State Alexander Haig, an avowed anti-Castroite whose aggressive postures with hints of military overtones succeeded in increasing tensions. A turning point in the advancement of siege under Reagan came in 1981 with the birth of the Cuban American National Foundation (CANF). Created by millions in taxpayer dollars, CANF's purpose was to deflect growing negative public reaction to government initiatives for the continuation of siege, allowing for the new strategy of apparently turning policy over to a nonprofit organization made up of exiles more connected to the issue. While the CIA and other federal agencies had administered organizational coordination and financial aid to the disparate and mostly violent antirevolutionary groups in the 1960s and 1970s,[146] the CANF was the first attempt by the US government to present an ostensibly benign public front to the anti-Castro efforts. CANF became the face of antirevolutionary politics, permitting the policymakers to plead it was following, not leading. The tail does not wag the dog in this instance, regardless of the promotion of the concept among Cubanologists and pro-embargo supporters.

Ricardo Alarcón reasoned: "If there was no CANF there would still be the blockade and all other American policy against Cuba, without question. Reagan created the CANF as a lobby institution, based on the lines of the Israeli lobby. To help influence Congress on the continuation of policy. It is there to support US policy, it was not there when that policy was created. This was set up to have an excuse to have a Cuban-American face on US policy, it is more elegant to confuse the public; that it is a family dispute between the Cuban-Americans and the Cubans in Cuba, that it is not the US government's fault. But it is entirely the continuation of consistent US policy against Cuba and CANF is simply the face of it."[147]

Anti-Castro reports and recommendations were soon being drafted by CANF, invariably adopted by whatever administration happened to be in power. A prime function of the group has been to maintain Washington's eye on the prize, circumventing efforts from those misguided politicians or officials who mistakenly believe the siege is counterproductive and ineffective. CANF was developed to be an important means to the continued reach for the end; the concept remains although its premier standing has since been overtaken by the more direct methods of powerful Cuban-American members of Congress, who in the majority are staunch CANF allies.[148] Since its inception the CANF has promoted itself as the democratic expression of the Cuban-American community, despite polls of the last decade indicating it more represents the extreme right wing that favors nonengagement, rather than the moderate majority. The group is an important tool for the American government to exploit its strategies through the appearance of an independent public NGO instead of direct agencies such as the CIA or State Department, as was the dominant feature of the early years. Using the façade of democracy to justify that the process is simply bowing to the will of this powerful lobby, the reality is that CANF is the servant to government wishes that do not change. The strategy of regime change is government spawn, thus permitting the continuation of CANF's effectiveness, and while the organization may have the hand on the steering wheel of policy, they are not the engine.

Founded in Florida by Cuban-Americans Jorge Mas Canosa and Raul Masvida, CANF historically has developed closer ties to the conservatively dominated Republican Party, a natural fit for the first generation of exiles who lost the most financially and politically. The Democrats, however, have also benefitted considerably from the largess. CANF has been blessed with a tremendous amount of influence-peddling assistance, receiving millions of dollars in the past 20 years from various government-funded agencies, including the National Endowment for Democracy (NED).[149] In a political system where money rules the rulers, the small collection of extreme right-wing Cuban-Americans that make up CANF's leadership has been able to masterfully manipulate the safeguarding of anti-Castro policies through the judicious use of bipartisan campaign donations. Besides private assistance, it is taxpayer funding that sustains the organization, which then turns much of that money back into the political system to ensure the government's desire to maintain siege is upheld. It's an extremely lucrative roundabout that no one wants to get off.

The organization, which on its own website states its objection to outside forces imposing change on Cuba, has supported a number of attempts to destabilize the Cuban government, directly and indirectly. One of the most expensive has been Radio and TV Marti, of which Mas Canosa was head in the 1980s of the presidential advisory board for the radio portion. The nonstop antirevolutionary media streams emanating from the United States have provided comfortable livings to those directly involved. How effective they have been in reaching the average Cuban on the island is less obvious. The signals are consistently blocked, and few inside Cuba have the opportunity to listen in. CANF's few political opponents increasingly challenge the cost efficiency of the multimillion dollar annual expenditure, and the corruption it often seems to attract.[150] CANF's connections with the propaganda efforts are not as serious as its alleged links to terrorist activities, through Luis Posada Carriles and the 1997 bombing campaign aimed at tourist facilities in Havana and Varadero. Carriles stated in a series of *New York Times* interviews that funding for the campaign, which killed Italian tourist Fabio Di Celmo and injured dozens, came from CANF with the knowledge of the organization's top man.[151] Former members made similar charges.[152] In the past decade CANF, under the current President Francisco (Peppy) Hernandez,[153] has somewhat softened its stand on absolute nonengagement with the Castro government, resulting in a split among members in 2001 and the formation of a more reactionary element under the Cuban Liberty Council.

The influence of CANF has waned over the past decade, taken over by the direct political pressure from the collection of Cuban-American congressmen, former and current members including Ileana Ros-Lehtinen, Lincoln and Mario Díaz-Balart, Bob Menéndez, Marco Rubio, and David Rivera. They and other non-Cubans such as Robert Torricelli, Dan Burton, and head of the Democratic National Committee (DNC) Florida Democrat Debbie Wasserman-Schultz lead the fight against any weakening of sanctions. If CANF is the steering wheel, the prosiege politicians are the horn.

While the pressure of siege continued unabated under Reagan, it was the collapse of the Soviet Union in 1990 that provided American policymakers with what they believed the best opportunity to destroy the revolution. From 1991 to 1994 Cuba endured its great depression, known as the Special Period, an economic plunge that saw the country's GDP shrink by an estimated 35 percent as more than 80 percent of its trade ended. It forced the government into initially increasing the centralization of the economy to ensure as much as possible the fair distribution of resources in the time of crises. Havana became a dark city, devoid of public transportation, gasoline, electricity, food, and hope. The government scrambled to recover, leading to a reluctant opening in foreign investments through joint ventures, particularly in tourism. Cuba had been involved in attracting outside capital since the 1970s and guaranteed rights of investors since 1982, but the island's dire situation compelled the government to double the efforts.[154]

The country experienced great social upheaval, which it has yet to fully recover from—a breakdown in many community standards, rise in thefts, and a population predominantly in Havana moving toward an attitude of individual survival over neighborhood responsibility as daily life became increasingly hard. A wave of immigration based solely on economic disruption swept thousands to new lands. The people's trust in the government to provide was shattered, and the administration itself was drowning in its attempts to plug all the holes in the dyke. The Special Period remains the defining moment of the revolution, splitting Cuban society from the comparative stability before the upheaval to the disruption of most communal norms and practices after. Citizens sold cars, jewelry, and anything else they could get their hands on to obtain food. Good people stole and cheated to survive. Young girls offered themselves to the influx of sex tourists to support their families. Revolutionary society built on trust, community assistance, and a sense of belonging was ripped asunder during "this run for your life" time.[155]

Soraya Castro, an authority on Cuban-American affairs at the University of Havana, remembered, "Cuba was not the same in the 1960s, under the Soviets it was different, there were things on the shelves, there was a strong sense of community. The Special Period, I love that term; it was the biggest crisis ever, we lost so much in such a short time. We lost all our trading partners overnight, after 40 years of dealing with the Soviet Union and the Eastern Block, we had to rearrange all our trading relationships. It was a struggle to obtain the basic needs of the people, a terrible time that led to social changes still being felt."[156] A substantial percentage of the urban generation that has grown up under the Special Period has a more cynical outlook on the future of the revolution and its social roots—connecting closer to commercial comforts and aspirations as a consequence of government failures, the increased contact with foreigners, tourists, family members in Miami, and the interaction with new electronic technologies. Cuban youth are expressing the same singularity of consumer validation in their lives as any first world counterpart, and are being increasingly targeted by American counterrevolutionary efforts to exploit rising discontent.[157] As Cuban society continues to work toward community-based integration, the battle against siege expands to a conflict with the encroachments of contemporary age, by what philosopher Charles Taylor once decried as "the malaise of modernity."

At the time of the Soviet collapse the George H. W. Bush administration placed extraordinary emphasis on forcing the former benefactor to break all commercial ties with Cuba, most importantly the remaining financial subsidies. The tactic proved successful as the Russians decided they needed Western aid more than expensive Cuban sugar. Representing billions over the previous three decades and one-quarter of the total GNP, turning off the trade, and then the grants, created dramatic distress on the nation's cupboard. In first half of 1991 Cuba received none of the expected rice, 7 percent of the lard, 11 percent of the condensed milk, and 18 percent of canned meat.[158] Daily consumable intake was reduced an average of 1,000 calories. Nerve diseases related to nutrition deficiencies—optic and peripheral neuropathy—were being reported in thousands by 1993. The starvation component of siege could now finally take effect. "The Soviet Union should stop feeding Fidel Castro," President Bush remarked prior to a meeting in Malta with Gorbachev,[159] a throwback to the early 1960s when depriving Cubans of sustenance was a major part of official policy. Freedom to starve developed into the definition of political liberty. "We are closer than ever to our goal of returning freedom to Cuba," Bush proclaimed in 1992.[160] "We are going to see a Free Cuba very soon," CANF head Jorge Mas Canosa promised.[161] While Cuban inefficiencies contributed to the situation, Soviet collapse and the tightening of siege meant difficulties to purchase goods, fertilizers, equipment, and technology worsened.

By the early months of 1992 most of the country fell dim and motionless, electrical blackouts of eight hours a daily occurrence. A 30 percent cut in petroleum left few cars on the streets of the capital, forcing *Habaneros* to riding a million heavy, cumbersome bikes donated by the Chinese. The city and the nation became fitter as it was slowly starving. Then came two more blows.

As Cuba opened up to the world following the end of the Soviet Union, instead of encouragement, the noose was tightened. No prospect was offered to endorse the island's international outreach and changing national market strategies. The objective from stateside was to guarantee Cuba had no prospect to recover, to force the leadership to direct the rapidly diminishing resources to combat augmented American aggression, to make the citizen's daily hardships all the more difficult, if not impossible, to survive.

Cuba's spiral into its economic black hole was seen as the occasion to deliver the death blow. Policymakers came up with a dual attack—the Torricelli Act passed October 1992 and the Helms-Burton Act of March 1996. During the early years of the republic the onerous Platt Amendment was the primary internal organism designed to ensure continuation of American stewardship. In the 1990s Torricelli and Helms-Burton were instituted to apply sufficient external pressure to destroy the Cuban Revolution and bring the nation back under US purvey. Platt, Torricelli, and Helms-Burton were all based on the established historical perception of the inability of Cubans to run their own government without American predominance in ensuring the "right kind of people" are in charge, as Governor Leonard Wood observed in 1902.[162]

Initiated by Democratic senator Robert Torricelli, the first thrust was aimed to reestablish the prohibition of US subsidiaries from selling to Cuba, calling back the draconian regulations from the 1960s that had lapsed under Carter. At the time the legislation was enacted the volume of that trade reached over $700 million—90 percent comprised of food and medicine. The law, known as the Cuban Democracy Act, additionally prohibited ships entering Cuban waters from stopping at American ports for six months. The purpose was to deprive Cuba of as much trade as possible, just as the island, so dependent upon vital maritime traffic, was expanding its economy to fresh markets in the capitalist world. Less than a year later all commerce with the subsidiaries stopped.[163] The act led to the ending of remittances to Cuba in 1994, and sending food and medical packages could only be authorized for strictly humanitarian purposes, the definition of which was controlled by the Treasury Department. The act officially permitted financial, material, and other forms of assistance to the development of an internal opposition, which the government perceived as wholly created by foreign design, by decree rendering it illegitimate. It was the continuation of the revolution's justification to crack down on "dissidents" on the grounds they were being cultivated and controlled by an external, and in this case, enemy power, giving aid and comfort to Cuba's fiercest adversary. It was the definition of treason according to Cuban officials, a description that would hold in most every other country in the world, including the United States.

The subsidiary section of the act was taken from the previous amendment of longtime Castro hater, Republican senator Connie Mack, but the overall push of the legislation was to make sure to keep the "foot on the snake, don't let up," so promised Torricelli.[164] It effectively did make matters worse with the Cuban side estimating an annual loss of more than $200 million.[165] The hand of the CANF apparently was fully behind the direction and implementation of the bill. "Anything the foundation wants it gets," according to one Torricelli aide, commenting on the passage through Congress.[166]

The man who gave his name to the new tactic to strangle the Castro government had previously been a cautious proponent of the revolution. The veteran congressman from New Jersey visited Cuba in November 1988 and apparently came back commenting on the living conditions being "quite good compared to other Latin American countries."[167] Coincidentally, shortly after his trip he was contacted by CANF head Jorge Mas Canosa, which led to a series of meetings, a strong friendship, followed by substantial campaign contributions from the organization. The former proponent of ending the embargo quickly turned into a rigid and vocal adversary.[168] Torricelli's legislation was based on a form of blackmail under Track II, which allowed for the provision of aid to nongovernment organizations "that promote peaceful changes towards democracy in Cuba." Transformation expected to be enhanced through the regulations that permitted the tightening of food and medicine to the Cubans, which the Americans would then supply "for humanitarian purposes" once the change condition—the end of the regime—was met.[169]

Even the American mainstream media, usually reliable proembargo allies, recognized this had gone too far. In a June 15, 1992, editorial the *New York Times* criticized, "This misnamed act (the Cuban Democracy Act) is dubious in theory, cruel in its potential practice and ignoble in its election-year expediency...An influential faction of the Cuban-American community clamors for sticking it to a wounded regime...There is, finally, something indecent about vociferous exiles living safely in Miami prescribing more pain for their poorer cousins."[170]

On March 12, 1996, the second blow fell. North Carolina Republican Jesse Helms, then chairman of the Senate foreign relations committee, and his fellow representative from Indiana Dan Burton presented legislation designed to finally bring down the walls. The Cuban Liberty and Democratic Solidarity Act, known referentially as the Helms-Burton Act, permitted American citizens the right to sue for property lost to the revolution (Title III), including those Cubans now US citizens (unheard of previously), and attempted to prohibit any foreign company, US subsidiary or not, from trading with Cuba by imposing sanctions and denying entry into the United States to top officials from the worst offending foreign companies operating on previously held US property (Title IV).[171] The first affected by the restriction was Ian Delaney, head of Canadian nickel operator Sherritt International, operating a mine on what Americans claimed were"confiscated" lands in Moa.

Title II contained some of the most demanding rules—proclaiming the siege would not be lifted until the return of all nationalized properties up to and including private homes abandoned by Cuban owners, along with the acceptance of the US imposed process for remuneration. On the political side the Helms-Burton combo outlined the imposition of a friendly government once the revolution was tossed aside, specifically prohibiting either Castro from running for office and dictating exactly how the "transitional government" would be ordered under American auspices. That provision made mockery of President Bill Clinton's public claim at the time, "The United States does not pick leaders or delete leaders for other countries. We let people make their own decisions."[172]

The international reaction was overwhelmingly hostile. The greatest pushback against the extraterritorial aspects of Helms-Burton was focused on Title III, seen to be in violation of the UN charter and NAFTA. Basic principles of state rights to exercise jurisdiction and control over matters within its territory were being compromised by the act, thereby making it illegal under international laws.[173] Canada and Europe became particularly aggressive in their condemnation.[174] Since passage every president has suspended that section of the act.

One segment of Helms-Burton retains lingering national political implications, that of the codification of Cuban policy, removing presidential authority to eliminate the blockade or travel restrictions. The battle for maintaining siege moved from the White House to the halls of Congress. At the time the Clinton administration protested they had no option but to pass Helms-Burton, demanded by the political and media forces following the Cuban air force shoot down of two small planes. The aircraft were conducting illegal over flights of Havana airspace, disregarding warnings from Cuba and FAA threats to suspend the licenses. Conducted by Brothers to the Rescue (BTTR), an anti-Castro group led by José Basulto, the flights were originally designed to pick up Cuban rafters during the height of the *balsero* (rafters) crisis of 1994, when the drawbridge was lowered to those who wanted to leave the worse affects of the Special Period. After the uncontrolled migration was halted, the Brothers switched from humanitarian efforts to dropping antigovernment propaganda leaflets on Havana residents. Cuba's experience with small planes releasing bombs, white phosphorous, harmful chemical, and biological materials on the cities and countryside was well within memories of the leaders reacting to the BTTR excursions. Although Cuban intelligence sources in Miami had passed on information that the group was testing antipersonnel weapons, and Basulto had inquired about the purchase of a Czech fighter jet,[175] there was no direct evidence the organization was doing anything but dropping paper. The Cuban government, however, wasn't going to wait forever to find out if more was planned. Approximately a dozen illegal flights were recorded over the capital, every one protested to American authorities, when Castro gave the final warning he would no longer tolerate this gross violation of sovereignty. On February 24, 1996, the Cuban air force brought down two of the unarmed planes, killing four and creating an international incident, outrage in the United States, and the forcing of Clinton's hand into signing Helms-Burton. Basulto escaped death in one plane by flying low under Cuban radar, apparently turning back before the others. Less than two weeks after the event the FAA finally got around to suspending the licenses of BTTR.[176] American coverage of the incident was one of a murderous, unprovoked action on the part of the Castro regime; in yet another manifestation of siege—control of information.

Certain Cuban officials reject the belief that after the incident Clinton had no choice but to sign Helms-Burton, claiming the President consistently expressed public support for the new measures, "making it clear his willingness to work with Congress to make the blockade more effective," National Assembly President Ricardo Alarcón remarked.[177] The act had been approved by both houses in October 1995, and while the administration had expressed serious concerns regarding some aspects, Alarcón reasoned, "those could have been resolved beforehand. When the violation of Cuban airspace took place on February the administration used this incident as an excuse to speed up approval of a bill that had already been agreed upon and over which a consensus had been reached."[178]

Jessie Helms was content to see his efforts fulfilled by whatever means available. The unreconstructed Southern conservative, famous at various times for his opposition to civil rights, gay rights, abortion, and affirmative action, was determined to witness the last of the revolutionary leader.

"Farewell Fidel, that's the message in this bill,"[179] assured that Castro would be forced to leave either "in a vertical or horizontal position."[180] Helms himself passed away July 4, 2008. The partner in legislation, Dan Burton, was best known for his support of the National Right to Life Committee, eclipsed only by his passion for golf. A longtime friend of CANF, he has made little comment on the issue in the past decade, other than voicing support in 2007 for ending travel restrictions for Cuban-Americans.[181]

America's two new weapons of siege were in place by the end of 1996. Another came less than a year after. Since the dissolution of the Soviet Union the Cuban stratagem of reaching out to the free world markets included an important tourism component. In short order the industry became one of the island's greatest revenue sources, all in hard currency, as thousands then hundreds of thousands of Canadian, European, and Latin Americans flocked to the virgin beaches, the history, culture, and the warm welcome. It wasn't long after the counterrevolutionaries responded. Following a number of threats from suspected terrorist groups Alpha 66 and Omega 7, a six-month-long bombing campaign hit tourist facilities in Havana and Varadero. Starting in April 1997 more than a dozen explosions damaged hotels, discos, tourist buses, and Havana's most famous bar, the *Bodeguita del Medio*. Italian tourist Fabio Di Celmo was killed when a blast destroyed the lobby at the Hotel Copacabana, a dozen more were injured during the operation. The world-famous Tropicana nightclub was also targeted, the plan thwarted only when the man designated to plant the device turned out to be a government agent.[182] The Cuban government became so frantic it invited the FBI to examine documents purporting to show further terrorist attacks being planned by anti-Castro groups in Miami. Thanking their counterparts, the FBI officials then went back to Florida and promptly arrested the agents sent by Castro to infiltrate the groups.[183] The Cuban Five were tried, sentenced, and remain in prison under difficult conditions despite worldwide condemnation and pressure from increasing numbers of high-profile international personalities. In an extremely rare ruling, the Work Group of Arbitrary Detention of the UN Human Rights Commission stated that the trial was not impartial and that sentences that went from five years to life imprisonment were excessively severe.[184]

The 1997 bombing campaign against the tourist facilities once again brought to the light Luis Posada Carriles, who boasted of his role to the *New York Times* in order to ensure sufficient publicity to discourage tourists from considering the Pearl of the Antilles as a destination.[185]

Cuba's reaction to the new legislative attacks and the terrorism against tourism was entirely predictable—maintaining security and surveillance systems while demonstrating even less tolerance for antigovernment activity. One of the desired repercussions to siege is to induce overreaction, to which the Cuban government graciously obliged during the arrest of 75 dissidents in 2003 under Law 88, passed in response to Helms-Burton and remarkably similar to America's Smith Act of World War II providing jail time of 20 years for publishing or possessing material that could be considered to be in support for the overthrow of government, or to belong to an organization seen to be working toward those ends.[186] Law 88 similarly declared it a criminal offense for any Cuban citizen to provide information to the US government or its agents that could be used to strengthen the embargo or destabilize the revolution. The dissidents were not arrested and convicted for having contrary political views, but for involvement as illegal agents for a foreign power.

Cuba's civil rights restrictions and defiance against political change during this period remained expressed in ultrasensitivity to criticism from both friend and foe. The augmented pressures of siege, the increased terrorism, Cuba's economic descent into near collapse, attempts to control the population's interaction with foreign tourists and businessmen at the same time it sought ways to further reach out to the world led to internal stresses between the reactionary old guard and the new generation seeking expansion of social solutions under nontraditional methods. The tried and true methods of rejecting all forms of expression seen as counterrevolutionary or in the employ of the enemy was manifested in arrests, entrenchment, and the inability to consider alternative responses. Internal and external turmoil again became portrayed as a threat to the constancy of the nation, resolved through the old standbys. America's strategy to destabilize and induce an overreaction was articulated during the 2003 dissident arrest crises by Assistant Secretary of State for the Western Hemisphere Roger Noriega, who described how "we opted for change even if it meant chaos. The Cubans had had too much stability over decades and it's true that the U.S. bureaucracy and military preferred stability. But members of my team said stability is the enemy and chaos is the friend if you want to profoundly change a regime...Obviously, chaos was necessary in order to change reality."Noriega acknowledged he and head of the US Interest Section in Havana James Cason worked on their own initiative to foster instability, and the Cubans reaction could not have come as a surprise. The 75 dissidents caught up in the scheme paid for it with their imprisonment.[187]

Torricelli and Helms-Burton established the latest ground rules for encirclement of Cuba, terrorism upped the ante in violence, the arrests of the dissidents provided additional US justification, and the political end piece was completed in 2004 with the Commission for Assistance to a Free Cuba—the blueprint for how the nation would look after the successful conclusion of siege. The Bush Jr. administration developed recommendations to bring about the end of the revolution, establish American-style democratic institutions, and open the free-market forces on the island. The report covered the big and small picture, outlining in great detail exactly how Cuban society, economy, and political life would be structured. The commission was the twenty-first-century version of the Platt Amendment, demonstrating again America's historically consistent, if misguided, determination to inflict upon the unfortunate inhabitants its superior benevolence. Primary to the report was dismantling the social programs. "The Cuban economy and government budget after transition may not be able to sustain the level of earned benefits and the lax requirements for eligibility that the communist system permitted." No more health care, free education, pensions. Seniors were targeted for work well after retirement age through the creation of "retiree corps to give jobs to those without resources, if they are in good health."[188]

Castro met the commission using the standard strategy by those under threat from a powerful adversary—defiance. "Our people will stand up to your economic measures, whatever they may be. Forty-five years of heroic struggle against the blockade and economic war against threats, aggressions, plots to assassinate its leaders, sabotage and terrorism have not weakened but rather strengthened the revolution."[189]

The implementation of the most recent aggressions, combined with the devastating hurricanes and the world economic collapse of 2008 has made the island's recovery from the Special Period and its ability to combat siege all the more difficult. As has the inherent hesitancy to implement meaningful modification for fear of being dangerously exposed. Bureaucratic calcification in which the old guard refuses to give way to the ideas of the younger generation has been a factor in the ponderously slow movement toward meaningful reform, thankfully gaining speed since late 2010. The siege's ability to convince experienced leadership not to let go for fear of creating disruptive opportunities for the enemy contributes to stagnation.

Surviving these impediments has been accomplished by a variety of methods—the revolution's ability to touch the rest of the world with its human capital, its long overdue recognition of the inherent deficiencies in an over-regulated centralized economy, as well as accessing the new economic lifeline in Venezuela where President Hugo Chávez has become Cuba's most important ally in Latin America. The favorable oil deals, one-sided trade relations, long-term subsides, and outright financial aid have been important elements in keeping the walls strong. The domination of left and center-left governments in many other Latin American and Caribbean countries in the past decade, interconnecting through such social/economic associations as ALBA,[190] provides much-needed assistance and security from isolation attempts that have continued, as in the case of America's successful exclusion of Cuba from the Summit of the Americas meeting in March 2012.[191] Leadership has learned the lesson of commercial diversity and international connectivity, reaching out to new markets and cultivating its burgeoning relationship with the Chinese powerhouse and Latin America's emerging economies.[192]

Cuba's ability to endure over the past half century has corresponded with an evolution in American strategy. The direct hostility, exclusionary efforts, military action, and hundreds of acts of terrorism from the first decades has shifted to the systemic use of social punishments aimed at eroding the people's will to resist. The island is no longer under threat of invasion, and there is little chance American pressure will convince the large majority of the world to turn its back on the Caribbean nation. Internally after 50 years the socialist experiment is firmly entrenched within a viable society, and it is that acceptance that the current methods of antagonism are being applied against. Economic blockade, behind-the-scene application of the extraterritorial aspects of Torricelli and Helms-Burton, antirevolutionary propaganda, refusal to engage, and political demands for change make up the modern siege.

* * *

Voice is the master of reality. The iconic words of José Marti led his country into a second war of independence, and continue to be expropriated by both sides of the revolutionary divide as a consequence. Castro's legendary oratory skills established a fundamental role in commanding solidarity and forging true national identity. For the decades prior Uncle Sam's "forcible advice" determined authenticity; and when that was silenced the greatest nation on earth couldn't let go. The northern power has yet to accept the loss of Cuba's physical benefits, nor that of being in charge, either directly or through the strong men. Tossing aside America's voice (even before the Soviets came) raised the ire against the revolution and its supporters who had the temerity of no longer respecting what they were being told. It was an affront to America's self-image, of its assurance of the exceptional values it had instilled on the island. The United States lost control of its good sense and tossed aside pragmatism in favor of malice and vindictiveness. America's expression against the revolution became "hysterical," noted Theodore Draper,[193] based increasingly on frustration and incredulity to the revolution's tone.

The loss of its voice to direct Cuban society, the denunciation of its perceived superior political/economic system, the dismissal of its historical dialogue of right of possession—this is part of why America treats Cuba differently. Why China can be a favored trading partner and Vietnam forgiven; why far worse governments by any measure are accepted as friends and allies. Why the United States persists with a counterproductive, vindictive 50-year-old policy, why it continues to think of ways to tighten the siege despite the occasional lapse into rationality and understanding that it has not, and will not, work in bringing down the revolution; but it has only accomplished the opposite. "US threat to Cuban sovereignty and to the safety and well-being of the Cuban citizenry has long served to justify the Cuban government's restrictions on civil and political rights, especially of travel, speech and assembly," University of Denver professor Arturo López-Levy revealed.[194]

Fidel's concept of revolutionary objectives inevitably clashed with American perceptions of its affirmative relationship with the island. The punishment became permissible in response to the seemingly undeserved insult and injury. Taking into account the power differences, America's wrath is unprecedented in its length and intensity. Its rage worked against the goal; the revolutionary government having a less complicated time to convince itself and the population of the necessity to break from America's historiography, to move rapidly along the socialist path and eventually fully into the Soviet method, embracing along with it the social restrictions and controls as the only alternative for survival. Watching all this transpire and not being able to predict or control what was happening removed America's political effectiveness, leaving only aggravation and rage.

The revolution became framed as "an insult to American prestige, a challenge to American dignity," thundered South Carolina representative Mendel Rivers.[195] Forgiveness would not be forthcoming until Fidel Castro and his lot were removed. "I cannot allow my country to continue to suffer the constant humiliation and opprobrium heaped upon her in an irresponsible manner," so demanded Massachusetts representative Silvio Conte in 1960.[196] Castro equally understood emotions can be a powerful motivator to achieve an end. "They deprived the Cuban people of their sovereignty; they treated the Cuban people like little children to whom they said: 'We give you permission to do just this, and if you do more we will punish you.' The Platt Amendment was imposed and we either behaved ourselves—behaved in the manner convenient to the foreign country—or we would lose our sovereignty."[197]

The United States was convinced it made Cuba what it was; a stable, prosperous little country and a showpiece for countercolonial benevolence, which later turned into a playground for American desires. The island nation formulated and validated burgeoning America exceptionalism, the guiding foreign relations matrix used by the United States ever since. So if Cuba did not meet American expectations, in fact rejected all aspects, then the prestige of the United States suffered. The only option to prevent that was for the Cuban Revolution—which directly challenged US reputation—to be seen as an aberration. It had to be made to fail in order to restore America's status. How? Siege.

The revolution defended itself against American siege strategy by declaring US policy had little to do with the Cuban people's desires and wants but was simply a method to return to hegemonic advantage. The siege is the manifestation of this collision of ideas—America's aspiration to return Cuba into their sphere of influence, Cuban determination to prevent that.It was the revolution that prevailed over foreign intention, reputation, and status. American exceptionalism butted up against Cuban patria and the two have been misunderstanding each other ever since. These immovable positions solidified into the constitution of siege and the defense thereof as the terms of engagement that continues to this day.

America recurrently demonstrates neither the capacity nor the maturity to show magnanimity to their former foreign charges who wanted to run the house their way. Every attempt the Cuban government has made to bring a higher degree of social equity has been met with policies to undermine the attempts, along with public derision and condemnation. The former guardians cannot unlock themselves from the self-absorbed perceptions of ingratitude or from the now discarded Cold War geopolitical realities where every conflict was seen in context of winners and losers, every compromise a manifestation of weakness. The United States convinced itself there was no other option but a relationship of aggression, which played exactly into the revolution's desire to portray its struggle as one between David and Goliath. US efforts to destroy true Cuban sovereignty, no matter what real or imagined slights directed against them by Castro, fell perfectly into the development of the dialogue of the fight for nationalism in face of imperial aggression. That construct and its social direction would have been extremely difficult, if not impossible, without the total cooperation of the United States through its policy of siege. The encirclement has concurrently assembled an effective container for the American side—the perception that punishment has to be applied to bring liberty to the Cuban people; then allow nothing out of the box to suggest otherwise. In conjunction are the prohibitions against as many Americans as possible to peek inside to see for themselves what's really going on.

Since the triumph of the revolution the call from Miami to "free" Cuba has been consistent. The word has a very different meaning depending on which side of the Florida divide it's coming from. In Washington it means political plurality, a free-market economy, corporate capitalism, private control of the commons. In Havana it means society based on community needs, true independence, and public ownership of all resources and social justice programs. Washington sees Havana's definition as spreading the poverty to all; Havana sees Washington's designation as a call for the return of class divide and foreign domination. Reconciliation of even this most basic word has yet to be accomplished, and is part of the current form of that "forcible advice" to which American expectations rest for the salvation of a postrevolutionary Cuba.

Following 1776 America was unencumbered in its ability to create a language of mythology, whereby for the first time in history the ascending forces of individual liberty and independence triumphed over colonial masters. That it was the rebels alone who accomplished the task and put the new nation on the path to greatness. Cuban revolutionaries of 1895 were afforded no such cultural necessity, as the United States confiscated the historical dialogue, purporting that they alone were responsible for Cuban freedom. The nationalists had to swallow the American version, suffer the indignity of ignominy and relegation, and wait till a singular Cuban voice could be heard. Castro spoke Cuban, to Cubans and for Cubans, the overwhelming majority who responded with words of affinity. No other Cuban leader from 1902 to 1959 articulated with the same authority or resonance to national ambitions. When Castro finally gave the Cubans the opportunity to speak of their history, their revolution, in their voice, the Americans as best they could made sure it was not heard outside the island. The siege then becomes not only an instrument for economic depravations, but one that has for 50 years done its best to guarantee the dialogue is consistently one sided, that the American public hears only what the government tells them about Cuba. The failures of the revolution, and there have been many, are spoken of consistently within American administration and media circles. Cuba's current attempts to resolve economic and bureaucratic deficiencies are rarely heard, or discounted, and the US official policy to exacerbate those shortcomings in order to make conditions so terrible the people will revolt remain a rare thing to discuss openly.

Language accomplished America's neocolonial dominance by elucidating the requisite of imposing its moral order on a so-called inferior people who welcomed the benevolent uplifting, all the while denying any imperial management. The exercise of power for the good of others justified controlling the parameters of sovereignty and social/economic structures. Fidel Castro rejected those definitions, angrily informing America that its control of the island had been for its interests; that Cuban independence had been a mere truth in the vision of America's reality. The power to the north reacted emotionally to the slap in the face it received from the bearded revolutionaries, and for the past 50 years has been taking its anger out on the island's inhabitants, in words and in deeds.

It is the voices of those who live with the consequences that should be heard most closely.

3

SIEGE AND SOCIETY

All of you must know that you have no greater friend than the United States of America.

—Message from then secretary of state Condoleezza Rice on the Interest Section ticker in Havana[1]

Six-year-old Rafael is a typical young boy—he'd rather play instead of doing his homework. For the moment he's ignoring the toys that surround him, attention focused on the portable television.

"How many times have you seen that today?" his mother Caridad Borges Vidal gently chides. "Four, five times, he loves that movie, what do you call it?"

The child breaks out in an infectious laugh, showing off wide gaps in his teeth. "Mommy, you know it's Toy Story. I love it, it's my best one." His interest immediately returns to the small screen, answering—somewhat impatiently—that he enjoys singing and dancing and wants to be an entertainer when he grows up. His mother reminds him he has to return to his studies in a few minutes.

Despite appearances, Rafael is not normal. The young Afro-Cuban has suffered from testicular leukemia since he was a year old. In September 2011 Rafael was admitted back into an isolation room at the William Soler National Children's Hospital in Havana, treated again for a disease the mother had hoped she'd seen the last of.

"He was here three years ago, we thought maybe that would be the end of it. He first was analyzed when he was over a year old. Then we had him checked again by a family doctor and it had returned. So we took him here." She does not tell Rafael anything more than "he touched something and that made him sick. He doesn't understand what is happening. So we just try to keep him happy,"[2] Caridad sighs briefly, revealing just a hint of the stress she's enduring.

Caridad, 47, lives in Havana, but mother and son are required to stay in isolation together, unable to leave the room for more than a few minutes a day to ensure the risk of picking up any infections is minimized. She admits it's difficult to be away from her husband and other children for such long periods. A teacher comes in twice a week and there are plenty of distractions but few others his age to interact with. "The hardest part is that there is no phone here in the room, it makes it difficult to talk to my husband and my children. They come over as much as they can, but it's not easy. Still, for the child." She looks over at her son, now completely engrossed in the movie again. "I try not to cry, I have to be strong in front of him, not to let him know how serious it is."

There is reason for concern, according to Dr. Alejandro González, head of the pediatric hospital's hematology department. His responsibility includes the isolation ward and he is familiar with Rafael's case. "The diagnosis is about 50–50, this is a recurring situation he has now, and that's not a good sign. We're keeping an eye on him closely, there may be a need for an operation."

The medical staff does their best, and William Soler is considered to be the finest children's hospital in Cuba, one of the most respected in Latin America. As everything in Cuba, shortages complicate efficiencies. Matters have been made worse since 2007 when the United States classified the facility as a "denied hospital."[3] The designation adds considerable difficulties in obtaining medicines, equipment, and technology, all part of the siege strategy. Since the early 1960s Cuba has been constrained in its ability to purchase food and medicine from the United States. Despite some easing of the rules, medical supplies continue to be hard to acquire, the battle lines drawn between those who indicate the embargo does not strictly prohibit purchases; antiblockade proponents retort that the stringent licensing requirements serve as an effective deterrent.[4] Cuba does its best to find needed medicines from other countries when American firms decide it's not worth the trouble to do business with the island; some products, however, are only obtainable in the United States.

One of the revolution's most valued social accomplishments has been its free and universal health-care system, and efforts to degrade that achievement have succeeded. Part of the reason to diminish the health-care reputation is to counteract the substantial amount of international political capital Cuba has achieved with its involvement in sending doctors and staff around the world, including commitment to Haiti more than ten years before the earthquake of 2011 and its continued assistance to that country's fight against cholera,[5] as well as treating millions of Latinos with cataracts under Operation Miracle in Venezuela and other Latin American nations. Recent US intentions to undermine the international medical programs have increasingly targeted doctors. The Cuban Medical Professional Parole (CMPP) immigration program encourages those serving overseas to defect and enter the United States immediately as refugees. A report in the *Wall Street Journal* revealed during most of 2010 CMPP visas had been issued by US consulates in 65 countries to 1,574 Cuban doctors whose education had been paid for by the financially struggling revolutionary government.[6] This program was initiated by the US Department of Homeland Security.

Dr. González acknowledges an element of the siege is aimed at his country's well-recognized efforts in the third world. "They don't want us to succeed, they want to downplay what we are doing. It's a way for our government to reach out to the rest of Latin America, and the United States does not approve." Dr. González is one of the coordinators of the facility's national treatment of leukemia in children, aimed at those aged 1–18, although adults also are admitted.

The State Department's decision to target William Soler has brought intended consequences. A quick list of medicines the department has been unable to obtain since 2007 includes antibiotics, medicines to treat pulmonary hypertension, anesthesia agents Sevoflurane, Dexmedetomidine, and Erwinia L-Asparaginasa, commercially known as Elspar and given to children suffering from lymphoblastic leukemia. US pharmaceutical company Merck and Co. refuses to sell the product to Cuba. Children suffering from retinoblastoma, cancer of the retina, endure additionally as Cuban ophthalmologic services cannot make use of Transpupillary Thermotherapy, available only through Iris Medical Instruments in California. Without the technology it is impossible to treat retina tumors and preserve the affected eye.

The restrictions affect companies outside the United States. "Vygon in England is being pressured by the Americans to end commercial relations with us. They have various items we purchase, such as products to study molecular alterations to help properly classify patient's conditions. One of the drugs to treat Rafael is Hydroxyurea. That drug improves the clinical picture of those patients with the disease. It's not expensive, but it is developed in the US, and is difficult if not impossible to get elsewhere. Patients like the little boy Rafael, maybe their situation would be better if we could buy it from America. But we can't."

While that treatment would not alter the life-threatening aspect of the disease, Dr. González quickly pointed out the inability to obtain other medicines have had far more serious repercussions.

"Children have died because we haven't been able to purchase certain items that are prohibited under the embargo, and since the hospital has been declared denied," he asserted. "Amplatzer devices, manufactured in the US and made from materials designed to avoid organic rejection, have become nearly impossible to obtain. The use eliminates the need for risky open heart surgery. In a few cases children waiting for the item have had to undergo the operation,[7] and they were unable to recover due to complications. It's not that we don't have the money, we're willing to purchase these things. It's just we can't. The Americans are always on the lookout for things we're trying to get, in order to persuade other countries or companies not to sell to us. Cubans are proud of the health system here, and we always want the latest and the best. The Americans are on the forefront of new medical technologies, they have the best, and they don't want us to have them," Dr. González commented without emotion.

Various international associations have recognized the impact of siege on Cuba's health care. Following the United Nations 2011 vote to end the embargo, World Health Organization (WHO) officials noted, "In the health sector, the consequences of the embargo have a negative multiplier effect on the cost of basic everyday health products, on the difficulties in acquiring health products, on the availability of basic services and, therefore, on the overall living conditions of the population... The embargo affects the individual health care of all people, regardless of age or gender, through its impact on Cuba's unified health system institutions, research facilities, epidemiological surveillance institutions and disease control agencies."[8]

Despite the added difficulties, the WHO consistently reports favorably on Cuba's commitment to health care and its ability to make the most of the dollars allocated, gaining better results while paying 15 times less for its universal health program as compared to the system in the United States.[9] One of the reasons suggested is the revolution's commitment to preventative measures as compared to reactive methods involving expensive procedures following diagnosis of a disease, more common to the American style. Cubans have developed the habit of attending a physician's care for the most minor of conditions. Early on the Castro government encouraged the attitude, dedicating considerable resources to health-care systems, the most extensive a nationwide immunization program providing 11 vaccines against 13 diseases, resulting in the saving of thousands of lives. Government statistics point to results since the first months of the revolution, initiated with the last reported case of polio in May 1962. That same year saw a vaccination agenda against five other diseases: diphtheria, tetanus, whooping cough, typhoid fever, and tuberculosis. An estimated $50 million annually is spent into manufacturing, importing, and acquiring supplies to support the process, which is undertaken via 700 immunization centers throughout the country.[10] Even those efforts have been targeted, according to Cuban officials who reported the US government seizure of $4.2 million allocated to Cuba by the UN Global Fund to Fight AIDS, tuberculosis, and malaria for the first quarter of 2011. Much of the funding was assigned to import AIDS medication, provided free of charge to some 5,000 HIV patients. The UN Global Fund is a $22-billion-a-year program that works to combat the three deadly pandemics in 150 countries.[11]

While international recognition gains medical diplomacy points, it's the ground-level work at facilities such as William Soler that sustain the system's viability. The hospital was built in 1986 as a means to reduce the already impressive infant mortality rates, which by that time were comparable to first world standards. The leadership, with direct input from Fidel Castro, has accomplished that mandate, according to Herminia Palenzuela, deputy director of the National Pediatric Cardiac Center—the main section at the hospital.

"By the time this was opened most infant mortality causes had been eliminated, vaccines were covered for all, many of the diseases that killed children before had disappeared, it was the step up in quality since the Revolution. So it was analyzed what to do to decrease it even more. They came up with two situations, congenital anomalies, representing 50 percent heart diseases, and prenatal problems. So we focused on heart diseases and developing surgery even in newborns," she said. In the year of the opening, congenital heart diseases accounted for three out of every 1,000 infant mortality incidents; "25 years later, in 2011 it was the 25th anniversary of William Soler, and they accounted for just 0.5 cases," Dr. Palenzuela stated proudly.

The hospital is in a constant state of activity. Corridors and salons are clean, yet sparse, everything in need of a paint job (as is most of Cuba). The staff is dedicated and interaction with parents is professionally informal. Adults have no hesitancy following doctors into restricted areas in search of answers, the insistence for information made more so as the young patients often have no concept of what they are going through. Explanation of the condition has thus become as much the responsibility of the adults as the staff. Dr. González understands the added emotional element, the parent's concern for their children, and most everyone's general knowledge of medicine turning all into experts, makes working at William Soler particularly challenging. "We have to be accessible to the parents, so they understand most of what is happening. The bond between child and parent is very strong in Cuba. And almost all Cubans, especially the mothers, are well informed about medical things, the system here teaches everyone," he smiled.

Cuba's difficulties in obtaining the latest medicines, equipment, and technologies add to the problem. An estimated 90 percent of all medical patents are under the control of American companies, and finding generic or alternatives is complicated and can be more expensive. The result is direct harm to doctors, and patients.

As Dr. Palenzuela remarked, "The blockade has affected us in all aspects of the Cuban health system. This center, we have a method where you take the patient who has a hole in the heart, and you can close it without doing surgery. It is simpler because surgery always has risks, particularly with children or infants. We were receiving from the US government licenses to receive those devices required to do those procedures." That ended when the 2007 classification of denial came down. "Prior to that we had approvals to purchase materials, catheters, coils, stents, devices like Amplatzer septal occluder. Dozens of children are waiting for this operation. Then the Treasury Department said the hospital is now on the list. And that changed everything."

While Dr. Palenzuela declares she has never heard a reason for the hospital's redesignation, the new conditions were explicitly spelled out. "We were told that for us to continue buying these materials we had to be inspected to make sure we weren't using it for the military, or on foreigners. How could it be used on the military? These are children we are treating. Yes, we have received foreigners but we give the service for free, very few foreign patients could pay, less than 10 percent. Many patients were from Haiti, other poor countries, they couldn't pay a thing."

The Cuban government, with the support of the staff at William Soler, rejected the new impositions. "We pay full price for these materials, how could anyone tell us how to use them? So the licenses were stopped and now we may have to be forced to operate on the patient or try to find different devices, which means buying it at two or three times more, or not being able to get it at all. If the blockade didn't exist we wouldn't have to buy anything outside the US. So now we have to try another type of device, and sometimes it might not be as effective. We're not a rich country, we have a limited budget. So now we have to buy smaller amounts, at higher prices, and sometimes we can't get anything. That means much more risk to the patient."

Dr. Palenzuela is not so sanguine when discussing the impact of siege on Cuba's health care. "I feel sad and angry because it affects children; they are innocent. It is worse with the children because they don't understand the embargo's effects, and we can never tell them. We don't even discuss this with the parents, it would only increase their anxiety. They are upset enough to see their children have these problems."

She related an incident in 2006 when the hospital purchased echocardiograph equipment from American-based Phillips at a cost of more than $1 million. After two years William Soler officials were informed Phillips could no longer conduct business with Cuba, which meant no spare parts. The equipment has not been used since. "No other country sells this, no subsidiary can sell it. We have Japanese equipment but it utilizes 2D technology, Phillips has 3D capacity. If I was a mean person, or thinking badly, I think maybe they wanted us to spend money on the equipment, knowing what was coming."

There is no doubt as to the purpose of the siege: "It is to artificially create shortages—food, material goods, technology, medical equipment and medicines. To make things so bad the Cuban people will get angry and want to change the government. The majority here want change, things to get better, but we want to do it within the system. But even the children here have been punished, their only fault has been to be born in Cuba. They have nothing to do with the changes brought on by the Revolution. So for those who say the blockade is not a big deal, they don't know what they are talking about."

Dr. Palenzuela is quick to stress: "Not every problem we have is the fault of the blockade, no one can say that. But without the embargo we could do so much better. I've been to the US before and spoke out against it, what it was doing to our health system. But the last few years I haven't been given authorization to return, maybe they don't want me back," she smiled ruefully. "I don't know what it is, they have an anger with us for supporting the Revolution. But what they do against the health system is the worst, it's a cruel thing."

It is also a trivial thing, to the point where keeping up on the latest medical techniques has come under siege. Director of Hematology and Immunology Professor José M. Ballester is one of the founders of the hospital. The 78-year-old finds time for most everyone, no matter how small the problem, and assured with a welcoming grin that "I'll work till I can't anymore. If I retire I'd die." He grabs a magazine from the clutter on his desk and tosses it aside, passing judgment not on its quality, but availability. "This magazine, Blood, it is a very important journal for us, the official journal of the American Society of Hematology. But we can't even get that, the blockade won't allow us to pay for it direct, we can't get it online. So we have to receive it from another country, it's late and more expensive. This is a small thing, but there are many problems regarding the blockade, scientific interchanges are limited, both ways, because of the restrictions. There have been many medical events in the US that I have applied for a visa to go and it has been very difficult. The Americans don't say no directly, but they delay until the day the conference finishes and then they give us the visa, that has happened many times.[12] Is it always coincidence? And it works the other way as well, sickle cell anemia, we have lots of experience with that, maybe more than even in the US. We can provide our expertise, they can learn from us but they never consider it." Cuba's promising pharmaceutical industry has for years been exporting a variety of drugs to dozens of countries.[13] The Cuban Molecular Immunology Center is meeting success in marketing its CIMAVAX-EGF vaccine, proven to be effective in patients with advanced lung cancer, none able to be sold in the United States.[14] Cuba's research in AIDS treatment is well-known; a trial vaccine may be on the horizon, with no chance of it reaching American patients.[15]

William Soler is not the only health facility suffering under the siege. One of the country's most well-known, the Frank País Hospital in Havana, specializes in orthopedics and traumatology. Staff has been forced to locate other markets to purchase components needed for maintenance of their hyperbaric chamber after the California-based Amron International refused to sell spare parts. Frank País, the only institution with a bone tissue bank in Cuba, endures further difficulties following the decision by American company Kapak not to supply high-density polyethylene bags used to package processed tissue.[16]

For Dr. González, a simply shrug explained how he copes with the added complications. "One does the best you can. The Cubans are different, we're not as good as we think we are, but we are not so bad as others try to portray us. We are an under-developed country, with lots of problems, but we always try to improve. We have a different system here and we are being punished for it."

While health care is a core priority of the revolution, it is but one facet of the nation's complex society. Education has played an equally important role, as has the various other segments including neighborhoods, youth, sports, women, seniors, veterans, unions. The siege has touched all parts. Education resources suffer, with basic school materials such as globes, PVC sheets, and educational materials more expensive, costing the government millions, according to officials. The University of Ciego de Ávila was forced to budget $100,000 extra when LKB-Pharmacy was unable to provide maintenance to protein purification chromatograph for the school's bioplant labs.[17] Matters seemingly unimportant as Cuba's inability to purchase Louisville, Wilson, or Rawlings sports equipment direct from American suppliers have incurred additional costs of close to $500,000.[18] Use of those items is often compulsory under international sports federation regulations.

Food has long been a target. Following the passage of the 1992 Torricelli Act making it harder for ships to transport goods to the island, approximately

1,500 tons of powdered milk from New Zealand was stopped, replaced at a higher cost from Europe. The same occurred with a shipment of soy flour from Argentina. While the Cubans looked for an alternative source, thousands of chickens were killed unnecessarily for lack of feed, resulting in a reduction in the country's egg production.[19] Fertilizers, pesticides, and equipment are consistently more expensive. Out of necessity Cuba has developed one of the world's most sophisticated organic agricultural programs, found throughout the island and in various locations in Havana.

*   *   *

The social strains brought on by the siege and the contradictory attempts to overcome it have consistently led to the misreading of events on the ground. Critics looked expectantly toward a Cuban reaction similar to the Arab Spring of 2011. Former secretary of state Condoleezza Rice spoke to the anticipation at a Dallas university in 2011. "Yes. Well, if I were Hugo Chávez, who has wrecked his country, or the Castros who've never even gotten to first base in helping their country, I would be worried about what's happening in the Middle East, because it is—even if the people of Cuba or Venezuela can't act in the same way, you can believe that there's a stirring within them to be a part of this great freedom movement."[20]

Rice and others have been wrong in large measure because the middle is not hollow. Middle East society was predominantly controlled by a leadership perceived to be foreign influenced (Egypt),[21] out of touch, and unconcerned with the masses (Tunisia) to the point of active conflict with populous interests (Libya), or where the population felt it had little outlet for grievances and few organizations to address them, other than the extreme religious option. Cuban society can be seen to be oriented for those who are willing to participate within the socialist organized parameters—which has led to the antagonist position rejecting revolutionary legitimacy based on resultant civic restrictions imposed by those same boundaries. Cubans who either become actively involved in the mass organizations or the increasing number of NGOs endorse the perception of having a stake in the revolution and the ability to contribute to government policy (whether that works in reality is open to debate). Participation functions as social entitlement, making a movement to overthrow the government at a grassroots level unlikely, regardless of the siege's economic harms. The mass organizations operate additionally to provide confirmation for declarations of democratic participation. These outlets for the public's voice helped maintain the sense of revolutionary merit during the worse disruptions of the Special Period following the collapse of the Soviet Union and defense against America's increased aggression. While the government has demonstrated its ability to make serious mistakes in half-hearted economic planning and social development particularly since the Special Period, the citizenship is more inclined to forgive and tolerate as long as the majority feel errors are mostly of omission instead of commission and that the sense of trying to improve standards for all, regardless of the failures, is the dedicated goal for both citizen and leadership. Since the Special Period the Cuban government has attempted to expand the individual's stake in the economic and social well being of the nation. A constitutional amendment in 1992 allowing direct voting for political members at local and national levels assisted in augmenting nationwide control and debate. Raúl Castro's reaching out to the population through a comprehensive survey showed a new willingness to attend to citizens' concerns. There remains depth to the logic of the revolution worth saving, and this combined with the still valid sentiment of protecting Cuban nationalism from the return to American hegemony facilitates movement in the direction of reform through engagement and not violent confrontation or social upheaval as was witnessed throughout Arab lands. The Middle East action was in part for the masses to take more control of national power; current Cuban reforms are to refine it.

"People want change, to improve things. But there are many groups the average citizen can become involved in, to express their concerns and suggestions to improve. It doesn't always work the way it should, and there is plenty of frustration as things don't get done, and the government sometimes does not listen, but it's the best we have and the majority I believe want to work to make it better," University of Havana professor of philosophy Thalía Fung offered.[22]

She has had numerous experiences dealing with issues complicated by American policy. Involved in various university-sponsored conferences, the articulate, well-respected Fung has seen many international academics shy away from attending, "The siege has induced some to vacillate on an approach to Cuba. It is a type of symbolic violence, for example there have been many from Europe, academics, express concern that if they come to Cuba they will be identified with a position that has a consequence, that the US will identify them with Cuba, without making any distinction between the position they might have and that of Cuba. I know of cases where progressive professionals have this fear of coming because of how they might be labeled by US propaganda which has so dominated international perceptions of Cuba. In 1997 we had a meeting regarding the environment, there was a person who had an extensive history with the subject, a well known Vice-President of World Watch. This person was invited to attend our conference. His links with the topic were strong, one of the top researchers in his field. We were expecting him to attend but at the last minute he said no, later it was found out he just didn't want to take the risk of being categorized for coming to Cuba, he felt it might affect his international reputation. This happens all the time."

How the siege has affected society is "a complicated issue" according to Soraya Castro, a specialist on Cuban-US affairs. For the past 25 years she has been connected with the Center for the Studies of the United States at the University of Havana, and is also involved at the Center for Studies of International Migration.

Castro is moving her office full of books and papers from its long-standing position at the university, a victim of the siege, she laughed. "Look up, it's terrible, parts of the ceiling are falling down, someone could get killed," a comment made out of a sense of embarrassment combined with genuine concern. "It is a very difficult time for us, the economy is bad, and that's why the hopes are directly related to the economic reform that has been approved in the Party Congress and other forums. Of course the blockade is not directly responsible for the condition of my office and is not totally responsible for the Cuban economy either, but it does affect so much of our economy and ordinary people's daily life."

She reflected that the state of the ceiling might be an allegory for what has been happening to Cuban society since the collapse of the Soviet Union and the tightening of siege. "The blockade has influenced Cuban society, it has been affected very negatively, particularly the past 20 years, the Special Period. Parts of what the Revolution was built upon are crumbling. The siege mentality has affected the way of living up to the point where we only think of another world out there, we just think how the United States government is going to react to what we do, to any changes we want to make. We have to do what is necessary, but there is always this thought of having to consider how the US will react, how they might use it against us, and that puts pressures and influences on our decisions. There is no Cuban history without the United States, since the Cuban Republic was born under US occupation, and it has to be taken into consideration whether you want to acknowledge it or not. People say it's paranoia, but it is paranoia based on historical fact. It is part of the Cuban national conscious how the historical relationship with the United States affects us here. And the proof is found in how the US government continues to react to Cuba; unlike they do with any other country. Their policies of aggression against us are unprecedented."

The congenial, engaging academic explained the polarization of Cuban society and how the government interacts with its citizens has its roots in the difficult relationship between the northern power and the small island. "The embargo, terrorism, Bay of Pigs, hostility, public commissions on how Cuba will be forced to change under US demands to abandon our social system here. So for god's sake how can you erase these real facts from the consciousness of the people, from those who make the leadership decisions? The government has always had to consider security, how to combat the siege, from an internal perspective. It has an effect on society, civil rights and relationships. For me and so many others, since I've opened my eyes for the first time I have lived under the embargo, American hostility, and the Revolution. I've known nothing else, I have no other reality. I'm not young anymore, I'm in my 50s, but I have no other reality to compare."

The siege sets up the environment to allow for the creation of various social restrictions, Castro assessed. "It justifies the closing of space for certain debates, things that are necessary for any society to advance. But you can see Raúl (Castro) speeches in the past two years he's not blaming all on the embargo, and is challenging Cubans to overcome it. To speak their minds and tell the government what we have problems with. And we are doing that, there is a great deal of discussion and suggestions how to improve. All under our socialist system, but the Americans believe it is all state controlled, ideologically driven, stagnant. Quite the opposite, Cuban life is organic, active, alive."

The greater danger to society, she worried, is the erosion since the Special Period of the revolution's foundation of community, brought on by growing class distinctions as a consequence of economic disparities. Cuba's new society was created equal parts on Che's "new man" philosophy as it was on a concept of social equality. Economic shortcomings brought on by siege and policy errors made everyone suffer from austerity even while the government's strategy was intended for all to enjoy prosperity. The inadequacies of commercial expectations in the first decades did little to dampen the sense of egalitarianism; of neighbors knowing and assisting each other when necessary. Until the upheaval of the Special Period altered the equation, when those with access to foreign dollars, tourist incomes, and remittances from Miami were visibly living better than the rest. The collapse led to a corrosion of community morals, of a dramatic intensification in administrative corruption, of an increase in crime as a way to survive and profit, and a lessening of the openness to assist a neighbor when one's personal predicament was so dire.

Castro commented, "There are those with access to foreign dollars who live better than others, and that was not the intent of the Cuban Revolution when it triumphed in 1959. But Cuban society has evolved and so has its realities, where you have doctors living on less than others who get money from their relatives in Miami or by other legal and illegal means. During the Special Period in particular, it caused stress where you are seeing more of the rich Cubans living better, and that produces tensions between people and the government and the system here. It is a difficult situation."[23]

The darkest days of the Special Period also had a harmful moral affect, turning honest citizens to the black market and its illegal activities solely in order to survive. "It was a terrible time for everyone, people stole to survive, people who wouldn't do it otherwise, but had no other option. The economy collapsed, we had nothing, and the Americans were thinking of new ways to make things worse. I had to do things, go to the black market, for my children to have something to eat. Those days the government didn't know which way to turn, we couldn't depend on the state for anything, people lost confidence in the system," a manager with an influential Cuban women's magazine explained.[24]

If US strategy at the time had been one of ending the travel restrictions and normalizing relations, the action could have precipitated the collapse of the government through inundation of tourists and the additional complications that would have placed on a government where management is paramount. "This government is always about control, and at that time they had none. Put the American mix into it and it would have overwhelmed them, they couldn't have handled it. Instead, the Americans increased the embargo, made things worse. That gave the government some breathing space, time to react and use the US to justify continuing the same things—they knew how to deal with American aggression. So making the embargo worse just gave the government the opportunity to recover, and keep the restrictions on," speculated Ramon Ortiz, a part-time cab driver in his 50s who works the Havana to Varadero run. His opinion is a common one among the urbanites whose faith in the system has diminished, but are hesitant of what the future might bring. Even though acknowledging the blockade has had a negative effect on Cuba's economy, the former scientist placed the greatest share of culpability at the feet of the government. "They put the blockade in all their luggage of blame, everything that goes wrong is the US fault. Sure the US has problems, so does Canada, any country in the world. So you can always take an international view. But I'm Cuban, I live in Cuba and I have to deal with that reality, and the reality is that the economy is a disaster, the government is terrible. I wish the US would end the embargo, lift the travel restrictions. But then would the government try to control that, put conditions on all US activity so nothing would help the average Cubans?" Despite the complaints, the revolution still stimulates a sense of nationalism, tempering anger without diminishing impatience. "I don't want 100 per cent capitalism, I don't want the US to come in and take over. But this can't go on, this government has to do something and my opinion is that these new economic reforms mean nothing. I don't see any difference," Ortiz said.

The social contract so vital to the cohesion of the Cuban Revolution has been severely tested and damaged since the 1990s, still finding itself under tenuous repair. The greatest stress to the refurbishing of the relationship comes from the younger generation who have known nothing but life under the difficulties of the Special Period. Add to the mix the powerful consumer influences outsiders are bringing to Cuba through tourism and business, and Soraya Castro worries personal values are being eroded from within. "You see the students here with all the latest things, and the others want that. It's the mentality, I don't understand it. It happens elsewhere and it is happening here. It's so hard for me to understand, why do you have to wear an expensive pair of jeans—many of the younger generation are moving away from what is important and becoming materialistic. It's the way of the world, but it's difficult to accept. Not all, but in the city, in Havana, it has really had an impact."

Eighteen-year-old Carmela Martínez, a second-year student at the University of Havana, has little problem appreciating what is important. "Our generation, all we see are problems here, never any improvement; the government isn't doing anything to help, there are no jobs. I don't know if I'll do what I studied for. Of course it's better to earn real money, working in the tourist industry, doing what you have to. And to want nice clothes, to go out and have a good time at a disco, what's wrong with that? My parent's generation, maybe that's different, they had good things in the 70s and 80s. For us, why should we support the government, what have they done for us?"[25]

That attitude is incomprehensible to Castro. "If I have a pair of sandals to wear, that's enough. Why do you have to have sandals with a 'name' on it? It is the materialistic approach that has touched us as well. That addresses only individual needs, less community oriented values, and does nothing to advance the society we have tried to build here, for the betterment of all. But that's what happens now, people don't see what American policies have done, they internalize the effects, and blame all on the government."

Thalía Fung agreed the younger generation has to be engaged if the revolution is to survive. "They believe the defects of the government are our responsibilities, that of the older generation. There is an ideological influence that has great weight, which we have forced on our youth to live through terrible internal misery, economic problems. And the younger generation wants the best and newest things, those things that the older generation didn't have. If you tell the younger generation all the problems the older generation had to go through during the early years of revolution, they don't care, they say it's just 'blah, blah, blah.' The parents don't want to deprive their children, and the younger generation wants to see a future for themselves. Those are important social pressures that are made worse by the state of the economy, and the siege. As Fidel Castro has proclaimed on numerous occasions, the revolution can only be destroyed from within."[26]

While Cuban society has bent discordantly under the conflict between individual desire and community accountability in part brought on by the economic injuries of siege and the government's authoritarian responses, the island's culture may have in fact benefitted from the worst times of blockade.

Rafael Hernández, director of the influential magazine *Temas* (themes) and a well-respected political scientist, suggested the most critical years of revolutionary history have coincided with periods of intellectual boom. "Intellectually the period of the early 1960s, the second half of the 1990s and lately, these are the times in Cuba of a tremendous level of activity and intellectual search. What do these times have in common? The early 60s Cuba was under incredible pressure, isolated, not yet fully connected with the Soviets, American aggression was at its height. The second half of the 1990s when the Special Period hit, the country collapsed economically and no one knew what was going to happen. The Americans increased the pressure with Torricelli and Helms-Burton acts. And now since 2008 the international economic collapse, and the damage the three major hurricanes did, it has put us in a very difficult time."[27]

Hernández is outspoken in his belief the transitions that have taken place in Cuba over the past two decades must be recognized not only from a social viewpoint, but from the cultural and humanistic as well. The current state of the artistic world on the island is going through an exciting time, he enthused, as compared to its restrictive past. The development of the Cuban novel form, the international recognition of music from Buena Vista Social Club to Pablo Milanés and Silvio Rodríguez, and the expansion of individual artists, film producers, writers, and dancers are but a few examples of Cuba's

cultural explosion on the world. The island's *Ballet Nacional de Cuba*, led
by internationally recognized dancers Viengtsay Valdés and Osiel Gounod,
is consistently in demand, and the children's theater group *La Colmenita*
received critical acclaim while touring the United States during 2011. Cuban
filmmaking has developed a well-deserved reputation for being daring and
critical, from internationally acclaimed works *Strawberry and Chocolate* to
more current efforts as *Juan of the Dead*, a zombie comedy that has a serious
social conscious. *Habanastation* has also garnered considerable attention for
its realistic portrayal of growing economic discrepancies in Cuba.

"In comparison, the most relatively secure time politically and economically for Cuba was in the 1970s to the mid 1980s, when the standard of
living increased and the economy was performing well in terms of relative
growth. When we were fully embraced under the Soviet system. But at the
same time we had narrower intellectual and artistic freedom of expression,"
said the energetic Hernández, recognized for his strength of conviction, ani-
mated opinions and independent thought. "Bad times create a special opportunity for intellectual creativity, this is not a social law but you can trace back
to the whole history of the Cuban intellectual and cultural process in the
past half century. This is more than a co-incidence. I don't know what would
happen culturally when we become a prosperous country,"[28] he commented
with an ironic laugh.

Cultural conformity was at its height in the late 1960s and much of the
1970s, particularly during a five-year period known as the Grey Years where
political ideology was the measuring unit for the validation of art. During
the period from 1971 to 1976 officials took a narrow view of what constituted Fidel's edict "within the revolution." Some artists and academics were
fired from their jobs and hounded into exile. Free-thinking poet Heberto
Padilla was denounced, arrested, and forced to make a public apology for his
thoughts even after winning a major local literary award. "Art as a weapon of
struggle," became an acceptable standard for top Cuban cultural officials,[29]
following closely the Soviet model despite Fidel Castro's warning in the
1960s that the enemies of the revolution were "capitalists and imperialists,
not abstract art."[30]

Nothing struck more of an indictment against the reactionary shift of the
revolution than the *Unidades Militares de Ayuda a la Producción* (UMAP)
camps from 1967 to 1969. The centers targeted homosexuals in particular,
although vagrants, counterrevolutionaries, juvenile delinquents, and certain
religious followers were also caught and sent for rehabilitation and reeduca-
tion in facilities reminiscent of Soviet labor encampments, revealed in the
1984 documentary *Improper Conduct*. Gays had come under scorn early on
in the revolution, with the closing of the periodical *Lunes de Revolución* amid
a wave of media censorship; its gay writers publicly disgraced and dismissed
from their jobs. In his autobiography Castro claimed the camps were used in
lieu of the mistreatment homosexuals were receiving in the military during
the Angolan War. They would do laborious tasks and be housed roughly,
but some saw it as better than joining the Cuban military, he reasoned,

as they would often still be publicly humiliated and discharged by homophobic elements.[31]

Castro later evoked siege imagery as the rationale for having his eyes diverted from this prejudice, taking responsibility in a 2010 interview with Mexican newspaper *La Jornada*. The treatment of homosexuals in Cuba at that time was "a great injustice, great injustice. If anyone is responsible, it's me...We had so many and such terrible problems, problems of life or death. In those moments I was not able to deal with that matter [of homosexuals]. I found myself immersed, principally, in the Crisis of October, in the war, in policy questions. At the time we were being sabotaged systematically, there were armed attacks against us, we had too many problems. Keeping one step ahead of the CIA, which was paying so many traitors, was not easy." Blame was also assigned on Cuba's macho history. As with many other countries, Cuba's attitudes toward the homosexual community have softened, eliminating all laws against gays or lesbians. Transgender operations are now covered by the health system and Raúl Castro's daughter Mariela is one of the strongest voices for gay rights. The problem of AIDS victims brought the treatment of gays into question in the 1980s when isolation camps brought down criticism from those who called the sanitariums "pretty prisons" while the government responded that the arrangement helped contain the disease and provided comfortable surroundings where gay men could live with each other in their final days.[32]

Further cultural components became targets of the defense against siege, the prerevolutionary diverse Cuban media one of the earliest to fall. By the mid-1960s it was completely taken over by the state after a short period of tolerance from 1959 to 1961. As privately controlled newspapers and magazines, mostly under American ownership, became increasingly shrill against the policies of the revolution, some calling for open revolt and an increase in siege, the government moved to shut them down. When *Diario de la Marina*, founded in 1832, began publishing reports from Miami calling for Castro's ouster and an American military intervention in 1960, he quickly ended its long history.[33] The media, Castro proclaimed, would not be used as a tool for counterrevolutionaries while the nation was under threat by those same forces.[34] A piece of social plurality was lost, victimized by the state's obsession with the importance to maintain solidarity of public speech under external threat and internal dissention. It has historical roots, Professor Arturo López-Levy observed, saying the country has a deeply ingrained "fortress under siege" hostility to speech that might give ammunition to the enemy dating back to the struggle to gain independence from Spain in the 1890s.[35] Present-day controls echo similar conditions and as one Cuban media critic noted, "The unanimity present in the Cuban media is the reflection of a siege mentality conditioned by US pressures, which work against greater pluralism and a broader public debate."[36]

The end of Soviet patronage, the country's plunge into its great depression, the social upheaval brought on by the Special Period, and the increase in American aggression energized an awakening of cultural expression,

Hernández enthused. "From the 1990s cultural institutions responded to this opening, and are still contributing more space, more support for expressive artistic views to be able to deal with controversial issues that Cuba has faced since the Special Period." There is a counterintuitive symbiosis at work: "The more secure a society is can be reflected in conventional or conservative cultural forms; the less secure can mean an increased cultural opening."

Internally, the movement toward increasing space for artists continues, with Hernández pointing to his current project as evidence. The quarterly published *Temas* was originated in 1994 as a vehicle designed to observe, critique, and reflect on social issues. The magazine is mostly unknown outside of Cuba (other than among international watchers) but gives refute to the claim that there is no media criticism of the government, or that intellectual debate is the exclusive property of Cuban émigrés, American government officials, or the myriad agencies and academic centers that focus on Cuba as part of the lucrative industry of US-based commentators and experts of the revolution. Funding goes through the government but that does not equate to editorial direction.

"Temas has never been a magazine presenting the official views of the government. It has always been something else. The content is decided by an editorial board, not by government decree. The board is comprised of Cuban intellectuals and artists, some of them outside of Cuba; and the vast majority well known social scientists and cultural investigators," Hernández explained.

The research-driven magazine has dealt with a variety of topics affecting Cuban society, including the economic difficulties, corruption, failures in government policy, future of the revolution, and the errors of leadership. Hernández stressed there is no censorship within the editorial staff, citing a topic many outside of Cuba would perceive to be off limits. "If I want to conduct an issue on the sexual market in Cuba, in regards to tourism, I need research done in Cuba. How the subject will be covered has to be decided. That's not censorship, it is how to decide what is more important and what lends itself to the type of research we do and the timing of it. All that influences what is written, it's the normal process any magazine goes through, not censorship." The so-called free press, owned by private concerns under the capitalist system, deal with filters and influences that determine content and self-censorship issues, he added, in areas such as environmental matters or economic issues.

Regardless of the progression used to determine the finished product, the magazine has consistently faced critical reaction from those "who are more conservative, and when we deal with issues that are critical, they think that can be used as a weapon against the Revolution. There are those who understand *Temas*, and there are others who think it shouldn't exist. That's from the siege mentality, that there should be nothing to distract from the sense of solidarity, nothing that should weaken our resolve against US policy or give them ammunition to attack us. It makes my work more difficult, but it doesn't influence what subjects we want to cover."

Without that sense of vulnerability, brought on and exploited by American hostility aimed at regime change, it would be easier to debate issues in an open environment. He further added, "So there is an affect of the siege. We have discussed topics, recently we did a full issue on transition in Cuba, the majority we interviewed said yes there are important changes taking place in the country. We have taken on issues that affect people, and treated them openly, so we can't use the US as a complete excuse not to discuss those subjects. But when the United States doesn't want anything from the Cubans except surrender, there is an influence and understanding of defense, of maybe being a little more cautious in order not to give a reason or opening to enable the United States to make us surrender."

While *Temas* may be considered unusual, it is not unique. Additional protoindependent publications with a critical bent include *La Gaceta* on matters of art; *Cataura* dealing with race relations; *Juventud Rebelde* on current daily issues. *Palante* is a cartoon humor magazine with a strong and loyal following for its political pokes at both sides. Criticism of bureaucratic failings and complaints of economic missteps can be heard regularly on *Radio Progreso's* "Puntos de Vista" and *Radio Rebelde's* noontime "Hablando Claro." Even the official voice of the government, *Granma*, has taken to publishing pages of letters from the public fed up with the difficulties and disadvantages of daily life. Internationally, Cuban Catholic Church publications *Espacio Laical* and *Palabra Nueva* have demonstrated the ability to challenge the Communist Party, encouraging current reforms to ensure they are neither compromised nor delayed.

As a man of words, Hernández encourages the constructive criticism that is a sign of the health of the revolution. He speaks harshly, however, of America's pursuit to command definitions and promote misconceptions. "The US has tried to control certain words against Cuba. They use the term 'civil society' to describe political opposition here. Transition, freedom of expression, human rights, travel restrictions, elections, democracy. These are words that have been politicized; the US brings them into the realm of the ideological. This makes it more difficult for the government here to deal with these subjects. There is a siege against words in Cuba, imposed by the Americans. To get back those words for the Cuban people, we can't allow the US government to steal those words. They belong to revolutionary tradition. This is our heritage, not capitalist heritage. This is the heritage of the Revolution. Part of our work is to try to exorcise those words and concepts and to return them to the values they belong; to the revolutionary socialist culture."

Examples abound of American attempts to impose its terminology upon Cuban society. Secretary of State Hillary Clinton added hers while pronouncing to a House committee in early 2011, "We share your commitment to freedom and democracy for the Cuban people. That's an absolute, ironclad commitment."[37]

Ownership of words and terminologies has been a hard-fought conflict the Cuban government has waged against their northern nemesis the past decades, revealed in Fidel Castro's efforts in his Battle of Ideas. Since relinquishing power in 2006 Castro has refocused the battle on the roots of revolutionary strength through the power of description in the struggle between socialist ideals and capitalist values. American attempts to undermine the walls through social sappers have met fierce resistance in the fight over language. "We must continue to pulverize the lies that are told against us...This is the ideological battle, everything is the Battle of Ideas," Fidel Castro proclaimed.[38]

The management of terms has consistently been utilized to promote siege for the benefit of the Cuban people, a principle Hernández strongly rejected. "Ridiculous, the embargo is aimed to hurt the population, not help them. That has been America's intent from the start."

Outside of the literary world, Cuban culture and society have shown an increased willingness to examine internal faults regardless of the potential utilization it might have for American propaganda. Television character Professor MentePollo and comic Mariconchi expose government absurdities and the affect on the individual. Punk rocker Gorki became well-known for their direct challenge to leadership. National icon Pablo Milanés created a stir in the summer of 2011 when he spoke directly and forcefully about racial difficulties and civil right restrictions in his country.[39] The singer continues to offer his critical opinions, accepting the embargo is not "totally to blame for our misfortunes. But the existence of the blockade has never given us the opportunity to measure ourselves. I would like to die with the responsibilities of our misfortunes very clearly."[40]

The church is also developing a new association with the government, emerging as a quasi-loyal opposition under the expanded social atmosphere under Raúl Castro. Roman Catholic Cardinal Jaime Ortega became the leader in the dialogue between the church and government that led in 2011 to the freeing of the dissidents arrested seven years earlier. Traditionally opposed to communism, the Catholic Church was marginalized and then shut out completely, the institution portrayed by revolutionary leaders as an intransigent force in support of those opposing the new order. After the Bay of Pigs invasion Cuba officially declared itself atheistic, a designation unchanged until the fall of the Soviet Union when the revolution proclaimed it was now a secular state. This softer position came in partial response to the visit of Pope John Paul II in 1998, which resulted in the government reaffirming the right to religious freedom, as well as reinstating Christmas as a national holiday. Both the government and church now have positive, beneficial interchanges and each side gained considerable standing following the second papal visit, this time Pope Benedict XVI in 2012, the visit also resulting in another holiday for the citizens, this time Good Friday.

Disputes such as church requests for parochial schools remain unresolved, but the institution has come out strongly against the siege, pointedly stating in 2006 following Fidel's illness that the Catholic Church would not allow foreign intervention into the internal affairs of Cuba. Cardinal Ortega additionally expressed his optimism that the religious revival in the nation will continue to have an impact on the direction new reforms are heading. "There is always a dialogue about the role of the Church with its pastoral activities and about the life of the nation under the economic changes planned for Cuba, changes that society is waiting for, that every Cuban hopes for, and that the Church has also encouraged, supported, and wished for."[41]

Tolerance of high-profile Cubans who publicly criticize but remain supportive of the system is an indication of Raúl Castro's determination to encourage divergence and overcome the muzzling effect of siege. Pablo Milanés has been outspoken in his criticism, including comments to the Miami media before his 2011 concerts, reiterating his complaint on travel restrictions the government places on its citizens, "Every Cuban in Cuba must have the right to leave the country without a permit card or going through a particular bureaucratic filer."[42] The interview was conducted with *El Nuevo Herald*, considered the harshest voice of the hard-right exile community in South Florida. While declaring his continued belief in socialism, the 68-year-old singer expressed a lack of trust for those who implement it, "If we think of socialism as a system to satisfy human beings from all points of view: the economy, love, the spirit, peace; we can say that none of the socialisms produced so far has achieved these goals."

Officials have not moved to stop the international star from giving concert tours around the world. Milanés, known for his complex, deeply moving ballads, considers himself a socialist. "My 53 years of revolutionary militancy give me the right, which very few exercise in Cuba, to express myself with the freedom that my principles require," he declared. Reaction to his candor was drawn exactly upon the political fault lines, with the counterrevolutionaries applauding his remarks and claiming that what he said in Miami he could never say in Havana; while supporters castigated the singer for being unnecessarily harsh in the exact place where his words would carry the most propaganda efficacy.

"Anyone who tries to say there is no criticism allowed in Cuba is not telling the truth. There is tremendous critical dialogue going on inside the country, on the economic and political changes, and we have had many Cubans up here speaking critically about the problems. The anti-revolutionaries want everyone to think that anyone who criticizes the government in Cuba will end up in jail. Ridiculous," CUNY Professor Peter Roman noted.

The criticism leveled by Milanés became part of a continuing conversation between the government and its people. There are lines, however, that are crossed at one's peril—primarily any denigration in public of Fidel or Raúl, or the top leadership. Personal attacks are seen to be damaging to the nation and a basic tool for American policy aims. The Cuban government's hypersensitivity to that condition persists and it has taken severe action, landing many in jail for taking that step. It led to the fall of two high-profile officials in 2009 when well-respected Vice President Carlos Lage and foreign relations minister Felipe Pérez Roque were sacked from their positions after a video showed them mocking the Castro brothers and deriding the advanced ages of the ruling circle.[43] While space for critical expression is expanding, the rules of the game remain elusive. Although in 2011 Fidel Castro challenged the usually timid state-run media to be bolder, with "objective, constant and critical" reporting, he immediately added a caution. "That doesn't mean that now each of us can just grab a pen and start writing whatever we feel like. Because he who makes mistakes must pay for it, no matter who he is."[44]

Recognizing the level of criticism the government is willing to abide is "a very difficult question to know where the line is, because the line depends on the moment," said Arturo López-Levy, a Cuban-born economist who lectures at the University of Denver.[45] Critical examination of a society, particularly one that underwent such radical change as Cuba's, is a vital element to progress. That normal condition has been corrupted by the pressures of siege and the demands it imposes for defense; the result is the government's consistency in shifting the boundaries of acceptability.

One fierce, unapologetic critic is the author of Generation Y, the internationally recognized, award-winning blog. Yoani Sánchez is as much a worldwide phenomenon for her writings as for the perception her fortitude demonstrates how fearful the government is to move against her, according to her fiercely loyal readers. Sánchez writes regularly for *Huffington Post*, has apparently interviewed President Obama, and her blog is translated into more than a dozen languages and claims millions of hits each month. Her work brought her a plethora of accolades in 2008—the journalism award Ortega & Gasset, worth 15,000 Euros, granted by conservative Spanish newspaper *El País*. She was selected among the 100 most influential people by *Time* magazine that same year.

Sánchez is implacable in her condemnations of all things revolutionary. In the past she has called Cuba "a huge prison with ideological walls," "a ship taking on water about to sink," where "creatures of the shadows, like vampires feed on our human happiness, inoculate us with fear of beatings, threats, blackmail." All of the island's problems are laid at the feet of the government. She went so far as to draw a threatening parallel between what might happen to Raúl Castro and the former Libyan leader. "In the bloodied face of Muammar Gaddafi our authorities have seen a prophetic sign of their possible fate, and now they are trying to shield themselves to ward off a similar outcome."[46]

Sánchez lived outside of Cuba for years, returning to Havana in 2004. Three years later Generation Y was born, with it the consistent denouncements of daily living conditions inside the country. Although at one point she claimed she was roughed up by Cuban security,[47] the government has done little to prevent her blog from reaching the outside world or to anyone with Internet access inside the country. Officials have, however, denied her permission to travel to pick up awards for her writings, a further example of how puerile the government has sometimes treated opponents.[48] Sánchez is considered one of the strongest voices of antigovernment sentiment living inside Cuba, and her writings carry great weight within those elements. Recognizing that the objective of American policy is to overthrow the Cuban government, Sánchez plainly admits that she shares the same goal: "The US wants a change of government in Cuba, but I want it too." She also reaffirms her will to impose "a sui generis capitalism" in Cuba, and her connections with the American government are well documented.[49]

American hostility has little influence over Cuban society, Sánchez asserts, assigning blame for most of the country's problems on the political structure. "Eighty percent of the economic problems are on the government, 20 percent on the sanctions...Much has been said of David and Goliath to describe the conflict (between Cuba and the US). But the only Goliath for me is the Cuban government that imposes control, lawlessness, low wages, repression, restrictions."

At the same time Sánchez publicly opposes American sanctions and travel restrictions "an atrocity. It is a failed policy. Although I've said it many times, it gets no press because it is bothersome that I have an opinion that deviates from the archetype of the opposition. I sent a letter to the U.S. Senate advocating for allowing U.S. citizens to travel to Cuba. It is an atrocity to see that U.S. citizens are prevented from traveling to Cuba, like the Cuban government prevents me from leaving my country. In any case I think the embargo has been the perfect argument for the Cuban government to maintain intolerance, control and internal repression."

The government's closest response to the blogger has been Margarita Alarcón, daughter of National Assembly President Ricardo Alarcón. With a site of her own to give voice to the changes taking place in Cuba,[50] Margarita countered the claim American policy bears no weight on Cuban society or on the imposition of civil rights restrictions, specifically limits to free speech. "Censorship is something that the Cuban Revolution has been criticized for throughout the years. In the early days, this censorship was in part due to a need the government felt it had in order to protect the budding nation and its people from obtrusive negative propaganda which had already begun to take its toll...Today the government still feels it needs to censor certain information and outbursts in order to protect it and continues to do so for the same reasons as in the past. One of Cuba's biggest problems is that the country is never left on its own to resolve and deal with its own problems without outside interference, hence giving the government not only the possibility but also the excuse for censorship."[51]

Although the degrees of restriction consistently rouse controversy as to the role American hostility enforces, what has rarely been at issue is the extent to which the Cuban leadership restricts the actions of a certain brand of dissenter—defined by those citizens who have accepted financial or material aid from the US government with the intent of working toward implementing American policy goals. Few other matters bring the siege into sharper focus than these Cubans who are hailed in Miami as courageous opponents of an inherently evil regime while condemned in Havana as traitors being bought by those who wish to destroy the revolution.

Historically, citizens exposed—or even suspected—to be in league with the enemy at time of war or national security are treated severely. America has had its experiences with individuals or groups assumed of sympathy for the other side; those of German descent in World War I, the Japanese in World War II, and Muslims today. Political prisoners are also nothing new to the United States; Eugene Debs was incarcerated for opposing the war effort, Mumia Abu Jamal and Leonard Peltier considered the same decades later. Puerto Ricans agitating for independence have served lengthy jail sentences.[52]

"This response enables us both to secure our own safety and vent our fury at those we already view with suspicion or contempt. If we have to put some aliens or radicals in jail to increase our sense of security, then so be it. Indeed, all the better. This is not theory. It is the unimpeachable lesson of history," so wrote Geoffrey Stone on his work describing how modern societies succumb to the collapse of free speech and intolerance toward dissidence in time of war or national security, or against political movements seen in favor of tearing down the existing order, violently or not.[53]

Government response intensifies when confronting those in compliance with enemy goals. In 2003 the Cuban government applied history's paradigm when it moved against 75 opponents under surveillance by security agents. Charges were based on confirmation they had accepted money, material aid, and direction from the American government, coordinated through the Interest Section in Havana.[54]

The crackdown became one in a long list of events that seemed to authenticate the regime's fiercest critics. Executing three alleged hijackers of a ferry the same year heightened anti-Castro bashing. What was usually missing in foreign press reports was a semblance of context. The arrests were induced under specific legislation, the Law Against Acts of Terrorism,[55] designed to counter American hostility. It called for the death sentence for hijackings involving the use of armed force and violence. The executions came under fears of a new destabilization campaign against Cuba, based on concerns the country might be next on the hit list in America's war against terrorism following the invasion of Iraq. US diplomats were seen to warn Cuba, along with Iran, Syria, and North Korea, to "learn the lessons of Iraq."[56] State Department official John Bolton recklessly stated that the island government might have the capacity to produce biological weapons.[57] Concurrent to Bolton's pronouncements were calls from Miami for an invasion of their homeland to finally solve the Castro problem. The dissident arrests can be considered an extreme violation of freedom of assembly and expression, the executions a blatant abuse of human rights, but in Cuba's eyes were taken as the only internal solution to the ratcheting up of the siege under Torricelli and Helms-Burton, the increased pressure on its economy from American aggression at a particularly vulnerable time, and the tensions brought on by President Bush Jr.'s statements of being on the right or wrong side of the terrorists—with most in his administration unhesitatingly putting Cuba in the latter category.[58] Officials were becoming hyperparanoid to American intentions as the siege mentality was ratcheted up a few notches.

At the time of the arrests relations between Cuban officials and the head of the American Interest Section James Cason were at their lowest. Cason, a favored appointment of the Bush Jr. administration, came into the job with time-honored American defined terminologies that left no doubt as to his priorities. "All of our allies agree that their policy goal in Cuba is, ultimately, the same as ours: the rapid and peaceful transition to a democratic government characterized by strong support for human rights and an open market economy." He stated on the same day, "the Administration's top priority is to promote a rapid, peaceful transition,"[59] or as Cuban intellectual Manuel E. Yepe disassembled, "transition to democracy" means "return to obedience," citing Afghanistan and Iraq as examples.[60]

Soon after being installed, Cason began implementing his intentions, holding meetings with high-profile government opponents, providing books, tape recordings, and material to those calling themselves independent librarians and writers. Evidence later indicated many of the self-indentified journalists were paid by the Interest Section to write antigovernment articles to be placed in the international press.[61] Cason then took a tour of the island handing out anti-Castro material, publicly denouncing the government and exceeding all diplomatic norms, according to Cuban officials and outside observers.

"As a diplomat you are not allowed to go into a foreign country and try and subvert the government or engage in internal politics of that country," Washington lawyer José Pertierra commented. "You are not allowed to take money into that foreign country. It is not up to the US government to have any voice in Cuba. Cuba doesn't belong to the United States government. Cuba is an independent foreign nation and under international law it has the right to pick and choose its own form of government and decide to do things as it sees fit."[62]

The State Department's response to Cuban complaints of Cason's actions was dismissive, claiming the Interest Section was involved with helping locals who wanted to receive food, assistance, and hope. It was all quite innocuous, Vicki Huddleston, head of the Interest Section before Cason, said. "We were handing out radios am, fm, short wave, to everyone, dissidents, Cuban people, government officials, whomever was willing to take a radio got a radio and Cubans love the radio because they were more powerful than the local radios."[63]

Matters became so tense that Fidel Castro even threatened to shut down the Interest Section if the interference continued, a move that might not have been unwelcome. A report suggested that Assistant Secretary of State for Western Hemisphere Affairs Roger Noriega told a radio station he and Cason—conflicting with US policy—sought to create confrontation with the Cuban government leading to Cason being declared persona non grata. The expulsion, in turn, would provide the Bush administration with a pretext to close the US Interests Section in Havana, kick the Cubans out of their counterpart in Washington, and heighten the increasingly acrimonious relationship.[64]

The Interest Section became an intelligence Trojan Horse, seen as a method to try to break the revolution from within. It was countenanced, complained about, and confined. But it did not stop. The Americans became progressively more involved with the journalists, many who had no professional background. A number of negative articles ended up in the international press to the satisfaction of US officials: "We have trained hundreds of journalists over a 10 year period whose work has appeared in major international news outlets," thus damaging claims of the independent nature of the opposition in the country.[65]

As far as Pertierra is concerned those arrested "were not only acting under the direction and control of the United States government, according to the evidence presented at the trial and the testimony against them by the people who had penetrated the organizations, but they were also being paid by the United States embassy, to do the kind of independent reporting or independent library work that they were supposedly doing. The stories were overwhelmingly critical of the Cuban government, were published in American publications and controlled and directed by the United States."[66]

Citizens accepting financial or material aid, much less orders, from the Interest Section are putting themselves in an untenable situation, confirmed former head of the US Interest Section Wayne Smith. "It's illegal and unwise to send money to the Cuban dissidents. When the US declares its objective is to overthrow the government of Cuba and later admits that one of the means of achieving that goal is to provide funds to the Cuban dissidents, these dissidents find themselves de facto in the position of agents paid by a foreign power to overthrow their own government."[67] That's the definition of treason in most every country, Pertierra added. "The actions of the Cuban government are justified under Cuban and international law. Any country is permitted to defend its sovereignty against foreign interference and really that's what the case of the 75 is all about. Foreign interference by the biggest enemy that Cuba has, namely the United States and the government that is far more powerful, militarily and economically than Cuba."[68] He noted comparable laws in the United States make it illegal for citizens to receive financial aid from Al-Qaeda or any other organization expressing its intention to overthrow the government, no matter how innocent their public profile.[69]

The arrests and trials came down in March 2003 after infiltrators produced evidence the dissidents were accepting money and direction from Cason. Those convicted were sentenced to long jail terms of 10–20 years. Then foreign minister Felipe Pérez Roque provided the rationalization, "The decision of Mr. Cason to convert the North American interests section in Havana and his residence into practically a headquarters for the subversion of Cuba...These judicial proceedings have to be understood as Cuba's actions when left with no other alternative on the path of confrontation and provocation that the US government has chosen for its relations with Cuba."[70] Refusal to connect the Interest Section's actions with the arrests was immediate: "Castro has been slapping his people around since Jim Cason was in junior high school and he needs no pretext for throwing people in jail," so replied Assistant Secretary of State Roger Noriega. International reaction was unswervingly negative, with even long-standing friends fiercely critical.

A small number of media and well-respected agencies acknowledged, infrequently, the position of the Cuban government. British news agency *Reuters* commented, "the US government openly provides federally-funded support for dissident activities, which Cuba considers an illegal act."[71] *Associated Press* reported America's efforts to manufacture and support internal opposition has been a decades' long policy: "Over the years, the U.S. government has spent many millions of dollars to support Cuba's opposition. Some American funding comes directly from the U.S. government, whose laws call for ousting Fidel Castro and his younger brother Raúl, Cuba's new President."[72]

The massive international outcry became a public relations disaster for the Castro government, and the condemnations resulted in the expected reaction of a country under siege—lashing out at critics, the deepening of entrenchment, and heightened sensitivity against both friend and foe who failed to appreciate or accept Cuba's position.

Action against the 75 quickly emerged as another rationale for not engaging Cuba; the United State's determined to freeze the diminishing amount of contact with the Castro government until the dissidents were released. The anti-American rhetoric increased in step with the position, and both sides fixed into a hostile mode not seen since the early 1960s. The episode additionally revealed the reflexive capacity to utilize American interference to justify cracking down on internal opposition.

Government's action against the 75, however, was in contrast to the more cautious approach to such high-profile critics as Oswaldo Paya and Elizardo Sánchez, longtime vocal adversaries of the government. The two had previously run afoul of the law for their open antirevolutionary pronouncements, but were not arrested in the 2003 crackdown, due in equal parts to their international status and the pair's rejection of American largesse. Paya, who died in a car accident July 2012,[73] had publicly stated those taking US aid were counterproductive to the dissident cause, commenting that accepting assistance would have placed him in the position of being supported by a foreign power against his own government. "It is not right, nor do we accept, any external element, whether from the United States of America, Europe or anywhere else, trying to design the Cuban transition process."[74] Accepting aid only harms efforts to establish an independent opposition and gives the perfect pretext for the regime, he added, a sentiment reinforced by former President Jimmy Carter after visiting dissidents in 2002, coming away with the understanding, "they were unanimous in expressing...opposition...to any funding of their efforts from the US government. Any knowledge or report of such financial support would just give credibility to the long-standing claims of President Castro that they were 'paid lackeys' of Washington."[75] The tightrope the dissidents have to walk, according to journalist Tracey Eaton, is "once identified as an opponent of the government you'll lose your job, probably go to jail, have no means of support. So it's almost impossible to be a dissident without outside assistance." Eaton, who currently runs a blog set up to examine the amount of money the US government spends on Cuba projects, and its effectiveness, added, "It's an easy way for Cuba to label people as mercenaries, as paid dissidents. The money support is a complex matter, it can be seen to undermine the process to advance freedoms in Cuba, hurting the cause."[76]

Paya, as head of the Christian Liberation Movement, was best known for his efforts in 1998 with the Varela Project petition calling for the change of the socialist nature of the country.[77] The petition was presented to the government, which shortly afterward responded by one of their own showing overwhelming support for the current political system.

Sánchez has publicly denounced the embargo against Cuba. "For more than 15 years, I have criticized the embargo, and later Helms-Burton. I think it's wrong, and I think Washington has committed many errors in its policy towards Cuba since 1959." Even while recognizing the conditions for siege he refuted its influence, "The fundamental cause of poverty and lack of liberty in Cuba isn't the embargo or Helms-Burton, but its totalitarian government, which is by definition a violator of human rights."[78]

Emerging from the crackdown was the establishment of the *Damas de Blanco* (Ladies in White), an antigovernment group made up of the wives of those incarcerated.[79] The Ladies have a recognized public profile within Cuba, regularly holding public demonstrations in protest against the arrests and what they call the repressive nature of the regime. Internationally the group has also gained notoriety, receiving the Sakharov Prize from the European Parliament in 2005. Leader of the group Laura Pollan, who passed away in 2011, was often seen railing against the government's attempts to prevent the protest marches, sometimes resulting in serious scuffles with progovernment factions she charged were organized by the state.[80] The marches continued even after the dissidents, including her husband Héctor Maseda, were released in 2010. Protests shifted with the Ladies campaigning for the discharge of other prisoners convicted of violent crimes such as hijacking, asserting those were of a political nature as well.

The Ladies in White are not without controversy. Its leaders have defiantly admitted receiving substantial amounts of money and material from the United States. "We unconditionally accept help and support from the extreme right to left," Pollan revealed in an interview with American media. Vladimiro Roca confessed that the Cuban dissidents are subsidized by Washington, saying that the financial aid received is "totally and completely legal." Marta Beatríz Roque said that the financial assistance received from the United States is indispensable for dissident activity.[81] Roque, one of the most outspoken of the 75, had been arrested in 1997 for releasing a document: The Country Belongs to All of Us, accusing the Cuban leadership of being "in the unenviable company of Stalin, Mussolini, Hitler, Franco, Trujillo, Pol Pot and Saddam Hussein." The document criticized all aspects of the economic and political system, calling for a populous uprising. She had previously claimed that "prostitution and drugs were things that we did not have before 1959" commenting on increased number of tourists to Cuba and their impact.[82]

Financial support for the dissidents was confirmed in a communiqué from the Interest Section: "The US policy, for a long time now, is that of providing humanitarian assistance to the Cuban people, particularly the families of political prisoners. We also allow private organizations to do the same."[83]

America has a lengthy history of artificially creating opposition to help facilitate siege. Assistant Secretary of State Richard Rubottom Jr. stated in the early 1960s that "the approved program [destined to overthrow the Cuban government] has authorized us to offer our help to elements that oppose Castro's government in Cuba so that it seems as if its fall might be a result of their own mistakes."[84]

Money has been the main weapon to arm the dissidents, although sometimes that has proven to be the source of scandal, most recently in 2011 when funds destined for the Ladies and other opposition elements in the network formed by the Interest Section were frozen in Washington following several accusations of fraud uncovered by the Federal Audit Office in which well-known Cuban-American figures were involved.[85] Allegations of the group's deep connection with the US Interest Section were revealed following a report a Cuban intelligence agent had infiltrated the organization. Carlos Serpa, a contributor to Radio Martí, described the dissidents as "mercenaries"—a creation of outside forces. "I am a manufactured dissident. My case is an example of how it is possible to make people outside the country believe that there exists a 'great' opposition and proliferation of 'anti-Castro' groups."[86] Serpa claimed he invented news for Radio Martí, and condemned members of the Ladies organization for receiving US funding and fabricating reports of injury and harassment by Cuban security agents.[87]

There has even been controversy in death for the Ladies. When Laura Pollan passed away in 2011 various group members claimed Cuban hospital staff did little to help in the final moments. That charge was refuted by Pollan's daughter Laura Labrada, who told the *Miami Herald* that her mother received "very good attention" in the week leading up to her passing, and that doctors attempted "the impossible" in order to avoid accusations of disinterested care.[88] In the world of certain anti-Castro elements, the daughter's own words were proof of the total control over speech in Cuba. Seven dissidents then issued a statement implying that Cuban authorities may have killed Pollan, warning that "any supposed ailment" they suffer or their eventual deaths could be the subject of political manipulation by the communist government.

Even more contentious than Pollan's death was the passing of dissidents Juan Wilfredo Soto and Orlando Zapata Tamayo. The 42-year-old Tamayo died after a prolonged hunger strike in which critics claimed little was done to keep him alive, while Soto did not survive in hospital under charges that the Cuban police had beaten him just prior. Officials responded vigorously to the allegations, airing a news program attempting to explain the details of Tamayo's death.[89]

In the case of Soto, it was another dissident, Guillermo Fariñas, who told the *Associated Press* that Cuban police had detained and injured Soto two days before during a protest where he was yelling antigovernment slogans. Fariñas, who also went on a hunger strike and charged police beat him, said Soto was hospitalized and doctors told him he died of pancreatitis. Fariñas acknowledged that Soto had a number of preexisting health issues including diabetes, circulatory and heart problems, and gout.[90] The Cuban government lashed out at the "defamatory campaign" surrounding the death of Soto, insisting he died of natural causes.[91]

Fariñas is considered a high-profile dissident, winning the 2010 Sakharov prize for "freedom of thought." His run in with the authorities began in 1995 when he was sentenced to a term of three years parole and fined 600 pesos after violently assaulting a woman, a work colleague at the institute of health where he held the position of psychologist, causing her multiple wounds to the face and arms. In 2002 in the city of Santa Clara, in the province of Las Villas, Fariñas was charged with assaulting an old man with a cane, resulting in a sentence of five years and ten months. He carried out a hunger strike and on December 5, 2003, was granted an early release for health reasons. It was that year he joined the political dissident movement and founded the press agency Cubanacán Press, financed by anti-Castro Cuban-Americans, according to the *Associated Press*. He has since carried out more than 23 hunger strikes.[92]

Although the majority of government opponents inside Cuba attempt to present a uniform political position, there is considerable dissidence among the dissidents. When the church's role in assisting in the release of the 75 in 2010 was revealed, reaction among the dissident community was anything but uniform. Paya complained that the religious side had overstepped its boundaries, and should not "accept the role of being sole interlocutors with the government. Cubans should not be left as spectators"[93] to these talks, upset the dissidents were not involved in discussions. He left it unclear why he did not consider those such as Cardinal Ortega as Cuban.

The fragmentation of the dissident organizations is an accepted, if rarely recognized, situation. One revelation slipped through when Wikileaks published a 2009 document from current (as of 2011) head of the US Interest Section Jonathan Farrar. He frankly stated that the dissidents are "divided, dominated by individualists who work badly as a team, characters who are more interested in asking for money than to developing programs." The diplomat acknowledged Raúl Castro is currently in "a position of undisputed authority" and the role of dissents is "none", because "many opposition groups are prone to dominance by individuals with strong egos who do not work well together." Farrar added that "the dissidents are old and out of touch. In effect, thanks to the compensation received, the Cuban dissidents have a lifestyle that no ordinary citizen can afford."[94] The State Department promptly refuted the allegations, Farrar refused comment, and a clarification statement was sent to the press.

Nowhere did the rivalries appear sharper then during the 2010 deliberations in Congress to end one of the key pillars of siege—the travel restrictions. Based on strong bipartisan energies it appeared likely the House was going to pass legislation[95] that would have circumvented the restrictions and allowed American citizens to visit the island. The matter was then delayed sufficiently till the mid-terms, and with the Republican victory in the House the movement was laid to rest.

In the middle of the debates 74 dissidents signed a letter to the US Congress in support of the bill. Notables Guillermo Fariñas, Elizardo Sánchez, and even Yoani Sánchez endorsed the correspondence: "We share the opinion that the isolation of the people of Cuba benefits the most inflexible interests of its government, while any opening serves to inform and empower the Cuban people and helps to further strengthen our civil society."[96]

Reaction from the hard-right Cuban-American community in Miami was swift, unequivocal, and condescending. Accusations the signers were manipulated, dupes of the Castro government, had no right to comment on American foreign policy, and even that they were secret agents for the regime rained down on the dissidents' heads. Influential Miami bloggers called them "*vendepatrias*" (sellouts).[97] After Guillermo Fariñas received a scolding from Miami radio talk show host and severe anti-Castro flag-bearer Ninoska Pérez for his support to end a large portion of American siege strategy,[98] he steadfastly explained the position, reasoning that if Americans were allowed to travel freely to Cuba, it would "knock down one of the paradigms of *castrismo*"—a concept more important to the dissidents who live in Cuba, and of little value for those who don't.[99]

In Miami and ultimately Washington the siege remains paramount, even above the dispositions of the Cuban government's fiercest critics, those at ground level living inside the belly of the beast. The proembargo exiles knew what was better for the Cuban people from their location in the safe confines of South Florida, and the well-meaning but ill-informed protesters in Havana had best not overreach their position. As American politicians of the late nineteenth century assured themselves that the island residents were incapable of self-government, the new breed of Cuban-American imperialists in the Sunshine State conjured up the same descriptions against their unenlightened allies. One of the constant criticisms the Castro administration faces is for its exclusionist tendencies prohibiting alternative voices perceived to be in contradiction to the government's imposed truths—the rationale based on the need for uniformity in face of hostility and threat to national sovereignty. The other side revealed the identical segregation of opinion, less any justifications of threat. Continuing the punishment through application of siege takes precedence over all contrary judgments of those living on the island, even when it comes from opponents of Castro. Both Miami's hard-liners and Washington's enablers remain steadfast in their purpose of regime destruction, not reform. No one, not even those dissidents in favor of the ends if not the means, will be allowed variance from the methodology deemed sacrosanct by the besiegers.

The A-list dissenters letter was soon matched by another signed by close to 500 other Cubans, many in jail, supporting the continuation of the travel restrictions. Sent to then Republican Congressman Lincoln Díaz-Balart, a hard-line Cuban-American, the new communiqué was signed by prodemocracy activists within the island including Jorge Luis García Pérez, Nestor Rodríguez Lobaina, Reina Luisa Tamayo (mother of Orlando Zapata Tamayo), as well as Ariel and Guido Sigler Amaya. The correspondence was latched onto by proembargo proponents as the true representation of the wishes of the opposition, ignoring all others.

Since the time of their release in 2010, some dissidents have discovered their newfound freedom has not altogether been trouble free. Orlando Fundador and his wife chose to relocate to Spain and subsequently complained that "we ate better in Cuba."[100] He implied that he was forced by the Cuban Catholic Church and the government to leave the country, despite public assurances by the Cuban side all dissidents had the choice to stay or go, with many deciding to continue in Havana—such as Oscar Elias Bíscet, awarded the US Presidential Medal of Freedom in 2007. Other dissidents who left for Spain expressed displeasure with capitalist society, one stating how "a woman who received cancer treatment in Cuba and now has pain could not get an appointment with a (Spanish) doctor until next year."[101] Diosiris Santana complained of police brutality—against the Municipal Police force of Madrid during an incident outside the Spanish Ministry of Foreign Affairs where the dissidents protested the end of financial aid from their host government.[102] Local Spanish reaction was often negative to the newcomers, a few calling for the government to send them back to Cuba.[103]

Thanks in large measure to the siege, the Cuban government has persisted in the ability to categorize dissidents not in the role of reformers, but rather through the spectacle of organized adherents to a foreign policy designed to destroy. Even when calling for moderation it remains straightforward to discredit opposition efforts so long as American political institutions publicly proclaim the purpose of financial benefit and material assistance to the dissidents. Arrests continue, including the detention of protestors caught handing out antigovernment propaganda in the middle of Revolution Square in 2011.[104] Usual charges of antirevolutionary activity in compliance with US directions followed the action, and whether those arrested were guilty or not becomes close to irrelevant when the pretext has actual historical precedence, permitting the government's ability to call upon it consistently. The siege is the instrument for enforcement of social pressures to marginalize targeted opponents and critics.

As it does to most aspects of Cuban society, besiegement distorts the facility of the leadership to respond with a degree of impassioned rationality, in this case to put into perspective and context the recognized opposition. President Eisenhower's observation to "never confuse honest dissent with disloyal subversion"[105] is a demarcation near impossible for the Cuban government to distinguish while constantly under the pressures of siege. Furthermore, there is little incentive to distinguish between those in cohort with America's ultimate goal and those using analogous methods but who honestly want engagement for the sake of social improvement. Not when siege permits the government to control the classification of dissent, a far simpler position when the actualities of encirclement are so close at hand. A softening of that position has been to some extent evident under Raúl Castro with his wilingness to engage the church to resolve the release of those arrested in 2003, and his statements to the public to express their concerns and criticisms within the socialist parameters. Those who go "outside the Revolution" remain subject to harsh treatment, and anyone who does so in conjunction with American support suffers the full consequences. Until the siege ends, those rules won't.

Cuban historian Juan Antonio Blanco explained, "Some of the intolerance that you see in Cuba towards dissidents against the system has to do with the perception that these dissenters are allied with a powerful foreign country. We are dealing with an undeclared war that the United States is waging against us. So obviously you don't get the kind of tolerant environment you might find in Switzerland...A relaxation of the way that dissenters against the system are perceived would require a relaxation in the international environment so that we could accommodate dissenting views against the system in a different way."[106]

Those arrested, tried, and imprisoned in March 2003 were not punished for their views on how Cuban society should be constructed. The issue centered on the evidence the accused had collaborated with the only foreign power that has declared its intention of overthrowing the state. Treason was the overriding charge, not political disagreement. In Cuba, more than ever before, there is wide-scale and profound deliberation going on in the media, institutions, families, neighborhoods, mass organizations, and the different levels of people's power. Conflicting opinions on what measures are needed to improve the socioeconomic system are openly debated, with suggestions ranging from providing more authority to the local elected representatives to crack down harder on corruption, concurrently with a decrease in the power of the central government to solve deficiencies with industrial production, food distribution, and consumer goods. Discussions are encouraged by the revolutionary leadership owing to its desire to increasingly engage the population's participation in advancing the social order. These deliberations, however, do not have as a goal the fatal disruption of the current socialist system to allow for a return to a predatory, capitalist-based structure nor to convert Cuba once again into a satellite of the United States. The opposition groups that have chosen to align themselves with the American side have voluntarily disqualified themselves from this important dialogue as far as the government is concerned. The fact the opposition or dissidents revolve on the margins of mainstream society is not the fault of the Cuban system or an indication of one of its flaws, so long as the government continues to be able to bond them with America's siege.

The nation's handling of internal dissident has not differed much from how it treats outsiders who come to the island with the purpose, intentional or not, of working toward the aspirations of siege. A continuing case, one that has given the Americans yet another reason to maintain the condition, is that of the unfortunate Alan Gross.

Gross is a mild-mannered, thoughtful man in his sixties with a long history as a social worker involved in various development projects around the world. From the affluent suburb of Potomac, MD, just outside of Washington, he traveled to Cuba an estimated five times on a tourist visa to meet members of the local Jewish community. Gross apparently had little knowledge of the country, or the depth of America's hostility toward Cuba. He did not speak Spanish, but he did seem to carry items of interest. The last trip in late 2009 ended with Cuban authorities detaining and then arresting Gross for possession of illegal satellite communication equipment, including a Broadband Global Area Network (BGAN) unit. BGAN is a sophisticated piece of technology that can establish an independent Internet connection from anywhere in the world. All in the size of a backpack. With a cost of under $2,000 and connection time averaging $1 per minute, the equipment is well out of the affordability range of most Cubans. Once set up the signal is independent from any regulatory oversight, which makes bringing in a BGAN without prior authorization prohibited in Cuba, as it is in many other countries.[107] The small size and big capabilities to potentially connect directly with anti-government organizations or terrorist groups places BGANs as a device most authorities want under their control and knowledge, regardless if they are in siege mode or not. If a foreigner was caught coming into the United States with such equipment, he or she would soon find themselves facing charges under the Foreign Agents Relations Act,[108] which addresses most of the same issues the Cuban government leveled against Gross.

The American received a 15-year sentence for working on a "subversive" program paid by the United States that aimed to bring down the Cuban government.[109] During the trial it was revealed Gross received more than $500,000 from Development Alternatives, a government contractor that has been awarded in excess of $2 billion since 2000 from the State Department and the United States Agency for International Development (USAID).[110]

In its guise of providing economic and humanitarian assistance worldwide, USAID has long stood as a proponent of siege. Evoking the benevolent historiography of the need for Uncle Sam's helping hand, the website contributes its part to America's capture of social definitions to justify direct interference into another country. "The primary goal of U.S. foreign policy towards Cuba is to promote a free and democratic society in which the government respects the human rights of its citizens. To that end, U.S. foreign assistance empowers those in Cuba who are working towards positive change to advocate for fundamental freedoms and free market-oriented solutions to meet the needs of Cuban citizens."[111]

USAID's treatment of Cuba is not standard procedure of the otherwise respectable development agency. Usual practice is to connect with the host nation and obtain permission for program implementation. The Castro side has never given consent, nor has USAID attempted dialogue with Cuban leaders, part of siege strategy denying any level of legitimacy to the government. USAID programs are unwelcome and illegal, and Cuban law specifically addresses prohibition for its citizens to receive assistance provided by campaigns run by it or any other US government agency. Havana officials brand recipients as "mercenaries." Stratagems aimed at the island were approved under section 109 of the Helms-Burton law with the declared purpose of imposing a regime change in Cuba. Gross became part of that policy, a well-paid agent. Although USAID programs in Cuba are not run by American intelligence agencies, the secrecy and lack of contact with Cuban officials make them seem that way, according to Fulton Armstrong, who worked under President Clinton as National Intelligence Officer for Latin America and more recently investigator for the Senate Foreign Relations Committee. "The programs did not involve our Intelligence Community, but the secrecy surrounding them, the clandestine tradecraft (including the use of advanced encryption technologies) and the deliberate concealment of the U.S. hand, had all the markings of an intelligence covert operation," he wrote in a *Miami Herald* column. The Cuban government, he pointed out, was well aware of the program.[112]

Revealingly, the key to the authenticity of the program, according to the USAID posture, is that the revolution itself is illegitimate, harkening back to one of the basic tenants of siege strategy and contradicting the agencies' claim not to promote regime change. Asked to comment on the Cuban government's response that such programs violate its regulations an official responded: "Cuban law is capricious and subject to the whims of those who are controlling it at that time. So we don't use Cuban law as a guide to these kinds of efforts in that Cuban law also violates longstanding and international human-rights protocols."[113]

Throughout the incident details emerged in often contradictory and confusing fashion. Gross consistently explained his trips to Cuba were from a desire to connect with Havana's small but active Jewish community. Spokesmen denied knowledge of Gross, were not interested in his assistance, and were not involved in any illegal activity against the state. Jewish leaders spoke of a good working relationship with the government, as well as strong international contacts that provide them with whatever technology required, including computers and cell phones.[114] "We don't need the sophisticated equipment that supposedly Gross brought to Cuba. We have legal Internet," Cuban Jewish leader Adela Dworin declared.[115] Months afterward the Cuban side released details of the trial, which seemed to expose Gross's culpability. The information included the revelation Gross knew of the legalities of the operation, and enlisted others traveling to Cuba for religious exchanges to carry additional equipment and components. When Gross was arrested on his final trip he carried a SIM card intended to prevent satellite phone transmissions from being detected within 250 miles, a microchip usually provided to the Defense Department or the CIA.[116]

The arrest and jail sentence accelerated American reaction from both sides of the political spectrum and the standard media denunciations. The Obama administration utilized the incident to justify halting further interaction with Cuba. White House press secretary Robert Gibbs said the decision "compounded an injustice suffered by a man helping to increase the free flow of information to, from, and among the Cuban people."[117] Republican response, particularly from Cuban-American politicians, was predictable. "With Mr. Gross' sentencing, the Castro regime has effectively demonstrated the hopeless and dangerous naiveté of this administration's policy toward the regime," said Florida senator Marco Rubio. "Mr. Gross is simply a humanitarian who was seeking to help the Jewish community in Cuba access the Internet, and he deserves to be freed and reunited with his family at once."[118]

Invectives against the government carried levels of misinformation designed for sympathetic public consumption, much of it showing bipartisan message control. Florida Democratic representative Debbie Wasserman-Schultz expounded the inaccurate, yet soon to be accepted, reference position— "American Alan Gross has languished in a Cuban cell since December without access to medical care, for his crime of distributing cell phones to the Jewish community in Havana."[119]

The Washington Post weighed in on the subject mere days after the arrest, "The Cuban government has arrested an American citizen working on contract for the U.S. Agency for International Development who was distributing cell phones and laptop computers to Cuban activists."[120] At the end of 2011 the paper reiterated its stand that Gross brought nothing more than "computer and cell phone equipment" and that he should be released unconditionally.[121] The height of media manipulation in service to the half-century of antirevolutionary propaganda may have been embraced by Andres Oppenheimer, who wrote in his *Miami Herald* column: "Obama did not mention the case of Alan Gross, the U.S. contractor who was sentenced to 15 years in prison this month for taking *telephone equipment* [italics added] to Cuba, but other U.S. officials have asked for his immediate release in recent days."[122]

One more closely connected to the facts, his rabbi David Schneyer candidly assessed that "Alan was convicted and sentenced to a fifteen year term not so much for giving electronic equipment to some Jewish Cubans but because he was working for a company under a USAID contract, under a program designed to help undermine the Cuban government." Writing in an article to his congregation, he added, "While his physical health is holding up, the anger and frustration [Gross] feels as a result of the deceptions and falsehoods that both sides have subjected him to is clear."[123]

Gross pleaded he was a dupe. During testimony in the two-day trial, he "recognized having been used and manipulated," in reference to USAID and the State Department.[124] His entreaty is directly at odds with an earlier written note in a trip report that recognized "this is a risky business in no uncertain terms." The account by Gross, revealed in an *Associated Press* article, concluded, "Detection of satellite signals will be catastrophic."[125] Months later Judy Gross came to the conclusion that what her husband was doing was illegal, but claimed he was unaware of legalities prior. "We know now that he did break Cuban law. He did not know that until he got to Cuba and was arrested."[126]

According to Phil Peters of the Lexington Institute, USAID officials consistently warn that its activities violate Cuban law and anyone looking to involve themselves in such activities should be aware of the risks.[127] Gross's declaration of naiveté had been questioned by others, including University of New Mexico sociology professor Nelson Valdés, a longtime Cuba watcher. Referring to the *AP* article that revealed the extent of Gross's knowledge and involvement, Valdés said, "He was arrested only in his last trip. In that trip he took into Cuba a microchip that allows sending signals without detection. Apparently that is the smoking gun (for his arrest). His role was to set it up and make sure it operated, so that makes him even more aware and guilty. Gross had been here (Cuba) five times before, he was not here to provide cell phones. He didn't bring the BGANs, he didn't distribute them. Others did. So what did he do? He was needed here in Cuba to set things up, locations to provide wi-fi coverage in Havana. Once set up he was probably the person training the people to operate the equipment. All illegal in Cuba, as in most every other country in the world." Valdés remarked that Gross could have at any time informed Cuban authorities of his activities, "and to plead he was unaware not reporting such high tech equipment would cause concern is somewhat dubious from a man with such experience."[128]

Despite the debacle, USAID remains committed to involving itself in the internal affairs of the island, currently seeking to hire a Cuba program czar at a salary of $125,000.[129] Its international reputation took a hit in 2012 following a resolution from the political council of ALBA, the Venezuelan-led association of Latin American countries, calling for the immediate withdrawal of USAID from all member states.[130]

As Gross languishes in jail, giving interviews to American media pleading for his release and calling himself a "hostage,"[131] the possibility of his early discharge remains remote, with President of the National Assembly Ricardo Alarcón publicly stating a deal is unlikely, "Cuba won't unilaterally free Gross" and that expecting such a gesture "is not reasonable."[132] Hopes were raised slightly when Cuba announced the release of close to 3,000 prisoners in late 2011, but Gross was not among them. He is at the start of his sentence, not the end, Alarcón observed. For once there was agreement from the other side, Secretary of State Hillary Clinton stating in regard to Gross: "We've made no deals, we've offered no concessions and we don't intend to do so."[133]

Discussions have periodically risen of the possibility to swap the American for the jailed Cuban Five, agents sent to Florida to infiltrate antirevolutionary organizations suspected of terrorist activities. So far nothing has emerged, and as CUNY professor Peter Roman speculated, a straight swap remains remote unless a connection is made by the Jewish lobby in the United States. "They want Gross released, they are aware of his situation, some Jewish groups have protested in front of the Cuban Interest Section in Washington. But they have little knowledge of the Cuban Five and the Cuban government's desire to free them. If they were told the way to Gross is through the Five, then maybe there might be a better opportunity. The Jewish community is very influential in Washington, if they started putting pressure it might be a solution for both."[134]

The Gross fiasco is emblematic of the obstacles both nations have stumbled over, seemingly never able to get their intentions in synch. As senior associate for US policy at the Inter-American Dialogue Dan Erikson described it, "After 50 years, the United States and Cuba are like two countries stuck in a bad marriage. They don't communicate, they have serious fights, they have small fights which they blow out of proportion."[135] It is yet another manifestation of the consequences of siege, American University professor Robert A. Pastor commented. "Neither side has shown the slightest interest in learning from experience and have demonstrated repeatedly the tragic way in which both sides are condemned to repeat their mistakes. It's not just the Obama people. It's the new people under Raúl Castro."[136] Negotiation, however, is not the route to resolution, what is needed is a change in American policy, said Tony Martínez, an antiembargo spokesman. "Sadly, I believe Alan Gross may stay in jail a long time, as long as these programs continue. I see the key to unlocking his freedom lies in our ending these covert and subversive programs."[137]

His case exhibits how the weapon of information is utilized in the imposition and survival of siege. Prior to reports showing Gross was aware his activities were illegal and the steps he took to deceive the Cuban government, the default position in media and political circles identified him as yet another victim of the unjust revolutionary regime, that no consideration would be given to the Cuban side. Only when the evidence of his wrongdoing came from an accepted American source was there any accommodation, reluctantly, that what Havana was saying was the truth. America continues to retain the overriding supremacy to frame issues and allow the conversation to be controlled—a primary prerogative of those who hold encirclement. To the detriment of whatever validity of message the besiegers permit to escape from outside the walls.

Running through the Gross affair was the charge of Havana's terror with losing control of message, no more evident than its obsession with the Internet. Portrayed as a vital weapon against totalitarian regimes, Cuba's perceived efforts to drastically limit its access to the general population is cited by opponents as proof of the government's paranoia.

The Cubans argue the limitations are a result of restrictions Americans impose; that there is no specific law forbidding citizen access. It's a matter of technical availability and investment in infrastructure, not government censorship. Cuba is one of the last nations that contact Internet signals via the much slower and limited satellite systems. The reason, leaders declare, is that the embargo prohibits from connecting into the now standard, and faster, fiber optic cables, some that run a mere 20 miles offshore. The island's limited access is prioritized for government officials, educational institutions, and international business concerns. Locals have availability through expensive Internet cafes in hotels and outdoor areas, costing upward of $6 an hour in convertible currency, making them effectively unobtainable. There is a substantial black market mainly servicing generally inconsistent email functions for private individuals. Government estimates suggest approximately 20 percent of the population is online in some capacity, mostly through the state-controlled intranet services found in the more than 300 school and office computer clubs.[138] Less than four percent have private connections, the National Statistics Office reported in 2011.[139]

The situation could change drastically once the long-awaited fiber optic cable from Venezuela becomes operational, increasing capacity 3,000 times its current connectivity. The cable is as yet unused a year after the expected startup in late 2011, its financing under suspicion of a corruption scandal. Cuban officials have been mostly silent on the issue, but hope remains the cable will be up and running in 2013.[140] Both critics and supporters anticipate how the government will react to the increased capacity and whether expanded access will be offered to the locals.[141] The government maintains, however, there are no official controls, constraints but a matter of regulatory policy. "There is no political obstacle" for access to the Internet, affirmed Jorge Luis Perdomo, vice minister of communications and informatics.[142] Internet availability is expected to be treated the same way as when regulations on cell phones were lifted. That market exploded within less than a year, thanks to prior infrastructure preparedness.[143]

Johnathan Farrar, chief of the Interest Section in Havana, took an informal examination in 2008 and reported that visits to the Internet cafes are done without interference, and while Cuba redirects browser searches to Google.cu there is extensive availability to a wide selection of sites: "You can read on-line the Washington Post or New York Times. You can access the websites of international human rights NGOs, such as Human Rights Watch or Amnesty International, and even download the entire HRW 2007 report if you have patience and 20 minutes to spare. Access is by satellite, and speeds were only a bit slower than those in USINT or in the Chief of Mission's residence."[144] His report noted that certain pages are blocked, mostly those from dissident and antigovernment organizations such as the Center for a Free Cuba, or the *Grupo de Apoyo a la Disidencia*. "If the Google.cu browser is set on the 'Cuba pages' option, the results of Google searches are strikingly different from a search done using Google.com. Typing in USINT (Interest Section) using Google.com, for example, yields the USINT webpage as the number one site. Typing in USINT using the Cuba pages browser yields a long list of vitriolic GOC (government of Cuba) sites depicting skullduggery between USINT and the Cuban dissident community."

Communication has been an intentionally difficult proposition, facilitating the sense of misunderstanding in promotion of siege mentality on one side and the ease of controlling definitions on the other. Such naturally accepted contact points as telephone and mail services are subject to obstacles unheard of in the modern world. Ordinary telephone connections are handled by third countries, making Cuba one of, if not the most, expensive places to call. There has been no direct mail service between the countries since 1963 and recent talks of a resumption of delivery stalled over small details. The lack of avenues for discussion hardens positions and suspicion.

Information, particularly through the Internet, will continue to be a vital resource to be kept under government management as long as the siege remains. Officials recognize the social media's potential to be utilized as a tool against the revolution, citing the incident in late 2011 when an American-financed plan to spam Cuban cell phone users with text messages was denounced as a propaganda scheme, while US officials noted only registered users would receive the messages, including content from the anti-Castro Radio and TV Martí stations.[145] To the hypersensitive government conditioned to distrust anything from those laying siege, whatever is determined to be aimed at destabilization efforts is cause for concern.

More disturbing was the incident in which Internet experts were able to publish secret phone number of top Cuban officials, including the home phone number of Vice President José Ramón Machado.[146] The Miami-based outfit Fuego posted the information on the *Cuba Al Descubierto* website, with a warning that "technology is going to destroy them" in reference to the targeted individuals, adding they face a difficult future if the regime collapses.[147] Also published were the address and home phone number of Raúl Castro's daughter Deborah and her husband Luis Alberto Rodriguez López. The attempts do nothing more than solidify the determination to maintain power over such information streams and the internal opposition that exploit it. The strengthening of the response to siege is the result.

The Internet, government officials promise, will be developed and available for the betterment of Cuban society and not a weapon to be used in aid of American blockade policies. It is yet another social institution that has been shaped and distorted under the justification of protection while under national threat.[148] The release of siege would eliminate the rationale, if not the practice, but in the least would render truer the basic nature of the government devoid of the American card to play. Laws could then be subjected to a more realistic evaluation when distinguishing between civil rights restrictions and human right abuses in context to security as opposed to those structured simply to maintain an iron control over the population.

An ongoing clash of definitions has long been fought over the meaning of civil and human rights. America's first world position consistently emphasizes the human rights equation as advanced social development, freedom to assemble, multiparty democracy, free press, and market-based economics rooted in private property laws. The Cuban side ascribes a social face to US psychology professor Abraham Maslow's theory of hierarchy of needs, placing greater merit on human rights for a developing country as signifying proper housing, food, education, and health care, aspects the revolution has been able in the whole to adequately provide. Civil rights of political plurality, privately owned media, and freedom of assemblage are of less social importance to a poor country, goes the Cuban rationale, and by necessity are curtailed when the nation is under threat and siege. Both governments declare their argument the dominate one, contemporaneously utilizing the 1948 UN Declaration of Human Rights (UDHR) as the defining authority.[149]

While neither side should attempt to treat the declaration as "a menu they may freely select" from, Cuba watcher Arturo López-Levy noted, it is the United States through the embargo that "opportunistically violates the UDHR's essential principles of interdependence and indivisibility, conferring a higher value to the right of private property, a right that is at best equal and at worst less important than other rights…Now, owning private property is undoubtedly a human right, but it is not absolute and does not have any higher standing in the list of human rights on the UDHR." Additionally, calls for multiparty elections and free-market prescripts under the Helms-Burton Act, "this is also an arbitrary prioritization of a right."[150]

Cubans charge US grumblings on human rights is a political stick to beat them with, a wide-sweeping contrivance conveniently called upon for continuance of siege strategy. It becomes another point of hypocrisy, the government alleges, when the United States refuses to ratify such international treaties as the ban against cluster bombs and land mines.[151]

America using the issue for its own foreign policy ends is a concept examined by such academics as James Peck who noted, "Washington has shaped this soaring idealism into a potent ideological weapon for ends having little to do with human rights—and everything to do with extending America's global reach."[152] The siege itself has been considered a human rights abuse by a growing number of international agencies. For the past 14 years the UN secretary general has documented the negative impact of the US embargo on Cuba. In a recent report to the Human Rights Council, the personal representative of the UN High Commissioner for Human Rights described the effects of the embargo on the economic, social, and cultural rights of the Cuban people as "disastrous." The study, prepared by Marc Bossuyt for the Sub-Commission on the Promotion and Protection of Human Rights, opinioned that the embargo violates human rights law, "the fact that the United States is the major regional economic power and the main source of new medicines and technologies means that Cuba is subject to deprivations that impinge on its citizens' human rights." Legislation such as the Torricelli Act that "tries to force third-party countries into embargoing Cuba" results in the US government attempting to turn "a unilateral embargo into a multilateral embargo through coercive measures, the only effect of which will be to deepen further the suffering of the Cuban people and increase the violation of their human rights."[153]

Terminology and the capture of definition achieve no greater importance than in the one word rooted most deep in the American psyche—"democracy." Since rising to the top of the international stage in the past century the United States has standardized its historic and contracted definition as irrefutably self-evident. Acceptance and embrace by the rest of the world is the yardstick of arbitrary judgment. Those who do not ascribe to those basic tenants (with minor variations) are by default anti-American, nondemocratic, and of questionable legitimacy. The Cuban Revolution is all of these and therefore of no value. Its laws are to be ignored, an attitude that landed Alan Gross in jail. Legitimacy is entitled through definition and another aspect of siege—the ability to seal contrary information inside the castle—is strictly imposed. The aspiration of a designated democracy that subscribes to certain economic and political standards is being utilized against Cuba to create, then condemn, the opposite.

America and Western liberal democracy is now tied inextricably to strict political and economic conditions, in conformity with the selected human rights definitions. American democracy is of a particular strain, however, emphasizing the predominance of free markets directed by a plutocracy served by a political system increasingly championing minimum government regulations. Its political foibles reveal a formula where corporate influence drives an exclusive two-party system, where a president is chosen by an archaic electoral procedure that has seen the candidate with the most votes lose, and a private campaign funding structure where money has become the determining factor in election results and corporations have the same rights as people to the corruption of both. Added to the mix is an unelected Supreme Court that has grasped an undeserved role as final arbitrator of the legislative branch. American democracy is unique, yet it is used as the measuring stick to judge all others—the prerogative of the world's only superpower. It is an inconsistent utilization, and the United States' historic close relations with some of the worst offenders of democracy in the past 50 years are well-known. Classifications continue, as countries deemed anti-democratic and anti-American (Cuba, Iran, North Korean, Sudan, Syria) are treated most harshly. Nations in the developing world just as nondemocratic, or democratic in name only, are forgiven most of their human rights sins (Saudi Arabia, Afghanistan, Kuwait, Pakistan, Qatar). An emerging economic superpower (China) is a one-party communist state, as is Cuba, and a violator of human rights according to US standards, but provided with a favored trading designation. A country America went to war against (Vietnam) remains undemocratic under US terms but is now a close friend and trading partner. And then there are countries that meet the political plurality test but fail the economic portion (Venezuela, Bolivia) and so are designated in the anti-American category.

America's fluctuating application of democratic principles is understandably determined in large measure on the mantel of self-interest. Geopolitical realities are never consistent, nor could they be. It is a condition of empires throughout history. As the world's greatest power, those relationships are open to closer scrutiny and examples of hypocrisy come effortlessly. Nowhere is that more pertinent than in the case of Cuba and the justification for siege. The island's political and economic systems are America's gold standard of democratic anathema. Add to the mix the historic ownership issues, the revolution's victory over US imperialism, and Fidel Castro's 50 years of defiance and you have a provision of intractability when applying the definition of democracy. The political component of siege is thus based on Cuba's return to a form of political structure acceptable to American designation.

Others find little difficulty in recognizing America's shifting standards at work when it comes to the entwining of human rights and democracy. Arabs know it well, a contemporary expression found in Cairo's *Al Ahram* editorial, "Those who contradict the Americans will be branded undemocratic. Those who stand up to America will be seen as violators of human rights. In her speech (Hillary) Clinton admits that American interests are not always compatible with democracy. She says that America reacts to pro-democracy movements on a case by case basis, and that no two cases are the same. There is a difference, of course. That difference depends on the interests of America, not of the nations involved."[154] Or as former Chinese finance minister Liu Zhongli elegantly put it: "The United States maintains a triple standard. On their own human rights problems they shut their eyes. For some other countries' human rights questions they open one eye and shut the other. And for China, they open both eyes and stare."[155] For Cuba, he might have added, they take out the microscope.

Canadian author Arnold August has written extensively on the Cuban democratic process,[156] observing its workings for the past 20 years. He's also familiar with American impositions, "the attempts to control the terms of democracy. They define the term, they impose it on all others; but they are very inconsistent with it."[157]

The Cubans approach the subject of US-style democracy from their own singular, unpleasant familiarity. The viewpoint is rooted in the experience of American hegemony from 1904 to 1959 when the term "democracy" came to be associated with corruption, imposition of a foreign political and economic arrangement, denigration of nationalist ambitions, and home leadership beholding to outside interests. Cuba had traditional multiparty elections, the vast majority dissolving under charges of fraud and voter manipulation; final resolution was often achieved through the direct interference of American force to ensure candidates supporting continued US imperialism emerged victorious, as happened throughout the 1920s and 1930s. Supporting the foreign power were nationals, mostly from the commercial class, who could be relied upon to provide cover to demonstrate the façade of Cuban independence. There was no shortage of surrogates willing to develop US primacy over their countrymen—coming mostly from the economic and political hierarchy who were either previously tied to the Spanish masters, or those seeking ascendancy on the coattails of the new colonizers. It was an easy matter to toss aside *patria* for the economic gain brought forth by the northern business interests. Political control was similarly uncomplicated to attain through manipulation of the franchise; imposing literacy standards and land ownership requirements. The result was the lower classes, most specifically blacks, were in the majority unable to vote. In the 1930s an estimated 70 percent of Afro-Cubans and the poor couldn't read, and were thus denied entry to the ballot box. That particular civil right became restricted to the higher classes, assisting in the solidification of American political prerogatives. It was the disadvantaged, shut out of the process and any influence on future political events, who most agitated for independence and a voice in their own country.[158]

When there was no multiparty option, strong arm caudillos directed the process with the firm backing of the United States, most famously the 1952 coup that put Batista in the dictator's chair. Democracy US style in all its forms became identified as an imperial instrument to be defeated, not reformed, by the radical element of the revolution. The final act was played when Batista's planned November 1958 elections, forced under US pressure, turned into a kabuki dance with all involved recognizing the overt manipulation taking place to ensure the dictator's victory and continued foreign dominance. Less than two months later the revolutionaries ended the charade. The new leaders then demonstrated that democracy as America defined it linked directly with colonialism and the suppression of national ambitions. The term "democracy" as America promotes it has resonated at a completely different level within the Cuban leadership ever since.

"The US inoculated Cuba against the two party political system with its experience with US style democracy," Arnold August remarked. "The 1952 (Batista) coup was based on corrupt elements, Fidel was running as a candidate and his Orthodox party was winning, Batista was third, and so he pulled the coup knowing he wouldn't win, the US supported it and that was another example of the corruption and manipulation of US style democracy, and the Revolution didn't want anything to do with that, so they developed a new system. Cuba knows exactly what it means when US says they want Cuba to return to 'democracy.'"[159]

The multiparty political arrangement America controlled during the republic provided imperial validation for Cuban democracy; for the locals it represented the opposite. "On many occasions multi-party systems are identified with pluralism. But that is not necessarily the case: sometimes multi-party systems are precisely the way to deny pluralism. In Cuba during the 1900s we had plenty of political parties but no democracy. For us, the multi-party system consistently denied the possibility of an alternative road for the country," said Juan Antonio Blanco.[160]

America has condemned Cuban revolutionary society for its lack of plurality, but if Western liberal democracy is supposed to give people choice, then American policy against Cuba is antidemocratic to the core, for it offers no option other than the acceptance of US terms. That incongruity is not lost on either the socialist government or its citizens, reducing US criticism as a call to return to something already rejected.

Since the earliest days of the revolution anti-Castro forces have demanded a restoration of multiparty elections based on the promise Fidel made to reinstitute the 1940 Constitution. The young leader's declaration was reversed in equal parts based on political opportunism as much as the unavoidable response from the first signs of siege. Terrorism, implementation of embargo, isolation of the island, and avowal of regime change from the same forces calling for reinstitution of the Constitution convinced Castro to end consideration of a return to the political (he did implement the agrarian reform) components of the document, the suspension not coincidentally suiting his revolutionary objectives. It remained that way until the country's socialist Constitution was instituted in 1976 with a credibility-defying plebiscite of more than 90 percent approval.[161] By then the 1940 Constitution had long ago been tossed onto the social trash bin of American imperial ambitions. To vast public partisanship *El Comandante* announced early on there would be no need for multiple political parties; the legitimacy of the revolution sprung directly from the support of the masses and their voices, not their votes for nonrepresentative political organizations influenced by foreign priorities. "The revolution has no time for elections. There is no more democratic government in Latin America than the revolutionary government," Castro proclaimed.[162]

By 1961 American-style general elections were abolished, and four years later the Cuban Communist Party (CCP) was the sole political institution of the state. Fidel's leadership of the party for the next 40-plus years through its electoral process brought continuity to the country's political construct and became a vital component to the stability and success of the revolution under American aggression. Detractors merely called it dictatorial.

Then as now the Cuban interpretation of democracy has rested on the direct touch of the population above political organizations constructed for elite interests. The malfunction of this vision is evident in the ideologically driven direction of one man, where too often the masses have followed and not led. Whereas the early years saw spontaneous expressions of widespread enthusiasm and an expectation of real social participation, by the 1980s the large-scale rallies had turned the events into cheerleading exercises in resonance for decisions already made. Little opportunity presented itself for implementing individual social expression without the restrictive party structure.

The collapse of the Soviet Union and the economic dislocations of the Special Period brought with it the opportunity to create a truer demonstration of participatory democracy, a movement that was emerging years before the great upheaval, said former Center for American Studies researcher Hugo Azcuy. "The need for a more pluralistic expression of Cuban society has been accentuated in the recent years of the crisis, but its antecedents are in the second half of the 1980s, when people began to publicly question the copying of the Soviet institutional and ideological model that began in the 1970s. In 1990 there was an important public debate, which even had a mass character, about the need to introduce changes at the root of the institutional system. Among the most important steps in this process were the new space given to private, non-profit associations, and also to religious organizations. In the space of a few years, since 1985, when the Law of Associations was passed, and since 1987, when the Civil Code was passed, more than 2,000 associations and civil organizations were created, including the majority of those which function today as non-governmental organizations. These include a wide spectrum of cultural, scientific, sports and environmental groups. This pluralism represents a recognition that the diversity of Cuban society, which has always existed, cannot go on being expressed exclusively within the old mass organizations."[163]

Efforts have evolved to improve political inclusivity; in 1992 the government allowed the election of all members of the legislative National Assembly of People's Power (previously 55 percent were voted on, the rest appointed). Membership of the CPP is now no longer a strict requirement into the political sphere, although the party continues to influence candidate suitability in a percentage of assembly members. Election commissions made up of local residents, regardless of party affiliation, enforce the candidacy process under the organization of the national trade union *Central de Trabajadores de Cuba* (CTC).

The Party is not considered to be an electoral organization in the Western sense, and has little influence at the local level, Arnold August explained. "The vast majority are Party members at the National Assembly level, but there is nothing to preclude anyone, it's just the best and brightest move to the Party membership in the system. Nationally approximately 15 to 20 percent of Cubans are Party members. As far as interference goes, there may be some isolated incidents at the local level. I know personally one case of a dissident wanting to run for local assembly and the Party wanted to stop it, but the election commission that determines candidate requirements stepped in and said anyone can run. The Communist Party has not participated in the local elections since the 1992 reforms, the Party has a supporting role, but they don't choose which candidates to advance, and they are not vetting them at local or municipal levels." The party retains overall direction of policies and economics, and allocation of resources regarding schools, hospitals, and transportation. "But local participation directs party decisions. Citizens, delegates and government representatives are connected to decide what to do," according to English professor George Lambie.[164]

Cuban municipal elections take place every two and a half years and to the provincial assemblies and the National Assembly every five years. The last general elections were held October 2012. Anyone over 16 is allowed to vote. More than 8.4 million voters, 71 percent of the Cuban population, had the right to participate in the most recent municipal process where 35,000 candidates were nominated through grassroots organizations and chosen by individual electors under secret ballot. When a person is nominated, no election campaigning is permitted; instead, his or her biography and other personal attributes are posted in public places. At the municipal level a delegate or deputy is required to inform electors about his or her work and, as in other countries, can be contacted by people in the constituency. Voter turnout in Cuba is consistently above 90 percent, a figure used by the progovernment side as a declaration of the participatory spirit of their democratic process, and by the anti-side as proof of the state's manipulation of information and control of the population.

Delegates to the municipal and provincial assemblies and the 601 deputies to the legislative National Assembly are elected by popular suffrage. Elections held in 1992, 1998, and 2003 for the National Assembly were seen as referendums on the socialist system, garnering overwhelming support across the island. The executive branch head of state and the council of state are selected from among the deputies. The council then chooses its president, similar to the electoral college system in America. This is where the two Castro brothers have presided for so long unopposed, and where global criticism to the lack of political choice is usually placed.

Cuban democracy observer Arnold August has extensive knowledge of the international awareness of what does, or doesn't, go on inside the country. "The general perception is that elections do not take place, and the corollary is that Cuba is a dictatorship, one party, no elections, run by one person, Fidel and now Raúl. And those who know about the elections just dismiss them as being totally controlled. Democracy in Cuba is one of the biggest misconceptions about the Revolution. The information blackout has always presented Cuba as non-democratic but the truth is Cuba has a different system of democracy. When it comes to Cuba the Americans are blindfolded by competitive elements of their democracy."[165]

Proof of popular will to maintain the socialist system has been demonstrated in the participation of the electoral process, according to Cuban intellectual Jesús Arboleya Cervera. "I still believe that this is the best evidence. However, for some this is not sufficient and they argue the alleged lack of legitimacy of a regime that, in their opinion, does not meet the "democratic standards" required in the world."[166] Others challenge the basic tenants of standards imposed by outsiders: "Elections are not synonymous with democracy but represent only one aspect of democracy. The West has tried for decades to reduce democracy to the exercise of voting every four years. To me, democracy is the daily input of the population on matters that affect their lives and not simply the casting of a ballot for a menu of candidates backed by powerful forces," Juan Antonio Blanco reasoned.[167] Democracy should "not only nor even principally be, about multiparty systems, periodic supervised elections or other common topics in the regional discourse about democracy, but rather about popular participation, social justice, equity, national development and other elements that are of greater importance for the construction of stable democratic regimes and the growth of societies where human rights are more fully respected," according to Hugo Azcuy.[168]

As in all aspects of Cuban society the siege induces restraining pressures on political diversity, academic Juan Valdéz noted. "A scenario of negotiation and lessening tensions between the United States and Cuba could allow the Cuban political system to overcome these restrictions. If the United States would renounce its internal political activities in Cuba, this would mean that Cuba could allow a loyal opposition to develop."[169] Until the siege ends the opportunity to increase political space within the current construct remains difficult to attain. Arnold August warns, however, there should be no expectation if American aggression were to conclude, the Cubans would embrace all what has been rejected for the past half-century. "I don't think there is any relation between US pressure against Cuba and the political system they developed, there was the historical component where Cuba rejected American democracy, but the US siege is not influencing Cuba to keep what they have now; they want it, they want to better it. If the blockade disappeared and US ends the pressure Cuba will be in a better position to develop this system of theirs. I'm convinced Cuba will not move towards US democracy because they understand its failings and problems. Ending the siege will make it far easier for Cuba to improve their political system, there will be less economic repercussions. One of the major problems is that delegates at the local level have a hard time at the job because the economic resources are low. Complaints can't be solved because of the economic problems. And that puts pressure on the political system. If the siege ends, the economic system improves, as do the problems than can be solved by politicians."

Raúl Castro once said that Cuba is "the most democratic state" in history, "even without representative institutions" because it "represents the interests of the working class, no matter what its form and structure."[170] The younger brother has expanded this expectation of individual participation within the new political and economic environment, but the potential of an official political opposition remains remote, in part due to the convenience of invoking the genuine aspects of siege. The rationale is rooted in the belief that for Cuba's tenuous position, a cohesive political bulwark is vital to battle American hostility. Propping up the one-party state solution to battle siege was front and center at the Communist Party conference in early 2012, with Raúl Castro declaring, "In Cuba, based on its experience in the long history of the fight for independence and national sovereignty, we defend the one-party system instead of the demagoguery and commercialization of politics." Permitting additional parties would open the door to US interference, "the equivalent of legalizing a party of imperialism on our soil," Castro added.[171]

Cuba's political structure represents the leadership's commitment to the independent social organism it has constructed, stubbornly based in the historical rejection of the nation's political experience under US domination. Yet another component of the Cuban argument, expressed by Raúl, reveals that an unrestricted multiparty option would make available US money, influence, and propaganda to destroy the revolution from an interior position. Ingrained is the anxiety that exile groups or US government agencies (such as USAID) would financially manipulate how parties would be organized, ensuring the promotion of candidates favoring pro-American economic policies and infiltrating the process to wedge in US interests in order to pry apart revolutionary unity. History will not repeat itself, the Cuban President promised, "Our adversaries and even some of our friends, setting aside the history of permanent aggressions, economic blockade, intrusion and media hostility—as if this were a country with normal conditions not a country under siege—urge to restore the pre-revolutionary multiparty system of a Cuba under U.S. neo-colonial rule."[172] The blueprint for political infiltration is available for anyone who wants to read the Helms-Burton legislation, or the Commission to Assistance to a Free Cuba. From a historical perspective America has amply demonstrated its ability to influence and impact the electoral process in other countries: Nicaragua, Iran, Chile, Guatemala, Panama, among others.

Recent history provides added motivation. The global economic meltdown, the corrupting influence of corporations, questionable voter results, efforts to restrict lists among minorities,[173] and the rising discontent with the ever-increasing disparities between rich and poor give reason to question America's two-party corpocracy dominated by the unelected moneyed interests that vet nominees for both sides, reducing the options available to ensure little deviation in domestic or foreign policy.

It's not only the Cubans who wonder where America's democracy is heading, but such respected commentators as Bill Moyers, who complained in an interview: "I saw a poll the other day...52% of the American people believe that both parties no longer reflect their interests. And I am part of that 52%. I can no more defend the Democratic Party than I can praise the Republican Party. We have two parties serving corporate business America and no party that serves...ideally...that serves the middle class or working people...Our democracy is dysfunctional. It isn't working. It isn't solving a single problem. The Senate might as well not be there."[174]

When anti-Castro adherents call for multiparty elections and a return to American-style politics as a condition to end siege, the Cubans see it as a mendacious demand to reintegrate formulas of management that worked so well for a foreign interest, and so little for the health of the nation. Island officials point to the system not even working for many in the United States, its social contract apparently unraveling in a self-imposed race to the bottom, where names and faces change every four or eight years but the system becomes increasingly rigged for the favored elite. Revolutionary society continues to refuse the free-market prescription in its most radical forms as currently practiced by their northern neighbor, along with the democratic terminologies that work in concert with predatory economic formulas. The state's determination to meet the needs of a small developing country under siege through severe socialist programs, accomplishing it outside the Western notions of defined political party arrangement, has experienced failures and corruptions. As has the American example. Debate continues as to the legitimacies of either extreme, based on the fight to control the definition of the word "democracy." Siege is the battlefield, this time on the civic frontline. Cuban society, its functions of democracy, and how it has been defending itself against the policies of the United States continue to play out in the relationship between government and citizens, between security and liberty, cultural expression and political restriction, and the hopes of a better economic life for all.

* * *

Cuba under the revolution is neither the socialist paradise some wish it to be, nor the communist hell others portray it to be. It is complex, full of faults, based on an idealistic economic model that never had a chance to work as intended, and a political system that serves at a functioning level but is under constant pressure to validate itself in the eyes of both a powerful external adversary and to its own increasingly dissatisfied citizens. It is, as most societies, flawed but based on specific culture, history, and the expectations if not the realities of large segments of the population. Cuban society is unique in the default defensive position it has been forced to assume as a result of the constant drag on economic advancement and political progress from 50 years of siege. It is not the sole factor in the shortcomings of the revolution, but it is one of many determinant ones. That the society has remained intact, and has the ability to undertake a long-awaited reformation, is a testimony to the Cuban spirit and adaptability. And patience.

The siege pressures Cuban society on a daily basis. It seeks not moderation, but victory, based on the proffered facade of knowing what's best for this nation of 11 million. The siege is America's modern-day attempt at intervention, without Teddy Roosevelt's Rough Riders charging up San Juan Hill. Everything Cuban life represents, the good and bad, is used by siege proponents to justify why those in charge now should be removed, why all should be returned to the safe confines of America's embrace.

Cuban society is difficult to fully comprehend without the context of siege. It is impossible to criticize a swimmer's ability to accomplish his task if there is a concrete block tied to his feet. Consideration must be given to the weight he has to overcome. Eliminate the burden to determine if the society under revolution can perform the way anticipated. So far the politics, the economics, the besiegers all indicate no intention of untying the block. Cuba is changing dramatically on the economic front, and with it society will enact political reforms, but siege proponents remain impassive. It is by intent, the only sight welcomed that of the swimmer drowning.

4

THE POLITICAL ECONOMICS OF SIEGE

45 minutes of the blockade is equal to the material to construct a school for
special needs children.

Three days of blockade is equal to the construction of one hospital.

—Billboards throughout Havana

The siege against Cuba has come at deep political and economic cost.
Millions of taxpayer's dollars have been spent to break down the walls, those
policies in turn totaling billions in lost revenues to the island. Few have been
spared punishment for having what the United States deems illegal commercial relations with Cuba—from international businessmen, major financial
institutions, multinational corporations to small travel agencies and chari-
table organizations. Seniors, religious groups, and students have been fined
simply for wanting to see life in the socialist country. Punitive economic consequences would be impossible, however, without the purchase of the political will in Washington. Rarely have elected officials, up to and including
the president, shown the nerve to spend the political capital needed to alter
the dynamics of the relationship. The opposite holds true, as the revolution
becomes a favorite whipping boy when politicians need to cash in on public sentiment or entice campaign donations. "Cuba bashing is like ordering
pizza; it's cheap and easy and everyone likes you for it," Washington lawyer
José Pertierra remarked.[1]

Historically, the politics of economy controlled Cuba for 60 years, when
US capital decided how the island would be ruled and by whom. Investments
dominated by American money combined with capital flight out of the island
kept many in poverty. The political system sustained the economic advantages of the foreign interest and obedient national enablers. Post revolution
has seen US money do all it can to tear down the past 50 years, including
the effective use of political influence complete with its veiled extraterritorial
applications.

As in all things siege, the two sides approach the financial component
from absolute certainty. The State Department reports 5,911 Americans lost
$1.9 billion to the nationalization programs since the 1960s, conveniently
neglecting to acknowledge every Cuban effort to negotiate compensation.
Lawyers in Washington tried to resuscitate the matter, claiming the value

of the loss now reaches $7 billion, and Cuba should be levied a user fee on remittances sent to the island to cover the costs.[2] Unstated is the detail that US companies placed nationalized properties as losses and have long ago deducted the full value from corporate taxes, beyond what they would have received in compensation.[3]

Revolutionary administrators retort the blockade has cost the island $900 billion,[4] comprising of hundreds of tallies such as the $80-million-plus owed Cuba by AT&T.[5] Officials estimate the island's per capita GDP would be roughly double if the siege was lifted, increasing its ranking from 109th to 63rd in the world.[6]

More symbolically, the courts have taken up the blockade's financial battle—Cuban magistrates in 2000 ordered the United States pay $121 billion in damages, in a rejoinder to a series of US rulings from a Miami judge demanding a payment of $187 million to families of pilots shot down by Cuban fighter planes in 1996.[7] Reaching back into history, a New York federal judge in 2006 ordered $91 million in frozen Cuban funds to be turned over to the Florida relatives of two Americans who lost their lives in the Bay of Pigs invasion 40 years earlier.[8] Legislation against Cuban assets still held in US banks is an increasingly valuable aspect of the business of siege. Claims of more than $100 million have sprung up from dozens of individuals and with the Cuban government refusing to challenge, awards are handed down by default.[9] In an effort to protect its funds from such judgements, the Castro administration has moved billions into what are considered less vulnerable Chinese and Venezuelan banks.[10]

Judicial action against Cuba's economy has clearly defined political motivation. The financial power and its governmental support for siege cannot be separated; one does not exist without the other, the condition no more important than in the past two decades with the predominance of proembargo organizations led by Cuban American National Foundation (CANF) and the influential rise of Cuban-American congressmen. A proportion of the taxpayer's money allocated to such groups as CANF end up in the hands of sympathetic politicians through campaign donations.[11] Millions have been spent and made in sustaining the industry of besiegement; from such publicly financed agencies as United States Agency for International Development (USAID) and National Endowment for Democracy (NED), privately run antirevolutionary alliances, think-tanks, universities and Cuban study courses, publishers, bipartisan donations, Radio and TV Martí, and the dozens of other activities against the Castro government that have made many financially secure. The US-Cuba Democracy Political Action Committee (PAC) is a special interest group that effectively lobbies for "promoting an unconditional transition in Cuba to democracy, the rule of law, and the free market," classic command of antirevolutionary terminology. The PAC has donated millions in an effective bipartisan effort.[12]

Acquiescent lawmakers accept the private and public funding to work as political sappers, undermining the strength of the siege walls through the introduction and maintenance of legislation designed to destroy the will of the Cuban people and weaken the structures of solidarity. They are doing the dirty work to ensure the pressure is maintained, that whenever possible the country is weakened and siege strengthened. Some are driven by ideology, by financial and political opportunity, by the potential for future power and influence in a post-Castro scenario, or by the inability to forgive the loss of it after the revolution.

Money is the tool to reward the powerful prosiege interests and punish the weak who suffer under its force. The political hands that wield the economic weapons are centered in Florida, reside in the halls of Congress, and have the backing of government institutions to ensure the dollars continue to flow. Whether they are spent wisely is another matter entirely.

Since 1996 an estimated $200 million has been dispersed on anti-Cuba measures, Tracey Eaton asserted. The former Havana bureau chief for the *Dallas Morning News* deemed the figure accurate, easier to track than the millions more that have been tossed into the pile during the decades before—a total that represents hundreds of thousands for every man, woman, and child in Cuba. Eaton started in 2010 what is one of the few serious examinations of the financial aspects of American policies and their effectiveness, through his website, the Cuban Money Project.[13]

His intent was to open up the information block on how much and where all the money was going. "In the democratic process you apply to get information, I've sent many requests to the State Department and USAID, and many times I've hit a brick wall. My opinion is that they are intentionally denying the information I'm requesting. These programs are semi-covert, but I think it's important to discover where the money is being spent, and if it is doing any good."[14] An example of the difficulties he encounters occurred when requests for information regarding the activities of Freedom House in Cuba were denied.[15]

On occasion the politicians do attempt to expose and curtail the embargo gravy train. USAID, the government agency actively involved with Cuba-related activities for years, came under scrutiny in early 2011 when Democratic senator John Kerry, chairman of the Foreign Relations Committee, opposed the allocation of $20 million for "democracy promotion" in Cuba as wasteful and unproductive. A cursory examination resulted in promises of greater vigilance. The matter was then quickly agreed to, all that was allocated released, without further comment.[16] More commonly, financing to force openings in Cuba's civil society are rubber stamped, as was the case in 2006 when the George Bush Jr. administration approved $80 million, or two years later in the final months of his presidency when another $45 million went to private contractors, most allegedly ending up in the hands of supporters in Miami.[17] The move to channel the money into nonpublic organizations above foundations, universities, and nonprofits accelerated under Obama and brought more questions of impropriety.[18]

"We are asking hard questions about fraud, waste and what actually works to benefit the Cuban people," California Democratic representative Howard Berman said at the time of the House hearings to approve the $45 million expenditure. Berman has been opposed to the embargo, one of a few congressmen who see little benefit in siege even though he has been a major beneficiary of campaign donations from the PAC.[19] "In the recent past, our committee's oversight of these programs has uncovered outrageous abuses from personal shopping trips to hundreds of thousands of U.S. taxpayer dollars simply pocketed outright," he indignantly added.

One example of government generosity in 2010 saw the Bureau of Democracy, Human Rights and Labor under the Department of State call for proposals from organizations, NGOs, student groups, and media for projects on a variety of Cuba topics. Grants ranged in amounts from $1.5 million to develop freedom of expression programs, $500,00 for political prisoners, the same amount for religious freedom, and a mere $350,000 for women's issues.[20] All recipients were required to connect with Cuban counterparts, a condition most on the island would hesitate to fulfill for fear of being tainted as dissidents accepting dollars in order to advance American policies of regime change. In the past, groups such as NED, USAID, International Relief and Development, and Evangelical Christian Humanitarian Outreach have been awarded hundreds of thousands from such offerings.[21] Funds for directly disruptive programs were shown to take various forms, one revealed in a *Los Angeles Times* editorial reporting $84,000 was awarded to a US company to send thousands of unsolicited text messages to Cuban cell phone users.[22]

Certain accommodating media have likewise lined up at the money trough, directed by the government's Broadcasting Board of Governors (BBG) or the Bush administration's Office of Cuba Broadcasting.[23] Besides the millions spent on the steady propaganda emanating from Radio and TV Martí, journalists in Miami were alleged to have accepted payment to write damaging reports leading up to the trial of the Cuban Five,[24] including *Miami Herald/Nuevo Herald* reporters Pablo Alfonso receiving $58,000 and Wilfredo Cancio Isla $20,000.[25] It was indicated these journalists and others in the media had been on government payrolls to promote antirevolutionary propaganda, one example cited in a story by Cancio claiming Cuba used drugs to train its spies.[26] Paris-based Reporters Without Frontiers, known for its antirevolutionary bent, came under scrutiny when it was shown it had received funds from NED[27] and signed a contract, "terms unknown" with extreme right-wing organization Center for a Free Cuba.[28]

Although not considered a supporter of the Cuban government, Tracey Eaton has less tolerance for spending money to topple it. One of the most contentious issues is the funding to the dissidents. "There are incidents where the money has been wasted. Some audits have been done and it has shown a minuscule percentage has gone to the dissidents. That's not what most people would expect. There are many questions about the money spent on these programs—how effective is it? In regards to what it wants to achieve. Do these programs follow the regulations? Are these programs breaking the law, we don't know the answers as these programs are shrouded in secrecy." Of the hundreds of millions allocated, Eaton suggested, "I'd guess conservatively less than half gets into Cuba. The money goes to many other things, studies, office expenses, internet sites."

The industry of siege has benefited dozens, including the University of Miami, Center for a Free Cuba, Freedom House, Loyola University of Chicago, and International Republican Institute. The general conformity to these programs, Eaton complained, is secrecy. "I can't say where it all goes, I don't have the documents, the government is not forthcoming. If it's a non-profit organization you can access some information regarding spending money, and there is a range of things the money is spent on, salaries is a big one, all sorts of things. The government will say we've given Freedom House $2 million, or to whatever organization; but the taxpayer doesn't know anything beyond that the money was given. What the money was used for is a harder detail to find out. How do you judge the effectiveness of these programs without transparency?"[29]

When purchases are inspected, questions arise as to their purpose and destination. During a 2005 US Government Accountability Office report on funding to anti-Castro organizations run by Cuban-American individuals, officials revealed expenditures on gas chainsaws, a mountain bike, leather coats, Godiva chocolates, and Sony Playstations. Defending the acquisitions, Frank Hernández of the *Grupo de Apoyo de la Democracia* said, "That's part of our job, to show the people in Cuba what they could attain if they were not under that system."[30] Other expenses are more difficult to explain as when it was revealed in 2010 the US Interest Section in Havana hired a New York company specializing in snowplowing services to spend $100,000 on guard uniforms, as well as contracting for snow removal, a service of rare utility in the Caribbean country.[31]

Well-established entities known for their antirevolutionary attitudes have reaped considerable largesse. Frank Calzón's Center for a Free Cuba received $202,000 from NED in a five-year period under the Bush Jr. presidency.[32] Groups such as the Foundation for Human Rights in Cuba (FHRC) and Lawyers Without Borders are among those that have won $1-million-plus grants in the Cuban sweepstakes.[33] Their totals were part of $18 million in disbursements passed on to approximately 12 recipients in 2010, none receiving less than $400,000.[34]

FHRC is a nonprofit outfit connected to CANF, presumed title holder when it comes to receiving government funds for the fight against Castro. Even CANF officials, however, have come out for greater transparency in the use of funds when given to others, despite its own share of controversy in its dealings, financial and otherwise.[35] In a 22-page report dated March 2008, the CANF found that US democracy-promotion programs in Cuba were "utterly ineffective due to restrictive institutional policies and a lack of oversight and accountability" within USAID. Part of the report noted that "less than 46% of total USAID-Cuba funds from 1998 to 2006" helped build solidarity with Cuban human rights activists. Most of the USAID funds "were distributed among Universities and think-tanks for the purpose of studying different elements of the process of transition to democracy in Cuba."[36] CANF's concern indicated more on who was getting the money than on how it was being utilized.[37]

There are incidents to warrant unease. One who got caught was Felipe Sixto, a worker at the Center for a Free Cuba, an organization on the federal funding list, one of many dedicated to bringing "democracy" to the island. In March 2009 Sixto was convicted and sentenced to 30 months in prison for the theft of $579,247 from the center.[38]

While Eaton is reluctant to condemn the programs, "I can't say, I'm not judging if these programs are good or not," he recognized there is great controversy as to their efficiency and how it is distributed. "There is political disagreement in the US whether the money is being used wisely or not. Joe García (head of CANF) got a big grant, and some Republican law makers, Cuban-Americans who are extremely pro-embargo, complained about the money he got—they're used to having it their way, to control the money and where it goes. There is political influence but what is happening, it's hard to determine."

Dollars set aside to end the Castro government have long purchased bipartisan support that ensures whatever administration is in place, the strategy remains unassailable. Donations to the Republican side have historically far outweighed those given to Democratic representatives, based on the conservative anti-Castro elements from the first-generation exiles and the modern crop of Cuban-American congressmen in Florida who have followed in the path of supporting antirevolutionary policy. A rising star in the Grand Old Party who has benefitted from the economics of siege is Senator Marco Rubio, who ran into controversy in 2011 on claims he embellished his family history, telling emotional stories of how his parents were forced to flee from Castro's communist tyranny. It turned out they left Cuba in 1956, three years before the revolution.[39]

Rubio publicly supports the financial arm of siege warfare, although recognizing the necessity of a level of oversight. Encouraged by claims the Cuban people were about to rise up against the government in late 2011, Rubio in a telephone exchange explained to activists in Havana: "We will involve even more all the funds that the United States government has at its disposal to continue promoting more strongly the programs to free Cuba from communism and, at the same time, we are going to investigate how they are being administered now."[40] His comments added ammunition to Havana's claims dissidents are inclined to report what the hard-right wants to hear, all to keep the funding going. The Florida Republican, tagged as an important party up-and-comer with strong Latin American credentials, garnered attention politically when he supported an anti-Castro proposal in 2011 along with fellow Cuban-American congressmen from the Sunshine State, Ileana Ros-Lehtinen, David Rivera, and Mario Díaz-Balart (brother of former representative Lincoln). The plan would have ended the current provision under President Obama allowing unrestricted travel back to the island for all Cuban immigrants. Díaz-Balart introduced the legislative amendment that was intended to end the "abuses" of those who were bringing excessive amounts of money and goods to loved ones in Cuba, calling into question the definition of what it was to be an exile from Castro's control and worried over the weakening of siege. President Obama threatened to veto any bill that altered his openings, effectively curtailing the group's efforts and reminding all where the center of Cuban policy remains.[41] Another move to punish fellow Cuban-Americans was attempted by Rivera in mid-2012 through a proposed bill that would revoke residency status for those who travel back to the island before gaining full US citizenship, a process that usually takes up to three years. Critics called it an effort to dissuade Cuban-Americans who, after residing stateside for only a few weeks, were visiting their homeland loaded down with material goods and financial aid.[42]

While Republicans enjoy most of the financial rewards, the Democrats are not far behind in the race to gain from the economics of besiegement. Famously, former congressman from New Jersey Robert Torricelli spoke favorably of island society, then turned virulently anti-Castro following campaign donations from CANF. He ended up putting his name on an important piece of siege legislation in the 1990s.[43] A collection of Democrats in 2007 became known as the Gang of 66 for their prosiege stance coincidentally around the same time Party Majority Whip James Clyburn was presented with a $10,000 money contribution from the Cuba PAC.[44] The group was instrumental that year in defeating an amendment brought forward by colleague Charles Rangel from New York, which would have eased banking restrictions on Cuban purchases of agricultural products. Expected to be passed easily in the Democratic-dominated House of Representatives, the upset occurred when Republican Ileana Ros-Lehtinen called for a recorded vote and with the support of the Gang of 66 the proposal was soundly defeated.[45] Much of the credit for assuring the 66 crossed party lines went to South Florida Democratic representative Debbie Wasserman-Schultz. "I was as active as you could be," she acknowledged, and her efforts were recognized by friend Ros-Lehtinen, one of the fiercest protectors of siege strategy, who called her "a tiger."[46] Ros-Lehtinen is widely renowned for her virulent opposition to the revolution, once calling for the assassination of Fidel Castro.[47] Deeply involved in the effort to keep the boy Elián González in Miami, Ros-Lehtinen has closely associated herself with Orlando Bosch (now deceased) and Luis Posada Carriles, two Cuban-Americans widely recognized as the masterminds of the Cubana Airlines bombing in 1976.[48] No item remains too insignificant if felt to be of benefit to the island government. She took on the Cuban children's group *La Colmenita* while it toured the United States in late 2011, demanding to know from Secretary of State Hillary Clinton why the troupe received visas and if any taxpayer money was used to subsidize the tour. She further called for the end of all cultural exchanges between the two countries.[49] Ros-Lehtinen had previously criticized the Smithsonian Institute for arranging travel programs to Cuba.[50] Officials in Havana keep a close watch on her activities, out of fear and respect, particularly so after taking over the chair of the Republican-controlled House Foreign Affairs Committee in 2010. "She is so extreme,"

University of Havana specialist on American policy Soraya Castro remarked. "Ileana is a very sharp politician. She is at the top, managing the psychology of Cuban-American policy. Very charming, so much more than the others. But she is tough, and smart. For the past few years inside the Cuban community in Miami there is a move to the center, moderation from the majority who want closer movement to Cuba. And that is having an impact on relations and Ileana is fighting against that."[51]

*   *   *

Voting where the money leads is as American as apple pie, and when it comes to Cuba there is plenty for all to get a taste. Three North Carolina Democrats confirmed its worth shortly after receiving thousands of dollars in donations from the influence-peddling Cuba PAC, according to published information.[52] Representatives Brad Miller, Mike McIntyre, and G. K. Butterfield began to vote against easing restrictions as organizers of the PAC increased lobbying in Congress in 2004, with the trio benefitting. Since that time McIntyre and Miller received $14,500 each from the organization, while Butterfield collected $21,000—the totals reported by Public Campaign, a nonpartisan advocacy group based in Washington.[53] Butterfield voted in September 2005 to maintain the trade embargo against Cuba, where a year earlier, he had voted to end it.

Both Miller and McIntyre insisted money played no role in their change of view, stating concern about oppression in Cuba was the overriding factor. The two admitted consulting with Cuban-American colleagues in Congress with regard to the 2003 crackdown on dissidents. "I thought, 'This is not right, and it's not humanitarian, and it doesn't promote democracy, and I'm not going to support someone who is repressive and evil,'" McIntyre said. "Yes, I changed my vote. That's the reason I changed—the horrors they suffered."[54] Miller, who served on the House Foreign Affairs Committee, admitted he knew little about Cuban issues before entering Congress in 2003. After talking to fellow Democrat Bob Menéndez of New Jersey, son of Cuban immigrants who had helped raise money for Miller's campaign, he also turned hard in support of siege, even though he maintained a degree of ambivalence. "And while I think the Castro regime is an oppressive regime, it's by no means the world's most oppressive regime." Lifting sanctions would legitimize an ailing dictatorship, he added, lending his voice to a classic justification for siege.[55]

In the past eight years supporters of embargo have sent approximately $11 million to Congress, according to Public Campaign estimates. The organization has examined various facets, revealing in 2009 a total donation of $850,000 from the PAC to 53 House Democrats who publicly opposed any easing of economic sanctions. The report called into question the lawmakers' motivation for opposing legislation easing Cuba restrictions, calling attention to the reality of congressional members constantly forced to seek funding for future campaign races. The group noted the situation where representatives who benefit from the contributions are usually fierce advocates of proembargo strategy.[56]

At the time the Public Campaign report was released, the director of the Cuba PAC, Mauricio Claver-Carone, responded that easing sanctions will only benefit the Castro regime. "I will not apologize for the Cuban-American community practicing its constitutional, democratic right to support candidates who believe in freedom and democracy for the Cuban people over business and tourism interests."[57]

A later examination by the Center for Responsive Politics outlined the amount of dollars members on both sides of the aisle obtained through the PAC, all to point Cuban policy in the right direction. Totally $3 million between 2009 and 2010, the big winner was Democratic senator Bob Menéndez from New Jersey who collected $112,500 while he was a member of the Foreign Relations Committee.[58] Menéndez was a strong proponent of allocating additional millions to USAID. Close behind came fellow Democrat Howard Berman of California, who picked up just over $100,000. The top Republican senator Chuck Grassley was also at the $100,000 mark.[59]

Of all the politicians who have been touched by the Cuban issue in the past decade, one of the most recognized and controversial remains Debbie Wasserman-Schultz. A passionate social liberal and champion of women's rights, chairwoman of the Democratic National Committee, she played a vital role in derailing an attempt to end a major component of siege during the summer of 2010.

Wasserman-Schultz, following up on her success with blocking the effort to ease banking restrictions on Cuba,[60] was front and center in the failed attempt to permit all American citizens to travel legally to the island. During a session in the Democratic-controlled House of Representatives, it appeared enough votes were available to pass HR4645, the proposed Travel Restriction Reform and Export Enhancement Act.[61] The Senate was poised to pass similar legislation that would have ended prohibitions on Americans visiting the island, and President Obama, through Secretary of State Hillary Clinton, let it be known he would sign the bill. The act passed easily in the Agriculture Committee, but was then stalled in the Foreign Relations Committee, where it remained until September, long enough for it to have no chance to be addressed in the full House before the November midterms. With little other choice, the legislation was pulled from the committee by cosponsor Howard Berman who recognized the delay left no time to deal with the matter properly, "That makes it increasingly likely that our discussion of the bill will be disrupted or cut short by votes or other activity on the House floor...I firmly believe that when we debate and vote on the merits of this legislation—and I intend for it to be soon—the right to travel will be restored to all Americans."[62]

The freeze at committee level was accomplished in large part due to the strenuous objections of Wasserman-Schultz, with the support of a group of her fellow Democrats plus the Republican Cuban-American hard-liners, most notably Lincoln Díaz-Balart.[63] Following the mid-terms, Republicans took control of the House, Ros-Lehtinen gained position as chair of the Foreign Relations Committee, and the travel legislation was shelved. Wasserman-Schultz made her opposition to easing travel sanctions clear during her campaign to defer the matter,[64] evoking management of terminology to validate siege and denigrate Cuban reforms. "Declaring the embargo a failure and using it as justification to reopen trade and relations ignores the fact that the Cuban economy is on its knees. The paltry changes we've seen (allowing Cubans to buy and sell some goods) have been necessitated by their economic crisis. Ending the embargo now not only ignores the atrocities perpetrated by the Castro regime, it also hands the Cuban government a huge financial boost at the exact moment they need and want it most."[65]

Her perspectives on Cuba had been limited early on in her career, but opinions became strongly antirevolutionary in part through exposure from Republican hard-liners in her state. Wasserman-Schultz is well-known for close ties with Lincoln Díaz-Balart, Ileana Ros-Lehtinen, and David Rivera, the relationship moving her to announce she would not campaign publicly for South Florida Democrats in the 2008 elections, citing her friendship with their Republican opponents. Unsurprisingly, the decision resulted in a small political firestorm within her party.[66] On the financial front she has reportedly gained more than $22,000 from the Cuban PAC lobby group.[67]

Following her success in turning back the attempt to end travel restrictions, Wasserman-Schultz remained strict in opposition to any opening with Cuba. Attacking the President's measure in early 2011 to increase people-to-people contacts through licensed travel, she tied her objections into the Alan Gross affair. "This affront is magnified by the recent announcement by the Obama administration that the United States will be loosening travel restrictions, which will pump much-needed money into the desperate Cuban economy, boosting the Castro regime. The United States reaches out to Cuba with a carrot, and we get back a stick. And a slap in the face."[68]

Politicians such as Wasserman-Schultz and her Cuban-American cohorts did not create siege, but serve as the guardians to ensure the forces of encirclement are not weakened nor the sufferings of those inside the castle walls eased.

If Wasserman-Schultz represents a turn to the hard line through political economics, specific commercial interests can create reverse influences. Republicans who have crossed over to the antiembargo division include Chuck Hagel from Nebraska and Arizona's Jeff Flake, for years promoting the cause to end blockade and move toward normalization with Cuba, established for pragmatic business reasons in their agriculturally important states. Jerry Moran of Kansas was one of more than a half-dozen Republican cosponsors of HR4645. The bill, aimed at ending the travel restrictions, was just as importantly designed to expedite Cuba's ability to purchase farm goods, easing some of the onerous terms the government has been forced to meet since 2000 when Congress passed the Trade Sanctions Reform and Exportation Act[69] to permit the purchase of food and medicine on humanitarian grounds under extremely strict licensing conditions. Castro refused to budge at first, but then changed his mind following the devastation of Hurricane Michelle a year later. Rejecting an American offer to donate emergency supplies, the Cuban government began negotiations and a full deal was finalized in late 2001. Since then food has been a wedge issue for anti-embargo proponents, using Cuba's purchase of more than $2 billion worth of US goods in the past decade as proof of the potential trade benefits if relations were normal, as well as to the anachronistic nature of the blockade.[70] Trade is steadfastly one-way as Cuban products—rum, cigars, medical technology, and other items—remain prohibited for the stateside market.[71] The restrictions on aquiring food and agricultural products has come under attack, notably from North Dakota Democratic Byron Dorgan who during a 2002 debate in Congress complained, "I think the poor, sick and hungry people in Cuba are the victims of these policies, and I personally believe that it is immoral to use food as a weapon."[72]

With the demise of HR4645 the complicated financial requirements to obtain US goods remains in place, despite some attempts to lessen the regulations. Conditions include paying up front, having no access to payment terms, and dealing with threats of confiscation of wire transfers to satisfy outstanding legal claims against the government.[73] As a result, and a consequence of the global financial meltdown in 2008, the Cuban side has steadily decreased purchases.

Prior to the machinations that led to the failure of HR4645, Moran spoke of the inconsistency in Cuban travel restriction policy. "This is giving Americans the freedom to make the choice of where to travel. It's also very hypocritical that we allow Americans to travel to China, but we have not allowed Americans to travel to Cuba. I don't understand the distinction; clearly China is a much greater threat, a much bigger country."[74]

The political realities at play as to how America treats China when compared to Cuba were clarified in 2000 shortly after the United States granted normal trade relations with the emerging economic powerhouse. During the discussions in Congress, House majority leader Richard Armey, a Texas Republican, made the observation that "free and open trade is not only the best way to make China a free and open nation, but it may be the only way. A market is simply an arena in which there is a sharing of information about market transactions, information about desires, wants, hopes and dreams, and economic conditions. But, Mr. Speaker, one cannot share that information about economics without also sharing information about culture, politics, religion and values. Information, Mr. Speaker, is the life blood of a market. It is also poison to dictators, because dictators know that it is the truth that will set one free."

When it was suggested that strategy might as well apply to the Caribbean nation, Republican whip Tom Delay responded with a strong defense of the embargo: "(It) has not worked the way it should have worked because we have not been turning the screws on him (Castro) and screwing him down and putting pressure on him, so that his people will rise up and throw him out. After all, Cuba is not Eastern Europe, this is not the Soviet Union, this is a tiny island." Immediately the retort came from New York representative José Serrano, born in Puerto Rico: "It finally happened. The last speaker let the cat out of the bag. Cuba is a small island, not a large European country. That is the problem. If it was a large European country or an Asian country, he would be lobbying, as he did, for free trade with Cuba, because he was the chief sponsor of lobbying on behalf of President Clinton for free trade with China. But he said it, Cuba is a small island, and for 41 years, we have been saying, you are a small island, you are insignificant, you speak another language, we are going to step all over you. It was never about what was right. It was about Cuba being a small island, and China being a big country."[75]

Favoring one country while punishing another with the same social structure is a standard geopolitical expression of immutable power dynamics. Cuba's revolution has permanently been put in the latter category. Foreign policy influences, but national political considerations play an equally decisive role. It is of no difference which side controls the White House or Congress as long as siege policy combines with Florida, home of the core antiembargo forces, retaining its status as a key swing state. Neither party nor president will stop pandering to one of the most important voting blocs who present the face of siege and promulgate its strategy fully. Barack Obama fell entirely under the influence when as a candidate he publicly declared Cuban policy a failure,[76] while once in the Oval Office he sang the same tune since Eisenhower. Calling the current economic reforms in Cuba inconsequential, Obama took up the habitual cry of bringing freedom and liberty to the Cuban people. And the default position to accomplish that remained the same—economic punishment bonded with appropriating millions of dollars to the supporters of siege. Obama succumbed to the mentality that money will help solve the problem of the revolution by approving a series of programs, including in 2012 a 34 percent swell in funding various proposals coming out of the US Interest Section in Havana, adding more than $4 million to that allocated the previous year.[77] The President then approved a 42 percent bump to the budget of the Cuban Affairs Office to $3,608,000 under the 2012 account.[78] Both agencies, recognized as leading Cuban policy from the State Department in Washington, received the increases while the department was cutting back on administrative expenses and many other foreign programs.[79] Some $11,742,000 in total was assigned for the operation of the two offices, part of $62 million for the ongoing plan to help bring down the revolution.

Of the millions spent to maintain siege, a large portion has been allocated to perpetuate the travel prohibitions and defeat such efforts as HR4645. If US citizens were permitted to travel to the island legally, it would have a detrimental effect on the embargo and all other antirevolutionary policies, Washington lawyer José Pertierra asserted. "The travel restrictions are the linchpin, remove them and slowly the embargo would fall. But there is tremendous political effort to keep those restrictions, because if the American tourist was able to come to Cuba they'd see for themselves what the country is about, the good and the bad. And that scares the hard right because they'd lose control of the message . . . Cuba is not afraid of having Americans come, they'd welcome them, they need the money generated by tourism. It is another lie that the government is afraid that it would destroy the socialist system. The Cubans would react and respond and continue, and it would be better for both sides."[80]

Restrictions on visits to Cuba provide sanctuary for the proembargo defenders to authorize politicians and media to regulate antirevolutionary perspectives for a compliant American audience. Equally important is the denial of substantial economic benefits the country would receive if US citizens were allowed to see what is happening on the island. Estimates range as high as more than $1 billion a year lost to Cuba's tourist sector,[81] based on predictions of one to three million tourists annually in the first three years.[82] There is loss to the US travel industry as well, including jobs in administration, as baggage handlers, and various support services. A glimpse of what the future could hold is available for anyone who sees the weekly planeloads of Cuban-Americans flying to Havana, or the hundreds of Americans traveling on expanded licensed programs. Since Obama cracked open the door for those groups, numerous cities other than Miami are now offering direct flights, and local officials have recognized the potential. When Tampa was permitted to operate a schedule to Cuba in 2011, local Democratic Congresswoman Kathy Castor called the day "historic, eagerly awaited and much worked for day for Cuban-American families and the entire Tampa Bay community." South Florida Republican representative Mario Díaz-Balart didn't take long to protest back: "It's become a huge revenue source for the Castro regime."[83]

Castor's commonsense is an atypical position. State officials flying in the face of their own economic self-interest is the usual occurrence when Cuba is put into the mix. Laws aimed at punishing local companies doing business with the island have come and gone, wasting time and taxpayer's money. In 2008 an effort to enforce local Florida legislation demanding US charter operations pay high bonds to operate flights to Cuba was smacked down by a Federal District judge who told the state not to meddle in foreign policy issues. The latest attempt came in 2012 at the passing of a bill banning the awarding of public contracts to anyone negotiating with the Castro government. The effort seemed to be aimed at Brazil's Odebrect that has been in Miami for years, and is now working on the Cuban port of Mariel to turn it into a valuable Caribbean shipping hub. A Florida judge froze the July 1, 2012, implementation of the law until the federal authorities have a chance to take up the matter.[84]

In another incident, additional jobs could have come to the state if a plan to expand the mode of transportation to Havana was approved. A proposal to run a ferry service from Miami to the Cuban capital, harkening back to prerevolutionary days, was rejected by OFAC, despite regulations allowing both "aircraft and vessels" to service the island. Officials of the Havana Ferry Partners complained the denial cost hundreds of employment opportunities.[85] While passengers were denied the option of arriving to Cuba via ship,

a maritime operation bringing humanitarian aid and noncommerical goods
was given approval in mid-2012, the first direct Miami to Havana shipment
in 50 years.[86]

Loss of revenue in Florida is reflected in the rise in costs to Cuba's existing tourist industry, according to Carmen Casals Sánchez, director of
international relations for the Ministry of Tourism (MINTUR). "Prices are
25 per cent higher given the necessity of acquiring certain supplies from
intermediaries and in more distant markets," Casals noted. Examples men-
tioned included food preparation and exercise equipment, as well as branded
items such as Coca Cola. Cited in the report was the loss of $11.5 million
from the ban on American yachts and sailboats visiting national marinas.[87]

The lack of an American imprint on Cuban tourism is an attraction for
some, disconcerting for others. Of all the places where the influx of US
money, along with millions of Yankee visitors, would bring a mixed blessing
to is Old Havana. The UNESCO-designated World Heritage Site remains
one of the purest examples of colonial architecture combined with a vibrant
urban community. Thousands of Cubans live amid some of the country's
most historic buildings and artifacts, a unique contingency where everyday
life intersects with the number one tourist attraction in the city. The incongruity is more apparent as millions of dollars of predominantly foreign investment have been used in restoration of tourist facilities and new commercial
endeavors, in contrast to the constant struggle of those living in some of the
neighborhood's dilapidated three- and four-story apartments, laundry hang-
ing from the balconies, streets littered with garbage, constricted avenues
in bad repair;, the reminder of the economic limits the Cuban government
faces. And of the impact America's siege has on the inability of the state to
access the financial resources necessary to solve both the commercial and
residential needs of *Habana Vieja*.

Old Havana has undergone a dramatic transformation since the collapse
of the Soviet Union, all for the benefit of tourism and the hard currency it
attracts. Restaurants of all types and quality have sprung up by the dozen,
shops entice crowds who walk the narrow cobblestoned streets with modern
merchandize, shoes, clothes, jewelry, fine chocolates, and Cuban literature
and art. Bars are filled with the sounds of Latin melodies, museums and
murals are discovered on every corner, and some of the most recognized
hotels in the country can be found, including Ernest Hemingway's favorite *Ambos Mundos* on Obispo, the main commercial avenue. Cuba's famous
bar, *La Bodegita del Medio* on Empedrado, is in the middle of the action
and always full. What is near impossible to find in Old Havana is any hint
of American capitalism. No McDonalds, Burger King, or fast food place of
any kind (except the stalls selling Cuban sandwiches for 20 pesos). There
are no restaurant chains, no Hilton hotels, no Trump casinos—nothing that
would give comfort to an American tourist looking for the familiar. Which
is considered both a positive and negative by the international visitors and
the locals who depend on their generosity. Old Havana is the epitome of
"consequence of siege."

Fortunately, it is recognized for what it has, not for what it has not. Credit for the remarkable reinvigoration of one of Latin America's most significant heritage destinations goes in large part to Eusebio Leal, the creative, dedicated Havana City historian. Leal is well recognized for using the limited outside investments and national funds to best advantage, described as a miracle worker who has transformed Old Havana from a drab, introspective barrio into a welcoming, vibrant tourist spot that has retained its legitimate historic relevance combined with amenities that envelope and augment the ambience. Leal, while uncertain of the impact American tourists would have on the area, has no doubt as to how they would be treated. "Lifting of travel restrictions will impact Old Havana and Cuba; but it is a very complicated thing. Cuba is a secure country for US citizens, the can come here and feel safe. I believe that always. When US tourists come they will be welcomed here. The Cuban people respect the US citizens, there are no kidnappings, this is not a violent society. It is not allowed for anyone to burn the US flag in Cuba."[88] Allowing the northern neighbor to experience the island for themselves "would start a new time between us, it would be positive for both sides, economically, socially, it would influence many things."

Leal tackled the issue of American government policy against Cuba as he has done with his work in Old Havana, direct and without compromise. "Cuba is called the universal sinner, the lies that are told about our country. We are criticized by the US, for human rights issues. But go to Mexico, it is like a butcher shop, so many killed. But it is Cuba that is blockaded for travel, you can go to North Korea, but you can't come here." As a historian, Leal acknowledged that America's relationship with Cuba hasn't always been so aggressive. "You have to distinguish the government from the people. We have issues that have split us, but in the history of America there is a chapter about Cuba, a positive chapter. American freedom fighters fought for the independence of Cuba, José Martí had many friends in the United States. There is no question as to the influence of US culture with Cuban, some of the most outstanding Cuban intellectuals spent time in the United States. America has played an important role in our country."

If businesses and tourists from the United States came to Old Havana, Leal is not certain the reaction a McDonalds would receive on the corner of O'Reilly and Mercaderes. "I'm not a prophet, I don't know what will happen in the future, how Old Havana will be changed. If in the future there were full commercial relations with the United States, you can't restrict the debates, the possibilities. A McDonalds in Old Havana, it should not be wholly discounted, nor accepted."

Americans who currently make the trip down to the socialist experiment, unless through licensed programs, do so illegally. There have been hundreds of thousands who have taken this route over the years, many facing the legal and economic consequences back home. The issue brings political ramifications, with freedom of travel proponents highlighting the absurdity of the situation. Former North Dakota senator Bryon Dorgan exposed a few examples in 2010 in a passionate speech to Congress, "It means we are punishing the American people saying: We restrict your right to travel. So Carlos Lazo, a man whom I have met and who went to Iraq to fight for his country and who won a Bronze Star because he was brave and was a great soldier, came back to this country after having served his country in uniform, was awarded with great fanfare a Bronze Medal for bravery, and then was told, when he was informed—he had two sons living in Cuba and his older son was sick—you have no right to travel to Cuba to see your sick child. Unbelievable." As jarring was the experience of Joan Scott, who went to Havana to distribute Bibles. "For that, her government tracked her down and tried to fine her $10,000. For going to Cuba to distribute free Bibles, this government is going to track its citizens down to try to fine them $10,000...I am tired of those stories. Those stories are an embarrassment about public policy gone wrong, and we need to fix it."[89]

Punishing those who try to circumvent the travel restrictions is a critical ingredient in the fight to keep Cuba untouchable. Policy does not limit itself to those who want to visit, but its long extraterritorial arm extends to individuals who promote trips to the island, whether they are aimed at Americans or not. And whether they are even operating in the United States.

Steve Marshall had most of his websites shut down in 2008 by the US government because he sold trips to Cuba. Marshall, born in England and living in Spain, promoted his packages to Europeans, doing no advertising in America. The sites, in English, French, and Spanish, had been online since 1998. Some, www.cuba-hemingway.com, were literary. Others, www.cuba-havanacity.com, discussed Cuban history and culture.[90] "I came to work in the morning, and we had no reservations at all," Marshall commented at the time. "We thought it was a technical problem." It was determined that his sites had been put on a Treasury Department blacklist, resulting in his American domain name registrar eNom Inc. disabling them. "How web sites owned by a British national operating via a Spanish travel agency can be affected by U.S. law," Marshall complained. Treasury spokesman John Rankin claimed Marshall's company helped Americans evade the travel restrictions to Cuba, and was "a generator of resources that the Cuban regime uses to oppress its people."[91] Published reports claimed the United States has blocked close to 600 companies and 3,700 domain names linked with the island.[92]

The economic warfare is equally vigilant in application to the reverse when Cubans find themselves accessing US-controlled facilities. The Hilton Hotel was prohibited from accepting Cuban guests at the IV Caricom/Cuba Summit in Trinidad in 2011,[93] while in 2008 the Sheraton Maria Isobel Hotel in Mexico City expelled 16 officials who were attending a conference, ejected on the orders from Washington. In another Hilton incident, the chain, owner of the Scandic Edderkoppen Hotel in Oslo, informed 14 Cubans that they could not stay there during a travel fair. The Mexican government subsequently levied a fine of $112,000 against the Sheraton Hotel for its action, and the aftermath in Oslo resulted in protests, threats of boycott, and demands for respecting national sovereignty laws.[94]

Nontourist activities have not escaped notice. Canadian citizen James Sabzali, while living in the United States, faced a 12-month conditional sentence and a fine of $10,000 for selling resins used to purify water.[95] French shipping company CMA CGM was penalized $370,000 when its subsidiary in Norfolk, Virginia, accepted payment for facilitating cargo services to the island.[96] OFAC even took on the United Nations, seizing $4 million from the Foundation Fund for Cuba's fight against AIDS and tuberculosis during the first quarter of 2011, Deputy Foreign Trade Minister Orlando Hernández charged.[97] Continuing controversy surrounds disputed Havana Club Rum and Cohiba cigars trademarks in the United States, island officials claiming millions in lost revenues from sales and market confusion. US entities fire back that the Castro government illegally confiscated and utilized prerevolutionary brands recognized worldwide.[98]

Of all the areas the US government is focusing its negative energies on, the financial institutions are garnering most attention—banks, account holders, and related operations. All have come under severe attack, increasingly so under the Obama administration. Since the early years of the revolution Cuba has had no access to the World Bank, Inter-America Development Bank, and World Trade Organization, denied funds and credits set aside for Latin America at a loss of billions of dollars.[99] Cuba has not been a member of the International Monetary Fund since 1964, leaving the institution after paying its debts. And now Cuba's ability to conduct normal business practices through the internationally connected banking systems is under threat.

American weight on banks not to do business with the socialist government has created hesitancy as when the Bank of Nova Scotia reportedly backed off loaning to Canadians wanting to invest in Cuba.[100] It has created specific hardship when Cuba is forced to pay high interest rates of up to 9 percent to the few banks that are willing to extend credit.[101] Additionally, it has resulted in some of the largest fines in the banking industry, amounting to hundreds of millions of dollars.

Incidents often delve into the realm of the absurd. British companies came under target again in 2008 when a health shop in Somerset and a London tobacconist were told by Lloyds TSB they had to stop selling Cuban products if they wanted to continue being served by the bank. The demands came after threats by the United States that it would prosecute international financial institutions with branches in America that held accounts doing business with Cuba, regardless of the country the accounts were in. Lloyds made clear it could no longer authorize payments from the health store to purchase Cuban sugar and the tobacconist, who had been in business for 100 years, had to switch to another institution or stop offering the product.[102] The Canadian Scotia Bank announced that it would no longer provide services for monetary transactions in dollars from the United States to Cuba through its branch in Jamaica.[103]

Even the dead don't escape the reach of siege. Under Bush Jr. regulations banks were restricted from sending no more than $100 to Cuban heirs of relatives who had died in America and left inheritances. In an uncommon show of rationality, the Obama administration permitted receipt of the entire bequest, ending what was called "one of the most ridiculous applications of Cuba sanctions that one could imagine."[104] That didn't stop OFAC from imposing a $22,000 fine on MetLife insurance company in 2011 for sending a check for a death benefit directly to a beneficiary in Cuba. It wasn't the payment amount, but the method that violated Treasury Department rules, a spokesman explained.[105]

Financial penalties have reached staggering amounts. A US judge approved a $298 million settlement by British bank Barclays Plc over charges that it had violated trade sanctions by not disclosing deals in Cuba, Iran, Libya, Sudan, and Myanmar. Credit Suisse Group AG, Lloyds Banking Group Plc, and ABN AMRO settled on fines ranging between $350 million and $538 million.[106] OFAC levied $100 million penalty against the Union of Swiss Banks for assisting the replacement by Cuba and other countries of dollar bills in poor condition.[107] The record holder is a $619 million charge in 2012 against ING for conducting commercial transactions with Cuba and other sanctioned nations.[108] American banks haven't escaped OFAC's wrath either. In 2001 JP Morgan agreed to pay $88.3 million for breaking sanctions, a portion based on violations of more than 1,000 wire transfers involving an estimated $150 million.[109] A majority of the assessments fall under sanctions against those designated as state sponsors of terrorism, a label particularly infuriating to the Cuban government. Under those regulations the United States has authorized freezing Cuban assets, more than $494 million in 2010 alone, confirmed the Treasury Department.[110]

The fines moved in harmony with aims to increase roadblocks toward Cuba's ability to use US dollars internationally, under such programs as the Cuban Asset Targeting Group created in 2004.[111] The pressure, derived from charges of money laundering was led in large measure by Ileana Ros-Lehtinen. In response to those and other measures to limit Cuba's access to US dollars, the Castro side replaced the American currency used by tourists with a national convertible peso (Chavito) and levied a 10 percent surcharge on the exchange of US cash for the peso. At the time Castro became determined to use fewer dollars and more Euros in the country's international commercial dealings, so far with mixed results.

Along with the fines, attempts to disrupt Cuba's financial actions extend to high-tech systems. The Society for Worldwide Interbank Financial Telecommunication SCRL (SWIFT) software programs that play a vital role in international transactions have become increasingly more difficult for the government to access.[112] According to island officials, SWIFT informed the Central Bank of Cuba (BCC) that a new version of software used by participating banks will not be available because it includes American technology and the owners are subject to sanctions under US law.[113] SWIFT was in the center of a European controversy following requests by US officials to be allowed examination of every transaction to suss out Cuban negotiations. So far that application has been denied.[114]

Besides the banks, various other financial services have done their share upholding anti-Cuban regulations. In the forefront is PayPal, a fully owned subsidiary of US-based e-Bay with operations worldwide. Its efforts are very efficient, according to Simon McGuinness of the Cuban Support Group in Ireland. He has first-hand knowledge of the problems sending money to Havana after his organization arranged to transfer in excess of €7,000 to a Cuban account to support its medical team in Haiti during the earthquake aftermath. The funds were first attempted to be sent through an Irish bank, "which I'd prefer if you wouldn't name in case the OFAC pulls the shutters down on them too," McGuiness cautioned.[115] The bank refused to send the money, citing embargo restrictions. The group then turned to PayPal and subsequently informed that all merchants using the service must comply with OFAC regulations, so sending money to Cuba would be in violation of the blockade, regardless if the donation came from a source outside the United States. McGuiness had no hesitation condemning the extraterritorial financial aspect of the blockade, referring to it as "a global system of extortion." He protested that OFAC has no jurisdiction to impose fines on those outside of US law, "but if international banks refuse to pay the fines imposed on them, their license to carry on financial business in the USA, or using the US dollar, will be withdrawn. The banks are therefore in the position of having no choice; either they close down or they pay up, exactly the choice offered by the Mafia in its extortion operation."[116]

PayPal has been busy elsewhere, shutting down the account of a German website that had been selling Cuban rum, despite EU Regulation No. 2271/96 making it illegal for any company in the European Union to comply with the embargo. PayPal operates in Europe through a Luxembourg-based banking entity.[117] Rum was again an issue in a matter demonstrating the worldwide reach of America's economic clamp against the revolution. In Chile it was reported hundreds of customers stormed liquor stores in an effort to buy up as much Cuban rum as they could. The reason for the 2009 "rum rush was the coming of Wal-Mart, which refused to sell Cuban products."[118]

*   *   *

There is something on the horizon, more specifically off the coast of Havana, that may change the rules of the economic siege warfare. This towering structure, well recognized in the Gulf of Mexico, is searching for a substance hundreds of meters below the surface in the usually calm waters of the Florida Straits, well within the island's territorial boundaries. Oil, the black gold that has altered the fortunes of nations overnight, is Cuba's potential salvation. If found in the quantities experts predict, ranging from five to 20 billion barrels of oil and 9.8 trillion cubic feet of natural gas,[119] petroleum could break besiegement by the sheer number of dollars gushing into Cuba's coffers. Not that getting the exploration started has been uncomplicated, thanks to the blockade. The administration was forced to

purchase, at considerably higher expense, a new deep-water drilling platform specifically in order to circumvent the restrictions on use of more than
10 percent American technology. Built in China at a cost of $750 million, with
mostly Russian parts, Scarabeo 9 was then sailed halfway around the world
in a months' long journey before ending up in Havana. Leased by Spanish
Repsol YPF, through a consortium including Norway, Italy, Singapore, and
others, the drilling began early in 2012. Repsol's initial drilling in May
2012 came up empty, leading company officials to consider whether to pull
out of further exploration. The failure is not unusual, experts insist, with
four out of five attempts unsuccessful in the search for new underwater oil
deposits.[120] Other lease holders will have the chance to find the oil in a process that could take years to develop, expectations that have both pro- and
antirevolutionaries on edge. Scarabeo 9 is capable of drilling in 3,657 meters
(12,000 feet) of water and will be used to explore the various offshore locations Cuba has sold off in 59 blocks inside an 112,000-square-kilometer
zone. Unconfirmed reports speculate that a number of blocks are still available and that the Cubans would not object to American interests securing
some of those, provided there was a change in embargo legislation. In the
meantime, Russia has become the latest player after arranging a second rig,
Songa Mercur, which started exploring Cuban waters in July 2012.[121]

When the oil starts flowing experts forecast it could be as high quality as Texas light sweet crude. If so, the island's economy will be transformed. It would release Cuba from dependency on the importation of more
than 100,000 barrels a day, mostly from a currently friendly Venezuela—
a relationship that has no guarantees in the future.[122] More importantly, the
island would emerge as an oil exporter over the next decade and enjoy the
benefits that would command on the international stage.

The natural resource has tremendous implications for Cuba's fiscal recovery, its role in the league of oil producers, and its relationship with the northern power. And so *oro negro* has become the latest issue in the interminable
battle to preserve encirclement. The prospect has sufficiently frightened the
proembargo side that laws in Florida have come forth attempting to prevent Cuba from drilling in its own water, based on potentially devastating
oil spills. As Tracey Eaton noted, everyone knows how high the stakes are.
"Oil exploration could be very important to Cuba's economy, in one aspect
it might result in less reliance on Venezuela. But it's been interesting to see
some of the hard-right politicians trying to sabotage efforts for Cuba to
develop that oil."[123]

At the forefront is the old standby, Ileana Ros-Lehtinen, who along with
fellow Florida conservatives Vern Buchanan and Bill Nelson have publicly
based their opposition on ecological risks to the state's tourist and fishing
industries. "We need to make sure the pressure stays on to keep these deals
from happening so that we can protect our shores from a potential Cuban oil-
drilling disaster," Ros-Lehtinen said.[124] Concern is rooted in the lack of faith
she and the others have in Cuban safety technology and measures, despite
the fact the rig will be operated by industry experts under internationally

accepted procedures. Cuban officials have stated intent to meet American standards, many hoping they exceed them in light of the BP disaster.

The US siege has worked against ensuring the platform is operating under optimum safety conditions, preventing the use of some American technical expertise. For the Cuban side the proper precautions are of paramount concern, ensuring nothing damages the pristine beaches and tourist facilities lining the north coast and in particular the key area of Varadero. The revolutionary government has gone so far as to indicate it would welcome US expertise in the project, a situation agreeable to oil expert Jorge Pinon at Florida International University in Miami. "For the U.S. offshore oil industry, Cuba is basically an extension of the Gulf of Mexico. In Cuba we can offer services from Houston, Freeport and Mobile," he said.[125] He added that in terms of responding to an emergency spill, having the US connected to the project would be vitally important. "The question to ask is, 'Does the company that's going to drill have a respectable record of environmental stewardship and does it have the know-how?' And the answer is yes. I'm not concerned with Cuba drilling for oil; I'm very concerned we don't have an emergency plan in case of a spill."[126]

Longtime Castro opponent Bill Nelson, an adherent in thwarting Cuba's attempts to develop the oil, surprisingly acknowledged the difficulties America's lack of involvement would have on dealing with a spill emergency. In 2011 he promoted an idea to talk to Mexico, Cuba, and the Bahamas to devise a plan in case of such a situation, an about face from a threat he made three years earlier wanting the United States to unilaterally withdraw from the Maritime Boundary Agreement that sets up exploration zones in the Gulf of Mexico, and then order Cuba to halt operations. He also favored applying sanctions to any company that drilled in Cuban waters.[127] As it stands the siege prohibits American engineers and expertise to be used, despite the fact drilling may come within 50 miles of Florida's coast.[128] Surprisingly, cooperation in the matter is not unheard of—Cuba allowed US officials to examine the platform at Repsol's regional headquarters in Trinidad before its final leg, the Americans pronouncing the rig fit and safe.[129]

The worry over environmental safety appears to be a convenient distraction. Ros-Lehtinen admitted that her no-drill bills have less to do with coral reefs than they have with averting an emerging oil industry in Cuba. "The U.S. must apply stronger pressure to prevent other companies from engaging commercially, and any other means, with this crooked and corrupt regime."[130] She further backed legislation that would deny visas and impose export sanctions and other penalties on companies involved in Cuba's operations, noting that "some deeply troubling drilling partnerships have already been established."[131] Significantly, any American attempt to block development would likely run up against the objections of Petrocaribe, a multicountry project formed to promote energy security in the region through exploration, refining, and distribution—backed by Venezuelan oil—of which Cuba is a member.

Regardless of the practicality of cooperation on the safe exploration of oil in Cuba, and the support it has from international organizations, the cries from antirevolutionaries continue in an effort to deny the desperately needed petro-dollars to the island. "This is part of a decade-long propaganda campaign by the regime in order to secure the oil industry's support for joining the lobby against the embargo," said Cuba PAC director Mauricio Claver-Carone. "We've been through this before," he commented on reports that Cuba is ready to drill. "It's the little boy who cried wolf."[132]

It is the possibility an oil-rich Cuba would be able to shatter siege that has the anti-Castroites worried, former history professor Robert Sandels observed. Even using conservative estimates as to quantities "would make Cuba energy independent, and eventually a net exporter. This would have an incalculable impact on its economy, and would send the U.S. sanctions policy into the dustbin of imperial miscalculations."[133]

Economics is one of the foundations for the constructs of siege strategy. Without the dollars to sustain it, the encirclement would wither and die. Politics and money, two interchangeable elements in the United States, combine efficiently and directly to besiege the island. With little hesitancy, the American government continues to toss in millions, regardless of the state of its own national economy, all in order to persist in punishing this small nation's defiance through the insurance of political will.

Whether the discovery of oil turns out to be the instrument to defeat besiegement, it is unquestionably a significant development with the potential to be the backbone for the reforms undertaken on the island since 2008. Raúl Castro has implored the citizens to change attitudes toward work, society, and socialism, and the transformations taking place are vital to the revolution's survival in the twenty-first century. Moreover, the changes represent in large measure the latest evidence of America's inability to deal with the reality on the ground in Cuba, to stop slamming its head against the walls.

5

A Changing Cuba—A Stagnant Siege

Why doesn't President Obama's administration take care of the U.S. problems
and leave us Cubans alone to solve ours in peace?
—Foreign Minister Bruno Rodriquez[1]

There is an unmistakable sense of anticipation sweeping over Cuba. In the
street corners of Havana, outside the hotel lobbies in Varadero, and most
importantly in the countryside and small towns, citizens are experiencing
the apprehension and excitement that accompanies wide-ranging transformation. In Cuba, where extreme outside forces and reactionary internal direc-
tives combine to make institutional change something not easily achieved,
what is happening is extraordinary. It is a revolution within the Revolution.

The island has come to grips with the economic repercussions and social
upheavals of the past 20 years, as well as conceding the limitations from
three decades of absorbing orthodox Marxist-Leninism and its stagnation
through centralization. The reformation enveloping the economy reaches
equally as deep into the political psyche. Significantly, the changes are taking on a permanency unlike the tentative reforms of the 1990s, thanks in
large part to the development of organized dialogues evident in the press,
academic and institutional spaces. The foundation sprung from the expressions of an estimated three million people who took part in Raúl Castro's
call for free and frank debate to ensure the survival and development of
Cuba's socialism.[2]

Openly discussing how "updating the socialist model"[3] will alter the
revolution is in direct challenge to the siege mentality, which for decades
equated such public displays and deliberations as seen as aiding the enemy.
The attitude of using the blockade as justification for suppression of opinion
and evasion of responsibility is being eroded. Those worried that the changes
will undermine Cuba's social justice structure and widen class divisions are
treated as legitimately as concerns the reforms are imperative for the country's future. Emergence of this debate is itself an indication of important
social change, *Temas* magazine editor Rafael Hernández commented. "When
we talk about debate or criticism we often talk about censorship, restrictions,
control, but we never talk about our own lack of a 'debate culture.' We must
foster a culture of debate from the start, because our society doesn't have it. We

often call a debate 'good' when the participants say the same as we think. That's not debate; debate is disagreement. And it's very important that in a debate we express divergent positions in a spirit of dialogue, of mutual respect. I think [Cuban] politics is going through this stage right now."[4]

It is impossible, he postulated, to expect no political changes to emerge from the economic shifts taking place. That speculation is coming true. A test case in separating ineffective and corrupting power centers is happening in the new provinces of Mayabeque and Artemisa. Previously the duties of the chairman of the local Assembly of the People's Power and of the territorial administrative board were held by one person; now they have been split. This aimed to disconnect the dual responsibilities that led to conflict of interest, with bureaucrats acting as both judge and jury under certain civil responsibilities. Citizen's complaints led to the restructuring, and if successful this attempt to introduce a greater level of political accountability and decentralization could be extended to the whole country in another example of the bottom-up movement of reform taking form in Cuba.[5]

Economic restructuring has been anticipated since 2009 when President Raúl Castro made it clear that the country could no longer stumble down the same path. Socialism had to discover a different route, one that did not abandon the civil justice programs but would accept that the state would no longer be makers of shoes or manufacturers of jeans; that not every aspect of the economy would be controlled by centralized, faceless bureaucrats who more often hindered than helped. Castro had apparently come to this realization when confiding to Venezuelan President Hugo Chávez, saying Cuba "had committed many errors," adding the Cuban leader lamented: "Here we nationalized even the funeral home, the barber shop, the sale of ice cream. That doesn't have any reason to belong to the state."[6]

In agreement was Ricardo Alarcón, President of Cuba's parliament, casting his voice to the altering relationship between state and commerce. "The Communist Party should have nothing to do with the economic management, with the administration, with the decisions made at the company level. Nor should the state or the provincial or municipal government. In other words, we have to develop the entrepreneurial autonomy or the entrepreneurial independence. The company is directed by its director. The conduct of the business is up to the business, not to the local government, not to the local assembly, not to the local party."[7]

To expedite the transformation the government called for more than one million workers to be shifted from the public to private sector.[8] In addition, the government announced its intention to abolish certain subsidies and the decrease in items on the ration card.[9] As he prepared the country for its shift to a single-party social democracy with market influences, Raúl declared, "We have to eliminate forever the notion that Cuba is the only country where one can live without working."[10] He resolutely assured the changes and ongoing discussions would "point the way towards the socialist future, adjusted to the conditions of Cuba, not the capitalist past," and that the revolution itself was at stake.

Raúl's comments were seen as trial balloons for the island's experiment with permanent entrepreneurship and revolutionary socialism; allowing for the opportunity to buy and sell homes and cars, open and expand private restaurants, food stands, taxis, barber shops, beauty salons, and repair shops; for farmers to be given the ability to control more of their own produce and markets—all for the benefit of the individual as well as the maintenance of accessibility to the state's social programs.

Anticipated regulations were made official at the Sixth Congress of the Cuban Communist Party in October 2010, with officials acknowledging the inefficiencies in the nation's economic model. These included: general low economic growth and productivity, particularly in the agricultural industry; deficiencies in investment; the gap between workers' incomes and the rising prices of goods and services; lack of connection between workers' productivity and salaries; excessive economic centralization; increased state restrictions on certain goods and services; the low level of housing construction; and the levels of foreign and domestic deficits. To counter these weaknesses the government outlined 300 adjustments designed to improve productivity by promoting private enterprise, establishing a more efficient tax system and balancing public finances.[11]

The current round of economic reformation was born from the advance and retrenchment of the late 1990s, when private entrepreneurship in restaurants and homes was tolerated then drawn back as the economy recovered. Individual restrictions remained firmly in place until the environment on two fronts took control in 2008—three hurricanes and one global financial meltdown leading to the realization that systemic internal adjustments were inevitable. Needing to demonstrate real commitment to address citizens' concerns, particularly the younger generation tired of talk but little action, the government developed a comprehensive strategy toward social/economic modernity. The latest round of reforms followed previous changes permitting Cubans to own cell phones, import electronic equipment, and ending restrictions on entering tourist facilities. All in an effort to eliminate what Raúl called "excessive prohibitions."[12]

The transformations of the past five years have come, relentlessly, assuredly, *sin prisas, pero sin pausas* (without hurry but without pause), in the tightrope balancing act between guaranteeing reforms are instituted for maximum economic benefit with minimum social disruption, while at the same time ensuring the besiegers no opportunity to manipulate the forces of change.[13]

The restructuring has grasped energy unto itself despite the government's resolve to advance methodically. Considered the most important of all the changes, Cubans are now permitted to purchase and sell (under certain conditions) residential properties and used cars. It has created sometimes incongruous situations.[14] Thirty-year-old Ladas that wouldn't fetch $50 in North America are selling for an equivalent $10,000 in a desperate rush to put even more private taxis on the streets of Havana. The housing market is an irrational conglomeration of expectation and reality as owners ask for thousands of dollars for small upstairs apartments in sleepy towns outside of Varadero, anxiously awaiting buyers who may never show up. Meanwhile, regal mansions near virgin beaches go for a fraction of what the property would command in Miami. Habaneros who have been saving for years now have the prospect to use the money, some of it obtained illegally, and the cash is appearing in large quantities, increasingly revealing the disparages between the haves and have-nots. Real estate and used cars have created a vast new stock of private capital in markets that will be controlled by decisions of individuals—much of it from outside the island as Cubans abroad send funds to relatives specifically for these purchases. The government benefits through a new income tax structure and percentage charges on all sales.

The seismic shift in Cuba's economy, complete with innumerable ripple effects, will occur greatest within the housing market. Under the old laws Cubans had title to their houses or apartments, but could not utilize them as a marketable item. The only option was to bestow them to heirs or trade them with another homeowner in the gray area system through a *permuta*, a typically unofficial Cuban solution to a problem.[15]

Within the new housing regulations there is no accommodation for authorized brokers, although dozens of entrepreneurs are already hooking up buyers and sellers through Internet sites and the most effective Cuban telecommunication system—word of mouth. The government is determined to retain the maxim that housing is to live in, not live from. Specific rules and regulations to affect that pledge include time frames when homes can be resold, and the limit of one city home and one country dwelling per person, discouraging accumulation of wealth and absentee landlords. Ownership exclusive to nationals avert direct foreign market access (recognizing much of the cash will come from relatives in the United States) although expanding the buyer class may be considered in the near future. Regardless of the restrictions, the release of millions of dollars tied to property sales will have an impact not just on the prime sources, but on ancillary markets, not the least of which will be the explosion of a legitimate building and repair industry. Demands for wholesale outlets are being answered by international concerns such as Brazil's TendTudo, planning a series of home improvement sites.[16] The key will be if materials, so often in short supply, can match expected demands and purchasing power of the thousands of already skilled Cubans who will move into the profit-making repair business. The state incentivized the industry by announcing subsidies to private individuals working in the renovation trade, capped at 80,000 Cuban pesos, the government's official cost to build a 2,500-square-feet house.[17] In total more than 160 million pesos have been allocated.[18]

"With a housing market, suddenly people have some wealth and that's a stake in the economy that generates activity," said Ted Henken, a Latin American Studies professor at Baruch College in New York. "This is a very positive step in the right direction."[19] The new wealth may come at a social cost, warn officials such as Mario Coyula, Havana's director of urbanism and architecture in the 1970s, who observed that the housing market could lead to a "huge rearrangement" in Havana and other cities as those who can afford to will move to better areas.[20] The potential negative social affects and financial disparities brought on by the reforms will be something closely monitored by the government in an attempt to circumvent the diminishing of revolutionary ideals.

While housing is soon set to become an economic steamroller, it's at the microlevel where the effects of reforms for the individual are having immediate impact. "My name is Juan," came the shout from the middle-aged Afro-Cuban worker between customers at the popular Café Pnocho food stand on San Rafael St. in the Central Park district of Havana. The street, a short pedestrian mall bustling with restaurants, shops, and commercial outlets, runs besides the venerable Hotel Inglaterra and next to the Capitolio in one of the busiest areas of the city. The spot sells *pan con minuta* (fish sandwich) for five Cuban pesos and large ham and cheese sandwiches for ten pesos. It's not uncommon to see lineups of 20 or 30 waiting patiently. The café is next to the state-run El Almirante, usually catering to far fewer customers willing to spend CUCs (Chavitos), the tourist dollar pegged at $1.08 USD that runs 24 times more expensive than one Cuban peso.

"Under the new economic changes this allows me to operate the food stand, we can sell in Cuban pesos and we can make money. See how popular it is here," Juan said, wiping his brow while grabbing a sandwich from the cook. "We work hard, everyday there's people waiting for our food. And I earn four or five times more than before,"[21] indicating he was a government worker on a 360-Cuban-peso-a-month salary.

Similar stands are popping up all over the city, a visual commitment to the permanency of the reforms and the expectations among those looking to enter self-employment. Since September 2011 when the government extended to 181 the categories and allowed small private firms to hire employees (not just family members), officials have been hard pressed to keep up with demand. It has been estimated that close to 500,000 licenses have been issued, majority for cabs, beauty salons, photographers, locksmiths, carpenters, and eating establishments in a direct challenge for the government to get out of the way. Onerous tax codes that were initially published have been drawn back for simpler and more affordable regulations.[22] Some private enterprises, known as *cuenta propias*, will be allowed to sell services to the state, under strict anticorruption rules.[23]

Other evidence of real change has direct commercial importance— establishments turning to the Cuban peso as the default method of payment. Since the opening of the tourist industry in the 1990s the island has dabbled with various forms of tender for foreign visitors, including the American dollar. In the past decade the dual-currency form has settled on the Cuban Convertible Peso (CUC), running 24 national pesos to 1. The Chavito, as it is referred to, has since emerged as the standard of use for a variety of local consumer goods from refrigerators, certain food, rum, cigars, car parts, services, and now the real estate and used car markets. The effort to return to the national peso is much appreciated, said Guantanamo resident Pedro de la Fuente, "They have opened restaurants, pizzerias, cafeterias and pastry shops and set up areas across the city where they sell sandwiches, snacks and soda. The population has welcomed this because before these things were available only in convertible pesos," he said.[24] The plan is to increase the availability of goods and services in pesos in a transition from the two-currency system, which the government hopes to eliminate in the next few years. With it will end the complaints from Cubans who argue the system makes too many items unaffordable on an average salary of 400 pesos a month, equivalent to 16 Chavitos in a reality where a stove can cost 300 CUCs.

Besides home and used car owners,[25] those who work the land will reap considerable benefit. An estimated 2.5 million unused acres has been set aside for anyone wanting to turn soil into profit as the government moves to augment development of the successful cooperative systems that have proven to be instrumental in increasing production.[26] According to a National Office of Statistics report from 2008, the state controlled 16.3 million acres (6.6 million hectares) for agricultural use, approximately 9 million (3.6 million hectares) determined fallow or underused. Landless Cubans can apply for 33 acres (13 hectares), while established farmers can increase current holdings to 100 acres (40 hectares). Private citizens qualify for leases in usufruct of up to 10 years, renewable for 10 more, while cooperatives and companies can seek 25-year renewable terms.[27] The government has identified raising food production as a national security priority, hoping to save hundreds of millions spent on importation, much from the United States. Considerable resources have subsequently been allocated to ensure the agriculture reforms have the best chance to succeed, as it represents the key component in the overall results of the transformations.[28] To that end *campensenos* have been given the right to purchase inputs and supplies from local stores instead of state appropriations,[29] as well as to sell produce directly to tourist facilities. This promises to undermine the control of publicly derided government entities such as Acopio, the giant buying and selling agency under considerably criticism for its centralized inefficiency.[30]

The concept of local cooperatives is gaining foothold in more than the agricultural sector. In a decision that gained little national attention, three provinces were granted rights to set up workers groups outside direct state control in a variety of industries, augmenting the government's efforts to move a million employees from the public payroll.[31]

Even the country's renowned health system has not escaped the drive for economic efficiency. A Ministry of Public Health report indicated some health centers will be downgraded or closed, administrators will be reallocated to patient care, and university places for nursing education will be reduced. "We intend to reorganize, compact and regionalize health services," the 11-page document outlined. "This bill will allow more efficient and rational use of the extensive and expensive resources at our disposal. This decision not only responds to economic reason, but also to the urgent need to achieve higher levels of efficiency and quality in everything we do."[32] Minister Roberto Morales ensured that no physician would be dismissed under the restructuring.[33]

Hoping to ensure the palatability of the wide-ranging reforms, an intensified sweep against local corruption that has cost the state millions has been implemented. Provincial administrations in such places as Sancti Spiritus fell under the effort to eliminate white-collar (or white Guayabera after the ubiquitous Cuban dress shirt) crime that has spread like a virus in government and commercial circles. Hundreds of party officials, state managers, employees, and even international businessmen have been caught in the struggle to decentralize, eliminate inefficiency and waste, and to maintain zero tolerance against those wanting to take illegal advantage. Much of it built in the early days after the Soviet collapse came from the desperation of survival rather than a culture of greed. Officials have made the fight against corruption a prime concern, to demonstrate the seriousness of the reforms, the ability to implement them fairly, and the intent to avoid the disruptions that occurred during Russia's and China's move to the market. "The creation of the Comptroller General in 2009 was a significant step in the first phase of Cuba's reform," said Arturo López-Levy, a former analyst at Cuba's interior ministry and now a Cuba expert at the University of Denver in the United States. "East Asia demonstrated the wisdom of creating an anti-corruption agency early in the economic transition from a command economy."[34] Many of the reforms were aimed at bringing legitimacy to the previously decreed illegal businesses, undercutting the black market and gaining financial benefits under the new tax legislation.

Few have been spared the battle against corruption. The country's multibillion-dollar nickel industry went through a cleaning with managers up to deputy ministers of basic industry arrested for "diverting resources." Minister Yadira Garcia Vera was eventually fired.[35] The hallmark product, cigars, felt the wrath when Manuel Garcia, Vice President of Habanos S.A, was arrested with other executives on charges of operating shell companies in order to divert high-quality *puros* and avoid paying duties.[36] Tecnotex, one of the island's top trading companies that purchases equipment for the military sector, saw director Fernando Noy and other top officials arrested in an operation that touched both British and Canadian companies doing business in Cuba.[37]

The eroding effect of corruption, the new Cuban reforms, and the impact America's siege has on both is a topic with intensely personal application for one of the country's most respected intellectuals, Esteban Morales. A prolific writer[38] and lecturer, Morales has garnering considerable international recognition along with some internal attention that wasn't quite as welcomed.

The quick-speaking Morales, who tumbles through a variety of ideas and concepts as rapidly as he downs his strong Cuban coffee, survived a disturbing experience where he came directly up against one of the most insidious aspects of siege mentality—the intolerance of criticism and punishment for a perceived indiscretion. Shortly before the government's anticorruption campaign, Morales wrote an insightful article titled "Corruption—The True Counter-Revolution?"[39]

"After 1985 the corruption started, and I said 10 years ago 50 percent of the economic leadership will go because of corruption. So I wrote this article in 2010, and it caused quite a stir," Morales laughed softly in the open air café across from his office in Havana. "Certain levels in government didn't like what I wrote, it is the mentality among some that you cannot expose the country to any criticism, regardless of intent or purpose. We are in a state of national security against the United States, so you can't give them any weapons to use against us."[40]

Those officials were sufficiently influential to take away his party membership, creating significant economic hardship. Morales, honorary director of the Center on United States Studies at the University of Havana, is highly respected and extremely popular among intellectual circles. The outcry that came from the community, and a direct appeal to Raúl Castro asking for an explanation, led to his reinstatement in June 2011, almost one year following his expulsion.

"I wrote Raúl, saying what was done to me was an injustice. He agreed, and he gave my membership back," the congenial Morales smiled. In the ultimate act of vindication, the younger Castro when announcing the government's plans to crack down on fraud announced to the country, "That corruption is the new counter-revolution, that's what he said," Morales noted with satisfaction.

Morales, considered from the old school style of economics influenced by the Soviet's three-decade exposure, is an expert in the ever-contentious relationship between the United States and Cuba. His insights into the economic reforms taking place on the island and America's response provides a consistent opportunity to lecture in Cuba and abroad.

"For me, the new reforms have helped because I can earn money for the lectures I give, at the University here and elsewhere. The reforms we are going through are important in so many aspects. There are the obvious changes in the real estate and cars, but the important impact will be felt by the support services. And by the blacks and mixed races, they will derive substantial benefits and that's a key element in making these reforms succeed."

Morales, an Afro-Cuban, judged the emergence of a service industry vital, "because it will affect the non-white sector and it will strengthen the perception of improvement for all. You understand that 85 percent of remittances coming into Cuba are from whites. I have no family in the US, so I have no remittances, but I can earn money giving lectures, good money. There are opportunities here now, the money will circulate and will benefit more people. Before there was no serious self employment, no service industry, now you can see increases there, it's a good thing. And these changes are permanent, there is no going back."

Concern over the development of unequal wealth distribution should not undermine the reform process, Morales stated. "The social benefits will continue, but yes there will be pressures regarding the emergence of different economic classes. But the equalization attitude is worse. Equality for politics and society is OK, but not in economics. Raúl Castro said the same—social equality doesn't mean economic equality, people who work harder can earn more. It has to be this way now, if you have more options it benefits more people. Civil society becomes more dynamic. My sense is these changes have to go faster." His reference to Raúl's statements came in a speech to the National Assembly in July 2008, when Castro made clear: "Equality is not the same as egalitarianism. Egalitarianism is in itself a form of exploitation: exploitation of the good workers by those who are less productive and lazy. Socialism means social justice and equality, but equality of rights, of opportunities, not of income." He identified the failure of "reinforcing social inequality that is not linked to the individual's or work collectives' labor contribution to society, excessive universal subsidies, combined with low wages, undermine the economic and ethical foundations of Cuba's socialist project."[41]

Morales describes himself as an optimist but acknowledged the reforms have already made things in Cuba more "complicated. In the middle of the world crisis, in our recovery from the hurricanes, we took a group of measures that put Cuba closer to a capitalist situation. Our socialism has become more complex now. Inside our society, there is the attitude of the people whether to go to capitalism or not. In general I believe people do not want capitalism, not what they see what is happening in the US and Europe. Modern capitalism is seen as not so stable, the problems within capitalism today is helping us determine what elements we want to use, to maintain our socialism with capital elements. The other aspect is that people want to develop our own variant, to improve things without giving up what socialism has constructed. And many look back to the good days, how we lived in the 1980s, and go back to that level of economic security."

That desire to return to the golden days of the revolution's economy has no attraction for the younger generation, he admitted, "they didn't live through it. They want more flexibility in their life, to be able to go outside the country and come back, to work outside and come back, to travel and come back. In our mentality the most important thing is to come back to Cuba, and these economic changes will impact those situations, especially for the next generation."

Providing that level of travel freedom will not materialize until "immigration is no longer looked at as a national security issue," Morales commented. Contradictory messages have emerged on the question of immigration, with Raúl expressing the mentality of siege when he seemingly dashed hopes for easing regulations. "Some have been pressuring us to take the step...as if we were talking about something insignificant, and not the destiny of the Revolution." Those calling for an end to the travel restrictions "are forgetting the exceptional circumstances under which Cuba lives, encircled by the hostile policy...of the U.S. government."[42] His remarks came as a disappointing walk back from previous statements, "Cuban immigration is no longer political it is economic," indicating there would be no reason to either prevent those from wanting to leave or from wanting to return.[43] Castro recognized that most of those leave for economic reasons and are "not enemies" adding removing travel restrictions would help "increase the nation's ties to the community of emigrants, whose makeup has changed radically since the early decades of the revolution."[44]

Justification for the travel restrictions go back to the early days of the revolution, designed to prevent those deemed criminal elements of the Batista regime from escaping. The problem, according to blogger Margarita Alarcón, was that no one "remembered to eliminate this restriction as time elapsed and it became part of the status quo."[45] The bureaucracy and expense Cubans have to go through to obtain permission to travel, including the expensive and onerous *tarjeta blanca* (white card) and letter of invitations, engender regular condemnation.

"The need for permission to leave should never have been invented in the first place," complained Victor Salgado, a 73-year-old retiree. "They should have eliminated this long ago. Why should I have to ask permission if I want to leave my country?"[46] Despite the obstacles, more than 200,000 Cubans made temporary trips abroad in 2008, a number proportionally comparable to other third world nations. Economics always play a part, as those wanting to travel must demonstrate family or friends outside cover their expenses, a usual requirement in order to satisfy the entry country regulations.[47]

The entire question of travel and emigration is under serious consideration, according to Ricardo Alarcón. The President of the National Assembly affirmed in April 2012 that the government will launch "a radical and thorough immigration reform in the coming months in order to eliminate this type of restriction."[48] While not specific in its scope, the changes could cover such laws that remove residence rights of those Cubans who leave the country for more than 11 months. Alarcón brought up the way immigration has been manipulated by US policy, most notably in the Cuban Adjustment Act, as a consideration to move deliberately.[49] "The immigration issue has always been used as a weapon of destabilization against Cuba since 1959 and as an element of distortion of the Cuban reality," he said, adding that the country is resolved to protect its human capital. "The training of doctors, technicians, teachers…is very expensive to the Cuban state and the United States does everything to deprive us of this human wealth."[50]

Even the expectation of relaxing the travel restrictions, seen as positive by most Cuban watchers, can be used to criticize the Castro government. University of Miami professor Jaime Suchlicki speculated that ending the constraints would be a way for the administration to shift "the burden of feeding and caring for a great number of Cubans" and that it would be used for anti-American propaganda if the United States refused tourist visas. His recommended response included tightening the travel by Cuban-Americans to the island, encouraging the US government to provide a limited number of tourist visas, and reducing the personnel at both interest sections in Washington and Havana.[51]

American policy has a part to play in the dialogue over travel and emigration, Morales asserted. "If US policy changed, our mentality towards things like immigration would change even more. We still look at the United States as a danger. But I also think the mentality in the US is shifting, it's taking a different form. Before we combated the US with a rifle, now we have to combat their aggression with the mind. There are many relations now between

US and Cuba; family connections, the information relations, there is such interest from Americans to come and see Cuba."

While the experience of Morales continues to command respect within government circles, a younger generation of economists are taking an active role in framing how the reformations are impacting the island and the potential interactions the new economy will have on the American giant. Based at the University of Havana, the Center for the Study of Cuban Economy is led by many who grew up under the Special Period, and so bring a different perspective from Morales.

Staffed by such respected researches as Omar Everleny Perez, Jorge Mario Sanchez, and Ricardo Torres, the center has come out strongly in support of the reforms, pressing for expansion and quickening the timetables. Everleny created attention by focusing on the long-standing failing of the economy. "The fundamental issue in Cuba is production. Prices are high and wages are low because we don't produce enough."[52] The reforms have to make sure that shortcoming is addressed, he added, otherwise the changes will do little long-term good. He's optimistic for the future, noting the reforms have brought a fresh perception to the importance of facing the challenges ahead. "Especially on the role of the non-state sector. Once implemented, these reforms will update the country's economic model."[53] He's also fully in favor of letting Americans come to Cuba, for their sake as well as to help solidify the reforms, reasoning by lifting the financial limitations imposed by siege it would eliminate the measures "that put the brakes on the normal development of an economy."[54]

The sense this is the best, and possibly last, opportunity for the socialist government to get the economy and itself on the right track is not lost on either generation. Esteban Morales accepts it is a critical point in the country's history, and the leadership "knows this is such an important time for the Revolution. Raúl has said: 'This is the moment of our last opportunity'—if we don't triumph now over these economic problems we will disappear." Throughout Havana and in the countryside signs proclaim it, officials speak of it, and citizens anxiously await it. Cuban consul general to Toronto, Jorge Soberon, spoke of the significance of the changes. "The updating of the Cuban economic model aims to strengthen our social system and to make socialism sustainable and irreversible, considering that it is the only way to guarantee independence and national sovereignty."[55]

Success will come down to a multitude of factors, among them the acceptance of the social cost and support for the government's determination to change the dynamics of the paternalistic worker-state relationship. As importantly, when the new money starts circulating from the sales of homes, cars, and ancillary business, the social disruptions will have to be addressed. There are, as well, ground-level factors to consider in order for the new market realities to operate efficiently. "The proper functioning of the private sector depends on non-discrimination and competition," Everleny described. "For this, a number of conditions will be important. Access to technical and material supply markets; access to sources of financing and insurance to cover risk; access to fair and competitive domestic consumer markets and export markets; regulations that do not impose undue burdens in their compliance or administration; and a tax burden consistent with the desired activity and size of the project. If these conditions are established, non-state employment will meet its expected contribution to the economy, above all in terms of job creation and the production of goods and services. I estimate Cuba could grow at a rate of 5 percent after the reforms."[56]

Others are not so optimistic, including José Antonio Ocampo, former undersecretary general of the United Nations for economic and social affairs and minister of finance of Colombia. In response to Everleny, the Columbia University professor worried that a tremendous social cost may be born, that the reforms are too little too late, unemployment won't be overcome, and "the reduction in real wages (and real pensions) will have an adverse effect on income distribution on top of the inequality that freer markets can generate. The dual price system is already generating inequalities associated with differing access to dollars from remittances and the tourism sector."[57]

Either way, without substantial government spending cuts there will be no chance of workers earning more, explained labor chief Salvador Valdés Mesa: "Until the country, through the measures it adopts, is able to reduce inflated payrolls, eliminate unnecessary free benefits and subsidies, which act against increasing the productivity of work, it will not be in a position to make salary increases from the current pay scale."[58] The target is to augment wages a minimum 10 percent over the next four years.

Inside all the economic reforms, there lies a political component. Officials recognize the two cannot be divided and have taken steps to ensure the latter is in place in order for the former to succeed. The once venerable Ministry of Sugar has been turned into a holding company; agriculture has been decentralized and the Basic Industry Ministry has reemerged as the new Energy and Mining Ministry.[59] Restructuring the political makeup of the economy is designed to increase efficiency, profitability, reduce bureaucracy, and to expose and eliminate the old corrupt practices. As importantly is the effort to shift the stratification of bureaucratic thinking, to alter the mentality of those who for decades have worked under prejudices entrenched in a system that made it more comfortable to act on perceived social conformities rather than risk personal attention to follow commonsense solutions. Raúl addressed the predicament in early 2011 when relating a "painful incident" of a woman who lost her job and took a 40 percent reduction in her income because she had not disclosed to her employer and her local Communist Party unit that she "professed religious beliefs and attended religious services some Sundays." After an appeal to the government her job was reinstated, the local officials reprimanded, and Raúl called her a "victim" of a "flagrant violation" of rights. He used the incident to promise the new socialism Cuba was trying to build had to incorporate not only a rethinking economically, but an end to the exclusionist tendencies of the past: "More than once I have said that our worst enemy is not imperialism, much less its salaried employees on our soil, but rather our own errors, and these, if they are analyzed deeply and honestly, will turn into lessons on how not to repeat them."[60] He followed with a warning against any opposition to the changes approved of at the Party Congress: "We will be patient and persevering in the face of all resistance to change, conscious or not. I warn that all bureaucratic resistance to the accords of the Congress, massively supported by the people, will be futile."[61]

The early shift toward implementing market practices within state enterprises has been painful and revealing, with long-entrenched managers discovering they are now being held responsible for wasteful economic practices. A report in the daily *Granma* blamed executives for the loss of millions of dollars based on the practice of relying on public budgets to resolve improper accounting practices. Manufacturing results were often measured more on output than on quality and cost considerations, and the reforms are increasingly requiring profitability, not illusionary production quotas, as the applied standard for state entities.[62]

More directly, the political fallout has seen Raúl propose term limits on leaders, including the president, of five–ten years, with the intent of rejuvenating a new generation of leaders. In conjunction the government is operating programs to increase the responsibilities of local politicians and the participation of its citizens. Acceptance that the party must step aside as the final decision-maker in the running of business, to let private workers and office managers decide what is best, is a dramatic shift in political thinking.[63]

The term limits are also an indication the Raúl administration comprehends the younger generation has to be given the reigns of not only the economic, but also the political power. It is not an easy matter, as the siege has helped create the illusion that the Old Guard knows how best to resist US aggression and to keep the revolution safe, drawing on decades of experience. The result is "the very top level of government and party leadership remains almost entirely in the hands of the revolutionary generation, of the oldest generation," said Philip Peters, a Cuba analyst with the Virginia-based Lexington Institute. "So the task remains to bring younger leaders into the top leadership."[64]

Cuba's managing of the changing of the guard has been done in typically convoluted fashion. On the one hand the selected second man to Raúl is first Vice President José Ramón Machado, also an octogenarian. On the other one of those charged with ensuring the economic reforms succeed is 52-year-old Marino Murillo Jorge, a highly ranked member of the Council of Ministers. He represents one of a number of younger-generation leaders expected to guide the new look of Cuban socialism in the coming years, including 46-year-old Havana Communist Party boss Mercedes López Acea and Lázaro Esposito, the 50-something regional party chief in Santiago de Cuba.[65] Heading the important Ministry of Agriculture is 46-year-old Gustavo Rodríguez. Whether a Cuban-style Gorbachev emerges from the faction may be determined in the next few years.

Even this matter can be connected to the siege, according to Ricardo Alarcón. "From the beginning, an essential part of the policy promoted by the United States was the physical liquidation of the Cuban leadership, but [the Americans] failed. Because they failed, there's a lot of us left. So what are we going to do? Self-destruct? In other words, do what the CIA couldn't do?" He added, however, there is recognition of "serious deficiencies in this subject and in the role of women, blacks and mestizos in leadership positions," and efforts to correct that were being made.[66]

There is little doubt it is time for the first generation of revolutionaries to let go, Cuban intellectual Carlos Fuenes said: "It is necessary to pass to the new generation in order to make socialism, because this socialism has stagnated. This socialism has already given everything it has, what it could give, its moments of glory, imperishable things that still survive in the memory and the daily life of the Cuban people. But we must have reforms in many aspects of the Revolution, but our leaders are not longer capable. Their revolutionary ideas are too old, have become reactionary and that doesn't allow for our socialism to advance. The new generation that comes now should be able to bring in a new form of socialism, a new revolution."[67]

The righteous stubbornness of the first-generation revolutionaries, who fought and won the social gains and survived America's worse, have entrenched their knowledge into dictating what is right to protect the country. Siege is an impediment to the initiative for change, when a society under threat can find it easier to follow those you know than the ones you don't, for fear the new will misstep and be taken advantage of by besiegers whose intent is to destroy, not reform.

Behind it all, eyes anxiously peer north. Island officials have forcefully indicated the economic reforms are not a consequence of American pressure, and Cuban watcher Arnold August concurred. "The Cubans are taking measures to improve the political and economic system, to improve the participation of the people which is the foundation of the Revolution. There is corruption, bureaucratic waste, and the Cubans admit that. The key to solve those problems is the people, they have to put these bureaucrats in their place and get rid of corruption. The debate is on the extent of how the Party will contribute. But it has nothing to do with what the US has done, or hasn't done. These are internal reforms developed to solve Cuban problems, nothing more."[68]

However, siege policy in response does not go unnoticed. It is incongruous, in line with most things in this complicated relationship. President Obama's alterations to ending restrictions for Cuban-Americans to visit their homeland and increasing licensed travel for Americans to visit Cuba on cultural, education, institutional trips for people-to-people contacts has been described as some of the most significant shifts since Carter's time.[69] Those changes, with its dramatically positive effects to the island economy, have come in large part under the radar. The President's official reaction has been traditional rhetoric, cautious to the point of dismissive. It has followed in line with the tone-deafness that came out of the White House following the release of the dissidents in 2010, in continuation of identifying unrelated incidents such as the jailing of Alan Gross with the condition toward normalization. President Obama's few comments have not been to encourage the reforms, but rather to diminish their importance and to continue to expect Cuban changes to meet US expectations.[70]

The President's public responses have been met with little enthusiasm among those who were expecting more. No sharper expression of that sentiment came from former head of US interest section in Havana Wayne Smith, who while describing his sense of frustration said: "Cuba seems to have the same effect on U.S. administrations as a full moon has on werewolves."[71]

Smith's inspired portrayal was in reaction to the consistent inability of Washington to recognize, if not appreciate, the reforms taking place in Cuba. In two separate comments to Hispanic journalists in September 2011, the President crystallized the position. "The Cuban government has said that it wants to transition, to loosen up the economy, so that businesses can operate more freely. We have not seen evidence that they have been sufficiently aggressive in changing their policies economically."[72] He added: "But there is a basic, I think, recognition of people's human rights that includes their right to work, to change jobs, to get an education, to start a business. So some elements of freedom are included in how an economic system works. And right now, we haven't seen any of that."[73] The President doubled down on classic siege terminology at the April 2012 Summit of the Americas, which Cuba was excluded from, over the protests of many other member nations. At a press conference he complained the regime had not taken steps toward democracy and "has not yet observed basic human rights," adding another brick in the propaganda wall of ignoring Cuba's perspective on the issue.[74]

The attitude reflects the indisposed stance Obama has taken toward engagement, despite Havana's willingness to discuss a wide range of topics including drug trafficking, immigration, and the country's economic movements. Since 2009 Foreign Minister Bruno Rodriguez has been waiting for a response to his proposed agenda. Rodriguez acknowledged, "I am realistic and understand that a bilateral dialogue could hardly begin with difficult issues of this nature," in reference to the embargo, but issues such as the environment, terrorism, and migration could be starting points.[75]

As far as Esteban Morales is concerned, the lack of encouragement is just more proof of the purpose of siege. "So many changes here, and so little response, so we know it is for a reason. We have always resisted siege because we tell the US you must respect us. Obama knows the blockade can do damage, but we can resist better now, we are in better condition. The United States always puts conditions on us, but Cuba never accepts. The only condition is there is no condition." Esteban acknowledged the positive aspects of allowing unrestricted travel for Cuban-Americans and eliminating constraints on sending remittances, but there is still the South Florida political reality the President has to confront. "Obama has to put his best face in Miami and that is the government part. It is the stick and the stick, no carrot. He has to say things to appease that hard element that wants no engagement; that wants to keep punishing Cuba."[76]

The President's hard position on the public stage is well-supported by media who desire no acceptance of Cuban developments to be utilized as a move toward rational relations. Although one of the goals of encirclement is to force the besieged to agree to conditions or be destroyed, anti-Castro stalwarts such as *Miami Herald* columnist Andres Oppenheimer can't accept yes as an answer, continuing to frame the issue as America benevolently reaching out to Cuba and the regime doing little in return.[77] Concurrently, any good Obama has accomplished comes under attack, with Washington-based agency Capitol Hill Cubans complaining of the ending of travel restrictions for Cuban-Americans: "However, the 100,000 Cubans in Miami traveling to the island multiple times a year do not have the right to finance the repression of the Castro regime against 11,500,000 Cubans, including our own families and friends. Thus, no matter how libertarian one might be (or purport to be), no one has the right to finance the repression of innocent people."[78]

Fortunately there has been pushback, from media, politicians, and influential study groups, that have looked at the reforms and found them of substance. With it comes the questioning of America's position. The Brookings Institute in Washington published an extensive and influential report in 2011, calling for the international development community, especially financial institutions such as the IMF and World Bank to reach out to the island and bring it "in from the cold." The report added, "In approaching Cuban economic reform, the United States should join with the international development community in nudging forward that irresistible flow of history," suggesting such economic reforms can develop political pluralism. The openings in Cuba provide "a golden opportunity" for engagement, noting "the unyielding Cuban-American lobby" attempts to block any outreach toward Cuba.[79] In a more direct appraisal as to what is happening in Cuba, Sarah Stephens of the Center for Democracy in the Americas reported, "Far from tinkering around the edges, these reforms are the most significant changes to the economic system to take place in Cuba probably since the Revolution." She warned that while much of the rest of the world expresses encouragement, the United States "stands on the sidelines, disengaged and increasingly irrelevant."[80]

Remarkably, a chink in the White House's armor of denial occurred when Secretary of State Hillary Clinton became the first high official to actually articulate what everyone else knew but left unsaid. In an exchange at a Foreign Affairs Committee hearing between Cuban-American Congressman David Rivera and Clinton, she attempted to connect Cuba's reforms with her President's agenda. "Well in the last three years there have been considerable changes in Cuba's economic policy which we see as a very positive development, we think having the Cuban people given more economic rights, to be able to open businesses, to have more opportunity to pursue their own economic futures, goes hand in hand with the promotion of democracy. I wouldn't claim that our movements were a direct cause but they were coincident with. Very often in oppressive regimes like Cuba, economic free-dom precedes political freedom."[81]

Even if Obama were to publicly support his secretary of state's admission and try to change the climate to one of supporting the reality on the ground in Cuba, the contentious history between the two countries remains an obstacle. Island officials often view with suspicion offers of cooperation from Washington, wondering if there is a hidden agenda to unravel Cuban socialism and implant Western-style free-market capitalism, or to circumvent security programs and the authority of the state. The matter remains, however, that US policy rarely avails itself of such opportunities to engage constructively.[82]

Josefina Vidal is head of the North American department at MINREX, the Ministry of Foreign Relations, and one of the most respected and influential experts in Cuba-US relations. While admitting the positive impact to the country's economy as a result of Obama's policy to ease travel restrictions for Cuban-Americans, she is wary of its potential ulterior motivations—a classic consequence of siege mentality. "It has been very good letting Cuban-Americans come to Cuba, and expanding licensed travel. It has been good for our economy, no question. But he didn't do that as a gesture to the Cuban people, he did it as a political promise to Cuban-Americans, he wanted their votes. We didn't see that as a gesture to the Cuban people, it was also to influence Cuban people with material goods, stories of how good things are on the outside, to influence Cuban people to look at the government here in a negative fashion."[83]

Her pessimism toward the Obama White House is not well hidden. "In many ways the Bush Doctrine is still being followed by Obama. In some ways it is worse. Financial transactions are more restrictive. The American government is going after anyone doing business here. Cuba has always been prevented from using US dollars, we've had no access to credit, and have always had to pay cash in advance for food payments, through a third country. We've had problems before when we used US dollars, and we understand they have the last word on their currency. OK, that's fine, it is their currency and they claim sovereignty over it, even if it is the international currency. But in the last few years transactions in any other currency is being blocked or frozen, no matter if it's the Yen, or Euro, or whatever. Banks are terrified to have anything to do with Cuban transactions. Businesses are afraid to come here."[84]

"There are more complications now," she continued. "When Cuba went to purchase medicines, there were further complicated procedures even to sell us aspirin. In the commerce department they have a list of products, considered dual use, that can't be sold to Cuba, things the US government says may be used for military purposes, or other applications. Obama didn't invent the policy, but he hasn't eliminated it and is prosecuting certain aspects as vigorously or more. Obama has added elements to the blockade; there are new rules for the Stock Exchange Commission, every company traded or exchanged now has to submit documents to SEC regarding any transactions or connections with Cuba. Things have become worse for these reasons."

The engaging Vidal noted the President had the opportunity "to introduce real change to Cuban policy, he had the support of the Cuban-American
community, intellectuals, businessmen, civil organizations, pro travel groups,
all in favor to institute real change. He said he wanted a new beginning
with Cuba, that if Cuba frees political prisoners, and makes changes in the
economy, allow more freedoms and we'll be ready to make changes to Cuban
policy. It has been four years later and there are no changes, other than
the re-establishment of travel for Cuban-Americans and remittances. The
changes we have made, we needed time to institute these changes and go
slowly, not to make mistakes and make sure the social infrastructure was
prepared. We couldn't postpone the changes anymore, but we also had to
consider the impact and the contribution of the blockade is still with us. We
did these changes because we decided it was best for us, not because the US
demanded them or influenced us to do them."

She addressed the ability of the United States to create straw man sce-
narios that Cuba must meet before the relationship can improve, regardless
of who is in the White House. The latest is the case of jailed contractor
Alan Gross. Vidal spoke of it during an interview with CNN's Wolf Blitzer,
after the host told her that high-ranking government officials indicated if
the Cubans would release Alan Gross then it would "set the stage for an
improved Cuba-US relationship" and help initial dialogue. She responded
by citing the various historical conditions demanded by the United States,
met by the Cubans, with no alteration in siege strategy. Vidal said Cuba has
reached out to the United States to discuss the Alan Gross situation, but has
received no response.[85]

Obama's stance can be seen as a continuation dating back 50 years, she
said. "It is both outrageous and surprising to realize that the blockade and
subversion policy applied by the United States against Cuba continues to be
guided by the logics contained in the memorandum drafted in 1960" that
outlined the intent to bring economic hardship, hunger, and the overthrow
of the government.[86]

Despite the frustration with Obama's seeming intransigence, the benefits
the Cuban government is deriving from his policies cannot be ignored, an
official at the Canadian embassy in Havana stressed. "Obama's rhetoric is
the same, but his actions have meant a great deal else. Allowing Cuban-
Americans to travel, freeing restrictions on remittances has sent billions to
Cuba each year. And that has saved the revolution," the official claimed.
"Obama is saying one thing but look at what he's doing. It has put so much
money into Cuba."[87] To make that money flow even faster, Western Union
announced a new electronic system to permit easier transactions into Cuba
from locations in the United States, in yet another incongruity of siege that
permits such actions under the same overarching policy that does its best
to thwart other types of financial transaction conducted at the government
level.[88]

If and when the United States finally decides the siege is of no further service, the impact on Cuba society may be scrutinized through the experiences

of another country. One that is often used as guide for the island's potential future.

With considerable caution the Vietnam model might have some application to Cuba, according to John McAuliff, executive director of Fund for Reconciliation and Development. McAuliff, who has long connections with both nations that go back to the 1970s, noted "Cuba is a different situation than Vietnam. There may be some things to learn from what has happened in Vietnam, but you have to look at the differences as well."[89]

McAuliff commented that ending the embargo against Vietnam provided the solidification for economic and political changes in a remarkably short period of time. "When the US embargo was lifted, there was a psychological impact. I'd say yes, the lifting of the embargo helped accelerate the economic reform process. The Vietnamese had already started moving to investment policies and expanded personal opportunities. Private enterprises opened, citizens were able to hire other people, there were some dramatic changes in a short period. Similar results might occur with Cuba."

America's relationship with Vietnam is a study in how two former bitter enemies can evolve into mutual respect within a few years. The United States had placed an embargo against North Vietnam in 1964 (under the infamous Trading with the Enemy Act) expanding the law to the whole country at war's end in 1975.[90] It lasted less than 20 years, President Bill Clinton terminating the economic punishment in 1994.[91] One year later relations were normalized, 1997 saw the establishment of a full American embassy in Hanoi and in 2001 most favored nation status was conferred by George Bush Jr.[92] Since then the Agency for International Development (USAID) has spent billions of dollars assisting a transition to a market economy, operating programs in the open and with the consent of the government. The two nations have cooperated on a wide range of issues, including hurricane damage, pandemics, illegal trade, and deforestation, and has promoted high-technology enterprise in Hanoi and Ho Chi Minh City. America has put no exclusions on working with members of the Communist Party or on those who fought against the United States. The position of the United States is to promote change through détente. Vietnam's culture, its history, and nationalism is recognized and respected.

Impetus for the relationship changer was the Sixth Communist Party Congress in late 1986 when the national leadership decided on major reforms to the state-controlled socioeconomic model. The changes became known as *Doi Mo*, normally translated as renovation. For decades Vietnam had operated under a Soviet-Marxist model, dependent upon huge amounts of foreign aid. When the conflict with the United States ended, the aid dried up, and the Vietnamese were faced with an impending economic collapse unless serious modifications were undertaken. *Doi Mo* was the result, its policy consisting of shifting from a centralized command economy to one embracing multisectors under a socialist-orientated market mechanism, in conjunction with the encouragement of international investment and a higher level of democratization for the individual. By the early 1990s things had turned around and Vietnam became one of the fastest growing economies in the world, rising to number three in rice export alone.[93] Its per capita income increased four times from 1985 to 2010 and the country became a full member of the World Trade Organization in 2007.[94]

America's support for the reforms, the release of the embargo, and the quick political normalization process had a definite, positive impact on the country's economic recovery, McAuliff recognized. "The United States is now Vietnam's largest export market—coffee and manufactured goods such as shoes and clothing. There is substantial American investment, many US companies operate in Vietnam." Some of the better know brand names flourishing in the country include Nike, KFC, Pizza Hut, and Dominos Pizza. "On the other side, millions of Vietnamese work in America and send remittances back, billions worth," McAuliff pointed out.

Similarities to the Cuban reality can be found, he added, starting with an unusual political coincidence. "It was the Sixth Party Congress in Vietnam that started the changes there, and the Sixth Party in Cuba in 2011 also defined the new economic direction. There is no reason why the same things couldn't happen in Cuba if the embargo was lifted. The country is much closer, there are much more historical and commercial connections." But the differences should not be ignored, McAuliff warned. Vietnam had a smaller state sector economy than Cuba has, so it was easier for the Vietnamese to switch over to market elements. Vietnam was implementing reforms prior, but the most rapid acceleration to their economy came when the embargo was lifted. Cuba is also attempting reformation while under America's more comprehensive siege, which adds pressure to achieve results in a short period of time under difficult circumstances. A major distinction is immigration. The wave of Vietnamese who settled after the war were dispersed throughout the 50 states, a consideration distinct from the high concentration of Cuban exiles in Miami. "That situation has led to the political and economic influence the hard-right Cuban-Americans have. You didn't see the same with Vietnamese immigration, so there was not as much influence to maintain that embargo."

The conditions on lifting the embargo on each country reveal the other key dissimilarity. American imposed but two demands on Vietnam—for its military to leave Cambodia and cooperation on MIA/POW information.

"The Vietnamese were getting out of Cambodia anyway, and they readily agreed to provide information on missing American soldiers," McAuliff said. "So it wasn't hard for them to accept those requirements." He stressed, "There were no internal modalities imposed on Vietnam as a condition to lift the embargo. And that's a big difference in how the US has treated Cuba. Historically America has known what's best for Cuba, so they require these changes to be made to the country's internal political and economic structure. That attitude hasn't changed."

On the political distinction, the Vietnam embargo was ended by presidential authority, while "Congress has more control over the Cuban embargo," cited McAuliff. Still, he is cautiously optimistic that Cuba might be able to reproduce aspects of the Vietnamese economic expansion if the United States would only let go. "Look at the agricultural lease system created, it's similar to what's happening in Cuba now. The re-distribution back to the workers. And in only a few years the Vietnamese were exporting rice to the world. I wonder if sugar could be Cuban equivalent regarding what is happening to the decentralization of the agricultural ministry. In Vietnam there has been a return of old capital investment, from Chinese-Vietnamese. And there is a parallel to Cuba regarding the Cuban-Americans and the investment potential they have. I'm sure the Cubans can learn from the Vietnamese situation, see their changes. I know they are looking at what is happening in Vietnam, but you always have to distinguish between the two. There is potential to see Cuba move towards the Vietnam model, but it won't be exact."[95]

Cuba and Vietnam have developed close political relations and the trade between the two is growing. In 2012 a multimillion dollar agreement was reached for Vietnam to purchase and distribute Cuban pharmaceuticals,[96] and more than 40,000 hectares of Cuban land has been set aside to boost rice production with Vietnam expertise.[97] Nguyen Phu Trong, head of Vietnam's communist party, visited Havana in April 2012 and commented on his host's economic changes. Acknowledging the reform process in his country was not easy, Phu Trong suggested the transition will be slow, but will bring improvements as long as there is acceptance of what he called "market economy with socialist orientation." Attitude adjustments and concern from those afraid of abandoning the old model were major obstacles to overcome in Vietnam, and he expected the same hesitancy from the island population. It seems that Cubans are "in the same phase. The change in mentality must be achieved at all levels, from the top to the base."[98] Three months after Phu Trong's trip to Cuba, Raúl Castro returned the favor with a visit to Vietnam where he was able to see first-hand capitalism and socialism working together.[99]

Cuba's successful reinvention of its economy will continue to be partially dependent on the signals coming out of Washington. Former President Jimmy Carter realized what the White House says and does has consequence to reality on the island, "I think one serious mistake that my country continues to make is the trade embargo." The siege has been "damaging to the well-being of every citizen in Cuba," and "impeded rather than assisted" reforms. "We should immediately lift the embargo," Carter said.[100]

At the least many Cubans would be content with hearing a similar message as that given by Hillary Clinton during a news conference in Hanoi in 2010, when speaking of the path to reconciliation between the former enemies: "Thirty-five years ago we ended a war that inflicted terrible suffering on both our nations, and still remains a living memory for many of our people. Despite that pain, we dedicated ourselves to the hard work of building peace. We have consistently moved in the direction of engagement and cooperation. Even on those issues where we disagree, we still reach for dialogue...These ties enrich us, and are proof of a peace that exists not only on paper, but is rooted in the minds and hearts of the American and Vietnamese people. And it is a credit to both our nations that this progress has been possible."[101]

Progress through dialogue and engagement is the elusive component to resolve siege. The present shifts in both Havana and Miami, however, may soon reveal the path to ending encirclement.

6

THE FUTURE OF SIEGE

> A revolution is not a bed of roses. A revolution is a struggle between the future and the past.
>
> —Fidel Castro[1]

The year 1958 was a good one for the United States. The nation towered atop the world; its military power predominate, its ideology prevailing; its commerce the envy of all others. The Soviet rival was behaving, China contained, and all was quiet in the backyard. Calm and compliant was Latin America, the mere sniff of insubordination smacked down—as befell Jacobo Arbenz in Guatemala four years earlier. Docile Cuba was the shining example in America's undeclared, compassionate form of imperialism. There were rumblings of local discontent with dictator Batista, but the strongman retained America's favor. So when the island exploded, when disobedience triumphed in the form of a band of scruffy *barbudos* (bearded ones)—that was too much of an insult to bear. Cuba's betrayal was particularly devastating, as for the 60 years prior it was well understood the island had been treated far differently from the others in the aftermath of the Spanish-American War. Puerto Rico had submitted to colonial status, the Philippines eventually, needing thousands of dead in a violent lesson in order to prove American benevolence. But Cuba, the Pearl of the Antilles, was bestowed with the blessings of liberty, independence, and economic advantages. She was given freedom to pursue her own path, as long as that path did not stray from American direction and purpose. The concept of Cuba rejecting the route and holding a revolution to toss out America's great gifts, this was inconceivable. The response became personal, hostile, unthinking, and deadly.

There was no chance the Cuban Revolution would be countenanced by the power to the north, despite its own history. Long before had the Americans lost their revolutionary fervor, overtaken by entrenched reactionary forces determining foreign policy objectives. Even if they were inclined toward their own antecedents, the direction of the island rebellion prevented any possibility other than conflict. For 50 years confrontation has ensued. Lives have been lost, treasure wasted, resources spent. It has come at a cost to America's standing in the eyes of the world. This Caribbean nation is the standard bearer for American pretense, damaging claims of moral authority and showing the United States to be penurious, vindictive, and revenge seeking. It diminishes whatever good the United States has stood for in the past, and corrodes its desires to persist in the future.

"The embargo is the perfect example used by anti-Americans everywhere to expose the hypocrisy of a superpower that punishes a small island while cozying to dictators elsewhere," journalist Moisés Naim declared.[2] The United States is not unaware of this position. Roger Fontaine, neoconservative from Reagan's Committee of Santa Fe, acknowledged: "The Cuban people have suffered enough. I don't think it is morally possible to make matters worse in the hope somehow, some day it will all get better. It's simply not acceptable to follow a strategy designed to make the lives of most Cubans so desperate that they will rise up in bloody revolt."[3] Or as the former President Jimmy Carter put it: "The embargo against Cuba is the stupidest law ever passed in the U.S."[4]

Yet intelligence has never been a determinant factor in application of siege. Even with familiarity of how others perceive it and recognition of its own dissemblance, America can't help itself. Vice President Joe Biden when asked if the United States was going to drop the embargo responded with an emphatic "no," then added, "We think that the Cuban people should determine their own fate and they should be able to live in freedom and have some prospect of economic prosperity."[5] The influence the embargo might have on the fate of the Cuban people, much less their economic prosperity, has been lost on Biden and most every other American politician since the day it was imposed. Equally blinding is the conviction that the rest of the world has no business in the debate. National Security Advisor Brent Scowcroft made it clear why the United States shrugs off such international meddlers as the United Nations who annually vote against the embargo. "My answer on Cuba is Cuba is not a foreign policy question. Cuba is a domestic issue. In foreign policy, the embargo makes no sense. It doesn't do anything. It's quite clear we cannot starve Cuba to death. We learned that when the Soviets stopped subsidizing Cuba and they didn't collapse. It's a domestic issue."[6] His insight provides a level of sagacity but does not explain why America continues this long unsuccessful siege warfare, ignoring the wisdom of such luminaries as Albert Einstein: "Insanity is doing the same thing over and over and expecting a different result."[7]

The Cuban Revolution has always worked against American sensibilities at a visceral level, and siege is the physical expression of the rage it has fashioned. Americans have yet to forget, much less forgive. During the decades close to a dozen presidents have drawn on that constant through application of the Cuba Doctrine. Developed by Eisenhower, the position calls for the destruction of Castro's social construct. Even President Carter, who came closest to overturning the doctrine, returned to its precepts when Cuba strayed beyond the allowed boundaries. The obsession with the small island has afflicted every chief of state with what Nixon described as a "neuralgic problem."[8] Unless and until one can be cured of this misery, ending siege will stay a needlessly complicated proposition.

Long ago siege ignored rationality for emotionalism. Throughout the years dozens of motives have been called upon to explain why the Cuban people had to suffer for their unfathomable enthusiasm for Castro. But the primeval impetus was, and remains, emotion. Seeing this insubordinate rabble denounce what America brought to Cuba elicited feelings of deep anger and belligerency. To watch them proclaim everything the United States represented to be no use to the new order, in fact in many ways the antithesis of what the revolution was hoping to achieve, was responded to by incomprehension, resentment, and promises of retribution. For a proud undefeated nation, one that just happened to be the most powerful on earth, the leader of the most admired social/economic system in history (so they proclaimed), and a close neighbor who brought so much benefit to these upstarts, this ingratitude was intolerable. Fifty years and more the indignation has remained the driving force for punishment. The closeness of the two nations made the break harder for America to accept, under the impression all was right in the land of rum and cigars. Siege was the answer to the insult based on the US perception of itself as the pinnacle to emulate, not the bottom to reject. Cuba's legitimate grievances of desiring actual independence and respect were concepts beyond America's ability to fathom. Lacking understanding, nothing was left except the bitterness of a relationship gone sour. US policy has resembled "a 50-year tantrum."[9]

So what the Cuban people were building had to be destroyed because it represented, according to Barry Goldwater, "a disgrace and an affront which diminishes the respect with which we are held by the rest of the world in direct ratio to the length of time we permit it to go unchallenged."[10]

It became an easy matter to justify policies designed to starve, propagandize, terrorize, and brutalize the population for the ungratefulness it dared to show the nation that gave so much and asked so little in return—at least in the eyes of the offended. Rationalities were created to deflect the real cause and meaning of the revolution, creating historiographies where good and evil were simplified in order to make the horrors to be inflicted upon the Cuba people palatable for the American audience.

While the international standing of the United States has suffered from its irrationality, the victims of siege have endured far serious losses. Under the protection of its Soviet patron, the government was able to moderate the economic damages, at the expense of a strict social condition that saw little tolerance for diversity under the banner of security from siege warfare. There was scant patience for debate or renewal while beneath the Soviet shield and when siege could be readily called upon to validate stratification. The dynamics changed following the end of the Eastern Block two decades ago when the island forced itself open to international tourism and foreign investment as a means to stop the economic bleeding. With it came an examination of social and economic systems incapable of coping with the new energies brought on by the crisis. At the height of the island's financial difficulties, American hostility increased and Cuba found itself having to protect itself anew from incapacitating siege strategies while trying to cope

from the affects of outside influence. While the damages from the Special
Period linger, society is recovering through emergence of divergent space
within the socialist system under new economic and political reforms. But
there is no questioning Cuba has long been injured by encirclement, no
more so since the country's economic collapse in the early 1990s. The great
depression left the nation economically crippled, seriously debilitating incentive for individual workers outside commercial aspects that touch foreigners. Unemployment was officially declared at zero while unofficially hitting
double digits. Lethargy was overcoming society where ideological enthusiasm was being thwarted by an inability to accomplish goals, particularly in
the younger generation. Weariness expressed itself in waste and corruption
at the workplace, while thousands rejected the fight for a future in favor
of flight from the country. The revolution has grappled to overcome this
Special Period, and the government under Raúl has made clear there is no
turning back, regardless of what the Americans do. So far the US response
has been to impede recovery efforts, from tightening of besiegement with
punitive legislation in the mid-1990s to efforts since 9/11 including the
cracking down of the island's ability to conduct international commerce. The
tightening of pressure ignored the political advice of such conservatives as
George Shultz, secretary of state under Ronald Reagan, who said in 2009,
"With the Cold War behind us, we should simply remove the embargo on
Cuba."[11]

Siege, often overlooked or diminished, is demonstrably not the sole source
for Cuba's deficiencies. As culpable have been the confines of the command
economy and political inflexibility—conditions well considered to be reflec-
tive of consequence to siege—that the revolution imposed. The siege has
permitted Cuba to circle the wagons and define permissible tolerance to
opposition; to develop political and economic rigidity and exculpate itself
from those deficiencies. It allows the effective projection of a small nation
bullied by a vengeful giant, a dynamic imagery recognized by the oppressor.
"Castro has found the embargo to be convenient to him," since he "uses it
very effectively all the time, making us the Goliath and Cuba the David," so
said former head of the US interest section Vicki Huddleston.[12]

Substantiation of Cuba's position is not difficult to ascertain. Leadership
has long perceived itself to be constantly on the defensive, sensitive to how
every action accomplished or contemplated will be treated by a foreign power
determined to exploit weakness. It is a large piece of the puzzle that has made
up the mosaic of the revolution, and should no longer be ignored or denied.
The siege, however, has always been ingenious in the ability to disguise, to
render its deepest affects near invisible. Many Cubans accept its presence but
not its impairments—a vital component to its effectiveness. Bringing the
siege into full light moves it one step closer to complete comprehension of
the harm it does, to recognize it is far more than the "irritant" American
proponents portray it to be.

The policy of constructing a barb wire around Cuba was born out of ven-
geance and anger. The plan was to have the ungrateful locals fear the power

of the greatest nation on earth, to hurt them, starve them, make them wish they never heard of Fidel Castro. The revolution reacted as America hoped it would—with rules, regulations, and restrictions seemingly rooted in malice, mistrust, and defiance—all responses that made it easier for the retribution to continue and increase. Siege created response, which permitted the United States to assemble the dialogue of revolutionary iniquity and the need to dismantle what they have consistently described negatively as "regime." For 50 years US policy has remained unchanged. Siege is the constant, regardless of how much the world, and Cuba, has altered since 1959.

The siege against America's former good friend has done its work effectively, inducing such sentiments—"Anything is better than this, let the Americans come in and take over"; "After 50 years when will the Communists leave?"; "Everyone wants to get out of Cuba, not one person wants to stay"— comments heard in Havana as a segment blames all on the fault of their government. Such is the genius that is this besiegement, its ability to remain well hidden but retain a determining factor on the opinions of nationals and foreigners. It works effectively to mute claims of its harm; in reflection the government having gone to the well of siege so often as an explanation to lessen its own inefficiencies that the real truth of its harm can be easily ignored.

Revealingly, many of the constraints Cubans live under have been experienced in various doses by an American society that has also perceived itself under siege after the events of 9/11. A demand for social conformity in the face of the enemy, mainstream media in compliance to state goals, intolerance to certain segments of the population, and civil rights restrictions under the banner of keeping the population secure. All have been in evidence since 9/11. A major criticism levied against the Castro government is its intrusive nature; Americans are realizing the same is happening to them as the government takes extraordinary measures to spy on its citizens in the name of national security. The NSA has built in immense secrecy the country's biggest intelligence center in Utah, designed to intercept and analyze communications from networks around the world. Emails, cell phone calls, Google searches, and personal data trails of each citizen will be exposed to government scrutiny in a "total information awareness" program the Cuban security apparatus could only dream of.[13]

* * *

Finding a conduit to resolution of siege has been historically elusive, although current circumstances may provide new opportunities. Changes taking place on both sides of the Florida Straits, combined with electoral expectations, demographic uncertainties, and a bit of timing could unite to finally allow the drawbridges to be lowered.

Cuban reforms in the economic section are already transforming the country's political paradigm. If the nation's petroleum reserves develop, Cuba could become a member of the oil exporter club and solve its financial problems in turn. The prospects are a crucial factor in the island's determination to bring itself into the twenty-first century under a modern, sustainable socialist model.

Things are also shifting in South Florida not in response but in progression. While the ultraconservative Cuban-American lobby and its congressional supporters remain the power brokers in maintenance of siege, the demographic construction of current Cuban immigration is altering the equation at street level. New arrivals from the island are signaling their desire for a move away from siege—visiting their homeland by the thousands, bringing remittances and material aid. They want engagement, not isolation. Once they become politically active, predictions are they will start voting for more moderate representatives who closer reflect their viewpoints on the homeland. Any loss of proembargo strength in Congress will help bring it down, as what nearly happened in the summer of 2010.[14]

The Cuban side acknowledges the altering realities in Miami. National Assembly President Ricardo Alarcón, when suggesting radical internal immigration reforms are coming (confirmed on October 2012), made note that the Cubans who have left in the past 20 years "do not present the same profile as the historical exile. This is now an economic emigration whose primary interest is to maintain a peaceful relationship with their country of origin."[15]

Evidence of the shifting attitudes toward those who leave the island is apparent through such conferences held in Washington between émigrés and Cuban interest section on how to change US policy.[16] Organizations representing the moderate position are materializing, such as Cuban-Americans for Engagement (CARE) born April 2012. One of founders Maria Isabel Alfonso is confident there is a shift in the air.

"We started this to let the hard right Cuban-Americans who favor embargo know they do not have my voice. We are open to a less conflictive relationship with the Cuban government, promoting better relations. The Cuban-American community is not monolithic."[17] Alfonso, who came to America in 1995, represents the modern Cuban immigrant who does not hesitate to criticize the island administration, but recognizes what the government has endured under American hostility. She fully supports the economic transformations taking place in her homeland, "and hope they are accompanied by other changes in the politics, without sacrificing the culture, education, social programs."

The professor in languages states two conditions to help advance normalization. "The US government should unilaterally end the embargo, it should not be used as a tool to pressure Cuba. And the Cuban government should continue with the changes and use that as a method to advance political reform." Despite the obstacles, she is optimistic. "I think in the next five years the Cuban-American community will have a key role in helping develop normal relations. The new immigrants want to engage and interact with government, for the benefit of all."

Even among the hard-liners there is a softening of opinion. Carlos Saladrigas, a longtime Castro opponent, is now preaching reconciliation using siege imagery, "Lets tear down the walls we have built on both sides, let us build the bridges that are needed," he said in a speech at a public forum in Havana in 2012.[18] His comments created little stir in Miami, another sign of the times. No longer is a *dialoguero* a term that could cost someone his life in Little Havana.

Further indication of a new reality occurred following the flap from Florida Marlins manager Ozzie Guillén and his offhanded comment of respect for Fidel Castro's ability to survive assassination attempts. While there was uproar, anger, and calls for his dismissal, it came from a predictable but narrowing group of old-time exiles and some media outlets. Twenty years ago Guillén would have been subjected to death threats, with the real possibility of having them carried out. His heartfelt apology calmed the waters, at the same time creating a discussion of what constitutes free speech in South Florida. Possibly the most revealing aspect of the incident was that fewer than 200 people, mostly in their seventies, showed up for an anti-Guillén/Castro protest at the ballpark, after strenuous efforts were made to draw a big crowd. In contrast it was remarked, "Twelve years ago—although a little boy is more symbolic and charged than a millionaire loudmouth—the Elián González tug-of-war brought thousands into the streets and ground the city to a halt."[19] The anti-Castro sentiment, while still bright-hot among the shrinking number of faithful, is losing its widespread appeal, even amid the media—where previously eight radio stations in Miami were dedicated to counterrevolution, now there are two with falling ratings.[20] The opposite is taking hold, with Miami TV host Carlos Otero, who left Cuba in 2008, regularly featuring music groups from Cuba such as *Buena Fe* with little negative feedback.[21] Unfortunately, reflections of an earlier, violent time in Miami can still occur. In late April 2012 a Coral Gables travel agency "exploded into flames" according to media reports, the owner and authorities confirming it was firebombed, most likely in retaliation for booking flights to Cuba.[22]

Although Guillén had innocently invoked Fidel's longevity, it is the revolutionary leader's mortality that could add another element to the mix of concluding siege. Antiembargo advocate John McAuliff, executive director of the Fund for Reconciliation and Development, speculated, "When Fidel dies it will have a psychological impact on the US, his passing may have an impact on the relationship between the two countries, because of who he is and what he has represented. When Fidel goes the energy of his unique historical perspective may lessen if not vanish." The passing of Fidel could afford the United States political cover to broach engagement with the island under the guise of having the person most associated with the revolution, the man who has poked his finger in America's eye for 50 years, no longer on the scene.[23]

Fidel's demise has been shown to be an uncontrollable element, as is the continuing fate of Alan Gross and the Cuban Five and dozens of other aspects that complicate the move toward normalization. Alterations to the status of any of those issues, combined with the growing energies of Cuban reforms and the temperate attitudes of a majority of Cuban-Americans has the potential to push siege on the path of closure. As does the international element. China is an active participant in the island's economy, and Cuba has warm relations with regional powerhouse Brazil. The socialist nation has never been more in favor with Latin American countries, at the same time the United States finds itself increasingly opposed over its stagnant policy. At the Summit of Americas held April 2012 in Columbia all members agreed on the need to include Cuba in this and other area organizations. Only the United States and Canada expressed opposition.[24]

With all facets potentially converging in the next few years, the final component remains in the hands of American politicians. Forces in favor of engagement continue to emerge, such as Democratic senator Jeff Bingaman describing Washington's policy as "out of step. It is past time to establish diplomatic relations with Cuba and end the embargo."[25] If Democrats find themselves in a strong position after the 2012 elections, the push for ending siege could reenergize. The most important voice in American politics remains in the White House, and it is there that the president retains tremendous powers to help bring the siege to its knees. Despite congressional control of the embargo's legal standing, the commander-in-chief holds measures that could go a long way to render blockade near irrelevant. Obama has made some movement, allowing unlimited travel for Cuban-Americans, and expanding people-to-people licensed trips for average Americans to visit the island. He's also, despite public comments to the contrary, expressed openness to a changed relationship with Cuba, although his conditions to a new dynamic have usually been framed within standard antirevolutionary terminology.[26]

While the steps taken are important, so much more could be done, according to Josefina Vidal, head of North American division at the Ministry of Foreign Relations (MINREX). "President Obama has had great ability to ease the siege, but has never used it. If he is elected for a second term maybe he will. In 2009 and 2010 with all the political coverage he had, Congress in the Democratic hands, he should have done more. But the President can still keep his prerogatives to permit certain transactions to Cuba, to reduce or eliminate certain aspects of the siege."

Specifically, the President "possesses sufficient legal authority to significantly relax the embargo"[27] through use of general licenses permitted under OFAC regulations. A major component is travel. Obama could substantially expand unrestricted family and educational trips, and define "family" and "educational" in the widest terms. He has control over 13 different travel categories including religious, journalist, athletic, and academic exchanges.[28] Lessening the constraints on American's capacity to see Cuba for themselves would substantially weaken other elements of siege policy.

McAuliff suggested the outcome: "Every American should be able to attest to a purpose of non-tourist educational travel, just as every self-identified Cuban-American simply attests to having relatives within three generations. Certainly some will take advantage, gaming the system, to just hang out at the beach. That happens already with the tens of thousands of Americans who feel morally justified to simply ignore travel restrictions—without OFAC fines since the last year of the Bush Administration."[29]

Obama might also bypass Congress to ease trade embargo constraints. This would allow more than just agricultural exports, permitting Cuban products to be imported into the United States, possibly the long-forbidden cigars and rum. More likely, medical products would be prioritized, such as Heberport, a treatment to heal diabetic feet that is being commercialized internationally.

Whether the President would use his authority to slice the siege into small pieces is something Vidal is unsure of: "Is it worth doing something about Cuba? We are a small country, not given much attention in the US, they have many other things to consider. I tend to be pessimistic."

She recognizes while Obama could act unilaterally, the legislative branch would be ignored at his peril. "You still need Congress to watch his back. You need Congress and the interest groups to support what he was doing, and it's not easy." Still, she can hope. "Imagine Cuba without the blockade—it will show our ability to advance more rapidly, without these restrictive policies. It will give us access to technology, to funds, to connect with US capabilities. To allow us access to the US market and for companies and tourists to come to Cuba. The siege has a negative impact on foreign companies wanting to do business here, so many decide not to because it's too much trouble, because they don't know what they have to go through to make sure they won't get into difficulties with the Americans, if they have any business relations with the US it's worse."

The siege works as a chilling effect on those considering Cuba as a commercial option. "The companies want to make sure they are not in violation of US regulations against us. And they don't know what additional complications will come in the future," Vidal added. Besiegement additionally cools cooperation on a number of important issues, such as drug trafficking operations, immigration, and environment disaster preparation. While there is some integration on these topics,[30] the siege more often acts as a brake for development of full operational efficiencies.

Pressures not to do business in Cuba are much in evidence. In early 2012 the US government went after Spanish telecommunications enterprise Telefónica over its Cuban affiliates.[31] Company officials had to spend considerable time to document its divestment of its interests in the island, and show it had no plans for future investment. Closer to home the feds investigated Esco Corporation, a privately held company that operates foundries in Portland and internationally. The problem was one of those plants, located in Canada, used nickel from Cuba. The unintentional violation may result in a multimillion dollar fine.[32]

For any chance of bringing siege to an end a long list of conditions must coalesce. If Obama wins a second term, if he sees value in spending some political capital on Cuba through his licensing authority, if Congress is of the mind to explore rapprochement, if Miami's moderation advances, if the economic and political reforms in Cuba expand and solidify, if they are recognized in Washington, if oil is found and Cuba overcomes its economic difficulties, if the island is allowed access to international financial institutions as an oil exporter, if the demands increase for engagement from American agricultural and travel interests, if thousands of US citizens come to visit Cuba and see it for what it really is, if Fidel becomes a figure to memorialize—then maybe practicality will have the chance to triumph over irrationality.

Yet there would still be one more piece missing. Understanding.

America would need to approach the Cuban Revolution and its 50 years of existence for what it is, not the self-delusional historiography it has portrayed it to be. When it comes to Cuba the United States has been steadfast in the conviction the Castro regime is illegitimate; that it has imposed such an iron will on its citizens they have no chance to express honest desires, and any articulation of support for the government is coerced. It is a position that can be accredited in part to siege strategy and the response to it. But it is disingenuous to believe in its veracity. The revolution has heard the voices of those who aspire for improvements within the socialist structure, no more so than the root of the transformations going on in the island today. Millions of citizens have had their say, the government listened and despite the constraints of siege, it has implemented far ranging reforms that touch the heart of civil life. There is a sense of leadership and citizens working within a divergence of opinions on how Cuba will construct twenty-first-century socialism. Additionally there is an historic element. With a long experience of rebellion against established power that did not meet the need of the masses, it would be hard to conceive the Cubans have suddenly become soft. What is closer to the truth is a readiness to take the steps indispensable for improvement, within what has been built—to advance economically while holding on to the social justice programs. Based on the belief the government, for all its ills, represents true Cuban autonomy. The siege itself provides evidence— one of its tenants is to make the people so miserable they would overthrow the government not because it was illegitimate or unpopular, but solely to bring relief from suffering. That is a prime objective of encirclement.

In any case, as Ricardo Alarcón remarked, "Why would Cubans submit to a government now after what it's been through historically? The people of Cuba in the majority support the Revolution still, no government can control all through oppression for such a long time, and the Cubans are not sheep, they of all Latinos would not put up with a government not legitimately representing their independence and sovereignty."[33]

The American's have never, either through willful ignorance or determined misunderstanding, accepted what the revolution has meant to the majority of Cubans. The rejection of US control in 1959 was an expression of what Edmund Burke argued, in his immortal work *Reflections on the Revolution in France*, that revolutions to be worthy cannot be predicated on nebulous conceptions of right and wrong, but on experience and tradition; that each nation must rely on their collective history, their own character and destiny.[34]

This is the Cuban Revolution, drawing on the tradition and experience of 400 years of harsh Spanish colonialism, then 60 years of self-deception under American neocolonialism. For all its faults, the revolution has remained a truly Cuban occurrence. It is their expression of national identity.

And it is something the Americans have yet to recognize. Instead siege has been the answer, and with it the arrogance of certainty. In the novel *Los Gusanos*, protagonist Blas de la Pena said: "You Americans will never understand us." The American blandly replies, "We don't really need to, do we?"[35]

America's siege has been built on emotion and maintained through ignorance, a political ideology closer to religious crusade. The condition makes it harder to conclude encirclement because it is based on faith that defies rationality. Enlightenment becomes the force to overcome dogma; for the people of the United States to understand what is really happening in Cuba, warts and all. To realize the system they are trying to build is different and infuriating to the capitalist way of life, but that it does not deserve more than a half-century of punishment.

The siege is not to be considered the glue of rationalization holding the revolution together. Decades-long effort to build a new society for those who continue to support it and the government that tries, despite its faults, to fulfill needs is where legitimacy endures. American policy, however, has been a method to excuse shortcomings, some justified, and its greatest effect has been in the delaying of advancement toward what the revolution hoped to achieve. It is a negative force that has warped and corrupted much of what was expected, coming at great civic cost. Ending it will not destroy the revolution, no more than continuing it will, only the ready convenience used by both sides for best advantage. Ending siege will not bring relief to all of Cuba's difficulties, only the opportunity to ameliorate them. Current Cuban reforms are designed to improve public life, and if siege is overcome as a result, it will be ancillary benefit. In the end terminating encirclement should be the goal for its own sake, consequences unknown but well overdue for those who have suffered under it.

The siege has been in place long enough. Cuba is moving into the future, it is now time for America to move from the past.

NOTES

1 AN UNSEEN TRUTH

1. Geoffrey R. Stone, *Perilous Times*, W.W. Norton & Company, Inc. New York, 2004, p. 419.
2. http://georgewbush-whitehouse.archives.gov/newsack:/releases/2001/09/20010920–8.html.
3. Paul K. Davis, *Besieged, 100 Great Sieges From Jericho to Sarajevo*, Oxford University Press, New York, 2003.
4. It led the then US secretary of state Madeline Albright to say the death of 500,000 Iraqi children as result of sanctions was "worth it." John Pilger, "Squeezed to Death," *Guardian*, March 4, 2000.
5. http://www.nytimes.com/2010/04/24/us/politics/24immig.html.
6. FOX hypes stories to claim "Christmas Under Siege": http://mediamatters.org/research/200412100006 (December 10, 2004).
7. Charlie Savage, *Democratic Senators Issue Strong Warning about Use of the Patriot Act*, March 16, 2012.
8. www.wired.com/dangeroom2011/07.
9. www.dhs.gov/xabout/laws/law_regulation_rule_0011.shtm.
10. Found in the former President's autobiography, *Decision Points*, Crown Publishing, 2010.
11. *Weekly Standard*, December 5, 2005.
12. http://news.antiwar.com/2011/03/07/obama-approves-indefinite-detention-without-trial/.
13. Janine Jackson, "Whistling Past the Wreckage of Civil Liberties," *Extra*, September 2011, p. 13.
14. Chris Anders, *Senators Demand the Military Lock Up of American Citizens in a "Battlefield" They Define as Being Right Outside Your Window*://www.aclu.org/ (November 2011).
15. http://www.aclu.org/blog/national-security/president-obama-signs-indefinite-detention-law. A New York judge tried to block the legislation in June 2012. Susan Madrak, *Federal Judge Blocks NDAA Indefinite Detention*, Crooks and Liars.
16. Jack A. Smith, "Our Civil Liberties under Attack: Big Brother's Getting Even Bigger," The Rag Blog, April 18, 2012.
17. Dana Priest and William Arkin, *Top Secret America A Washington Post Investigation*, December 20, 2010: http://projects.washingtonpost.com/top-secret-america/articles/monitoring-america/?wpisrc=nl_politics.
18. Ellen Nakashima, "One Tip Enough to Put Name on Watch List," *Washington Post*, December 30, 2010.

19. Smith, "Our civil liberties under attack: *Big Brother's getting even bigger*," The Rag Blog, April 18, 2012.
20. http://www.guardian.co.uk/world/2012/apr/18/cispa-unprecedented-access-internet-privacy.
21. Kevin Zeese, "FBI Raids on Political Activists," *Z Magazine*, November 2010, p. 7.
22. Maher Arar arrested on charges of alleged terrorism, later shown to be innocent. Monia Mazigh, *Hope and Despair: My Struggle to Free My Husband, Maher Arar*, McClelland & Stewart, 2008.
23. James M. Klatell, "Jose Padilla's Mental State at Issue," *CBS News*, February 11, 2009: http://www.cbsnews.com/stories/2007/02/24/cbsnews_investigates /main2510272.shtml.
24. James Bovard, *Terrorism and Tyranny*, Palgrave/Macmillan, 2003, pp. 108–109.
25. *New York Times*, February 12, 2006.
26. Jane Mayer, "The Secret Sharer: Is Thomas Drake an Enemy of the State?," *New Yorker*, May 23, 2011.
27. Chris Hedges, "Supreme Court Likely to Endorse Obama's War on Whistle-Blowers," www.truthdig.com, March 12, 2012.
28. Doug Mataconis, "Oklahoma Outlaws Sharia Law," November 3, 2010, www.outsidethebeltway.com. In January 2010 Peter King (R-NY), chairman of the House Homeland Security Committee, wanted to hold hearings in what many consider McCarthyism like proceedings, while fellow Republican Louie Gohmert (Texas) said on Frank Gaffney's radio show that it was a "creeping" threat: http://thinkprogress.org/2011/01/19/gohmert-sharia-hearings/.
29. Nouran El-Behairy, "Congresswoman claims Muslim Brotherhood infiltrating US government," *Daily News Egypt*, July 21, 2012.
30. http://thinkprogress.org/politics/2011/08/26/304306/islamophobia-network/.
31. FAIR Extra 4/03 and 5–6/03. Also see Paul Rutherford, *Weapons of Mass Persuasion, Marketing the War against Iraq*, University of Toronto Press, 2004. Judith Miller's *New York Times* uncritical reportage of the government rationale for war is well covered.
32. The Patriot Act saw only Democrat Russ Feingold voting against it in the Senate. Fellow Democrat Barbara Lee stood alone in all of Congress who voted against the authorization of use of force after 9/11.
33. FAIR Extra, October 2001; also http://www.therationalradical.com/dsep/bill-oreilly-afghanistan.htm.
34. *Toronto Star*, August 20, 2011.
35. "'I'd do it again' says police commander filmed pepper spraying the faces of women at Occupy Wall Street protest," *Daily Mail*, October 21, 2011.
36. Bill O'Reilly: Occupy Wall Street Protesters Are 'Drug-Trafficking Crackheads,' http://gawker.com/5849721/bill-oreilly-occupy-wall-street-protesters-are-drug+trafficking-crackheads
37. *Extra*, magazine of FAIR, October 14, 2011. Also http://sjlendman.blogspot.com/2011/11/americas-media-war-on-ows.html.
38. www.counterpunch.org/2011/10/18/wall-street-firms-spy-on-protestors-in-tax-funded-center/.
39. "Occupy Wall Street: NYPD Attempt Media Blackout at Zuccotti Park," *The Guardian*, November 15, 2011.
40. Rebecca Kemble, "8 Arrested in Wis. Capitol, Including The Progressive's Editor, for Using Cameras or Holding Signs," *The Progressive*, November 2, 2011.

41. www.peacecouncil.net/pnl/02/712/712CivilLiberties.htm.
42. Amnesty International: http://www.globalissues.org/article/263/amnesty-international-human-rights-backlash.
43. http://web.amnesty.org/library/Index/ENGPOL100112003; http://www.globalissues.org/article/427/amnesty-international-no-shortcut-to-genuine-security.
44. http://www.commondreams.org/views04/0317-12.htm.
45. Ibid.
46. Proposed Bill C-30 presented in 2012 by Public Safety Minister Vic Toews.
47. www.legislation.gov.uk/ukpga/2001/24/contents: Anti-terrorism, Crime and Security Act 2001.
48. http://www.notbored.org/england-history.html.
49. A survey by cableco NTL: Telewest and carried out by YouGov, polled more than 2,000 individuals. Just over 80 percent supported use of CCTV: http://www.silicon.com/management/public-sector/2006/11/23/cctv-ok-with-uk-39164280/.
50. Stone, *Perilous Times*, p. 551.
51. Attorney General John Ashcroft's Assault on Civil Liberties (updated September 2003): http://www.aclu.org/national-security/attorney-general-john-ashcrofts-assault-civil-liberties-updated-september-2003.
52. O'Reilly Factor, April 30, 2003. O'Reilly often threatened his listeners not to protest against the war, as it would be a sign of disloyalty, almost traitorous. www.globalissues.org/issue/245.
53. Stone, *Perilous Times*, p. 529.
54. Radio host Thom Hartman often speaks of it, quoting historic incidents where America has sacrificed liberty for security, ending up with neither.
55. http://www.angus-reid.com/polls. Of those polled, 77 percent supported the plan to strip citizens of US citizenship if shown connected to terrorism. *Most Americans Endorse Terrorist Expatriation Act* (May 20, 2010).
56. Ibid.
57. Hardoon Siddiqui, *Coming to Grips with New Anti-Semitism,* Toronto Star, September 17, 2011.
58. Interview with author, 2011.
59. Stone, *Perilous Times*, p. 557.
60. Godfrey Hodgson, *The Myth of American Exceptionalism*, Yale University Press, New Haven, 2009, p. 38.
61. www.law.berkeley.edu/files/SteinfeldPaperMarch14CSLS(3).pdf. Author email interview with Bruce Bedell of the On Line Institute for Advanced Loyalist Studies: C:\Users\owner\AppData\Local\Temp\Loyalist Institute Home Page.mht.
62. Author email interview with R. Wallace Hale, Loyalist author and authority: "I'm quite certain no Federal compensation was ever paid to any Loyalist, and can't recall any mention of compensation paid by any of the States, although it's possible there may have been rare instances. By the terms of the peace treaty, Loyalists were supposed to be able to collect any debts owing them by the revolutionists (patriots), but most Loyalists who attempted doing so received hostile reception. Usually, failure or refusal to swear allegiance to the State resulted in attainder and banishment, or forced expulsion by the patriots of the area. Leaving brought on confiscation of property."
63. Stone, *Perilous Times*. Amaury Cruz, lawyer, writer, and political activist living in Miami Beach, December 20, 2010, from consul email Montreal: "Indeed,

the equivalent of the crime of dangerousness was first established in the U.S. through the Alien and Sedition Acts of 1798. These have been reincarnated in the Prevention of Violent Radicalization and Homegrown Terrorism 2007, which was passed in the House of Representatives, but not yet in the Senate. This is the result of legislation based on 'fear and trembling, a disease unto death' (to quote Kierkegaard titles), either here or in Cuba. However, Cuba has lived for fifty years under an obsessive policy of regime change by the world's most powerful nation, the fear is not unjustified."

64. Stone, *Perilous Times*, p. 12.
65. Ibid.
66. Ibid., p. 171.
67. http://www.essortment.com/espionage-history-1917–1918–21257.html.
68. Stone, *Perilous Times*, p. 230.
69. http://www.bc.edu/bc_org/avp/cas/comm/free_speech/smithactof1940.html.
70. Stone, *Perilous Times*, p. 252.
71. Tim Weiner, *Legacy of Ashes: The History of the CIA*, Anchor Books, New York, 2008.
72. George C. Herring, *From Colony to Superpower*, Oxford University Press, New York, 2008, p. 770.
73. Interview with author, April 5, 2011.
74. Stone, *Perilous Times*, p. 533.
75. Interview with author, April 6, 2011.
76. Radio host Ed Schulz, in response to an incredulous caller (2010), commented he has never noticed any lessening of civil rights. Most people accept the notion that if the individual is not doing anything wrong there should not be any objections to the surveillance programs.
77. Interview with author, April 6, 2011.
78. http://www.consortiumnews.com/archive/bush.html.
79. Sources: State Department official source of Plame leak, CNN Politics, August 30, 2006: http://articles.cnn.com/2006–08–30/politics/.
80. Stephanie Miller radio show, March 18, 2011.
81. Jonathan Turley, "The Demon is Dead; So are Many of Our Rights," *USA Today*, May 6, 2011.
82. July 2010 online survey by *USA Today* (1,500 participants) indicated 94 percent were in favor of lifting blockade. Cuban UN report 2011, p. 87. An April 2009 CNN/Opinion Research Corporation poll showed that 64 percent of Americans surveyed think the United States should lift its travel ban on Cuba, while 71 percent thought the United States should reestablish diplomatic relations with the island nation. "Poll: Three-Quarters Favor Relations with Cuba," *CNN*, April 10, 2009.
83. *Cuba vs Bloqueo*, July 2011 Report by Cuba on resolution 65/6 of the UN General Assembly, pp. 88–89.
84. Noam Chomsky, *Making the Future*, City Lights Books, San Francisco, 2012.
85. Interview with author 2011.
86. White House release, September 2, 2010, Presidential Memorandum—Continuation of Authorities Under the Trading With the Enemy Act.
87. http://www.politisite.com/2012/02/24/.
88. *Cuba vs. Bloqueo*, July 2011 Report by Cuba on resolution 65/6 of the UN General Assembly, p. 54.

89. Comment made at meeting with intellectuals at Havana Book Fair, February 2011.

90. Lars Schoultz, *That Infernal Little Cuban Republic*, University of North Carolina Press, 2009, p. 4.

91. Keith Bolender, *Voices From the Other Side: An Oral History of Terrorism Against Cuba*, Pluto Press, London, 2010.

92. The most infamous was Operation Mongoose, after Bay of Pigs April 1961 invasion and ending in the October Missile Crisis 1962.

93. Bolender, *Voices From the Other Side*.

94. The Cuban government knew about the invasion, but not the specific dates or location. Thousands of Cubans were rounded up and imprisoned prior to the invasion based mostly on the accusations of their neighbors under the Committee for the Defense of the Revolution watch programs.

95. Stephen Kimber's account from his forthcoming book, *What Lies Across the Water*, indicated the FBI had been aware of the activities of the Cuban agents in Florida a few years prior to the arrests. The information received from the Cuban authorities did not reveal the identities, only apparently augmented what was already known. One of the five, René González, finished his sentence and was realized in 2011; he remains in the United States serving out his probation order in South Florida. His wife and others fear for his safety.

96. Posada and Orlando Bosch have long been considered masterminds of bombing of Cubana Airlines in 1976, killing all on board. Bosch died in Miami in 2011, Posada continues to live in the city despite international calls for US authorities to try him as a terrorist.

97. Don Bohning, *The Castro Obsession*, Potomac Books, 2005, p. 73.

98. Speech during UN General Assembly vote against the US embargo on Cuba. The vote is 179 to 4, with 1 abstention. http://www.un.org/News/Press/docs/2004/ga10288.doc.htm.

99. Department of State, Foreign Relations of the United States, 1958–1960, vol. VI, Cuba (1991), p. 885.

100. Noam Chomsky, introduction, *Voices From the Other Side*, pp. ix, x.

101. Aviva Chomsky, *A History of the Cuban Revolution*, Wiley-Blackwell, UK, 2011, p. 86.

102. Ann Louise Bardach, *Cuba Confidential*, Vintage 2003, p. 132.

103. Peter Schwab, *Cuba Confronting the US Embargo*, St. Martin's Griffin, New York, 1999, p. 100.

104. Yoáni Sanchez, Cuba's most famous anti-Castro blogger, has publicly stated her opposition to America's aggressive policy against Cuba, see later.

105. Interview with author, 2011.

106. Schwab, *Cuba Confronting the US Embargo*, pp. 171, 172.

107. *Correa Reiterates Condemnation of US Blockade of Cuba*, Quito, Prensa Latina, December 28, 2011.

108. Cuba offered compensation based on assessed tax values, American refused. In the 1970s attempts were made under Carter to negotiate compensation, which ended abruptly with the United States using Angola as an excuse, according to former head of the US Interest Section in Havana, Wayne Smith, author interview, 2011. See later.

109. Lars Schoultz, *That Infernal Little Cuban Republic*, University of North Carolina Press, 2009, p. 105.

110. http://users.polisci.wisc.edu/LA260/castro.htm. From a 1961 interview with the Italian communist newspaper *L'Unita*, explaining that the Cuban Revolution was not in any way dogmatic.

111. Dominica Republic, Honduras, Guatemala, among others were actively hostile against the revolution.

112. http://www.ciponline.org/cuba/cubaproject/Nov%20IPR.pdf.

113. Jeffrey Goldberg, *Don't Lump Cuba With Iran on U.S. Terror List*, Bloomberg View, January 16, 2012. The other countries on the lists include Iran, Sudan, and Syria. For details as to why Cuba is on the list, see http://www.state.gov /documents/organization/65476.pdf.

114. Speaking at LASA conference in Toronto, October 2010.

115. Interview with author, June 2011.

116. Arrested under Law 88 specifically passed to counter provisions in Helms-Burton Act that strengthened siege.

117. A nationwide series of meetings began in 2007 asking for feedback on ways to improve the social/economic makeup of Cuba. See chapter five in this volume.

118. www.radioguaimaro.co.cu/english/index.php/news/national-news/105-cuba -will-talk-with-us-raul-castro.html.

119. "Raúl Castro Comments on Cuba-U.S. Ties," Guardian unlimited.

120. Marc Frank, "Exclusive: Cuban Government Set for Broad Reorganization," *Reuters*, September 30, 2011.

121. *Quotable,* Cuba Triangle, Monday, January 3, 2011.

122. Venezuela, Peru, Bolivia, Argentina, Brazil with center or center left governments have encouraged positive ties.

123. *Cuba Experts Applaud Obama's Defense of Cuban American Travel in "Megabus" Negotiations,* Washington Office on Latin America, December 16, 2011.

124. Interview with Miami-based Univision, May 23, 2011.

125. Laura Carlsen, *Center for International Policy (CIP) Analysts Look at Obama's First Year,* January 27, 2010.

126. US OFAC Charges at Cuba, Prensa Latina, October 9, 2011.

127. From his famous Chance for Peace Speech, http://beyondterror.org/eisenhower .html.

128. Dwight Eisenhower, *The White House Years: Waging Peace, 1956–1961,* Doubleday & Company, 1965.

129. Wayne Smith, former head of the US Interest Section in Havana. Email interview with author, April 2012. In early 1960 secretary of state official Lester D. Mallory admitted, "The majority of Cubans support Castro."

130. USAID worker Alan Gross, arrested for bringing into Cuba prohibited high-tech communication equipment. See later.

131. Bernie Dwyer and Roberto Ruiz Rebo documentary, *The Day Diplomacy Died*, Two Island Production, 2009, for background and how Cuban state agents infiltrated the dissident organizations.

132. See chapter four.

133. http://www.cubaverdad.net/repressive_laws.htm.

134. Interview with author, 2011.

135. http://uscode.house.gov/download/pls/18C115.txt.

136. www.cafc.gov.

137. Interview with author, 2011.

138. Republican Marco Rubio Florida Senator, a hard-liner against any engagement with Cuba, born to Cuban parents but has never visited the island.

139. Numerous bills to end the travel restrictions and embargo have been introduced during the past five years, the most recent in summer of 2010. See chapter four.

140. Victoria Burnett, "An Airlift, Family by Family, Bolsters Cuba's Economy," *New York Times*, June 11, 2011.

141. Interview with author, September 2011.

142. Interview with author, July 2011.

143. *Miami Herald*, posted on Thursday, April 7, 2011, "For Cuba Policy, New Ally at the DNC, Calzon Receipt of Thousands of Dollars of Support Money from US Government."

144. http://refspace.com/quotes/Man_and_Socialism_in_Cuba.

145. Paul D'Amato, *CUBA: Image and Reality*, International Socialist Review, Issue 51, January–February 2007.

146. Wayne Smith, *The Closest of Enemies*, WW Norton & Company, New York, 1987, p. 87.

147. "Ibero-American summit Supports Cuba," *Prensa Latina*, October 2005.

148. Andres Zaldiva Dieguez, *Blockade, the Longest Economic Siege in History*, Editorial Capitan San Luis, Havana, 2007, p. 13.

149. Arturo López-Levy, *This Time is Different for Cuba's Economic Reform*, Havana Note, December 24, 2010: http://www.thehavananote.com/node/838.

150. Arturo López-Levy, *"Chaos and Instability": Human Rights and U.S. Policy Goals in Cuba*, NACLA Report on the Americas September/October 2011, p. 16.

151. Salim Lamrani, "Conversations with Cuban blogger Yoáni Sanchez," April 30, 2010: http://www.rebelion.org/noticia.php?id=104205.

152. An examination of Cuba's efforts to engage the United States in order to end the embargo can be found at Peter Kornbluh's website: http://www.gwu.edu/~nsarchiv/latin_america/cuba.htm.

153. http://www.globalresearch.ca/index.php?context=va&aid=18664 (April 14, 2010); Hillary Clinton said embargo to stay on until Cuba improves human rights.

154. "Cuba challenges US to lift embargo, 'even for a year,'" *Sydney Morning Herald*, April 26, 2010.

155. Interview with author, March 2011.

156. Interview with author, 2011.

157. Interview with author, March 2011.

158. Jeff Franks, "Raul Castro Turns 79 with Eyes on Future," *Reuters*, June 4, 2010.

2   Laying the Siege

1. Chalmers Johnson, *Dismantling the Empire*, Metropolitan Books, Henry Holt and Company, New York, 2010, p. 52.

2. Term as described in the title of Wayne Smith's remembrance of US-Cuban diplomacy. *The Closest of Enemies*, WW Norton & Company, New York, 1987.

3. Peter Blackwell, *A History of Latin America*, Blackwell Publishing, MA, 2004, p. 454.

4. April 28, 1823, in US Congress House of Reps Island of Cuba, p. 7.

5. Shout of Barie, near Santiago, signifying the call to arms.

6. George C. Herring, *From Colony to Superpower, US Foreign Relations Since 1776*, Oxford University Press, New York, 2008, pp. 20–30. Also *John Adams*, Simon & Schuster, 2001, by Pulitzer Prize winner David McCullough. Both explore the theme that France's overextending financial commitment to the American Revolution was a factor in their own revolution two decades later.

7. Evan Thomas, *The War Lovers*, Little, Brown and Company, New York, 2010, p. 352.

8. John Kirk, "José Maríi and the United States: A Further Interpretation," *Journal of Latin American Studies*, Cambridge University Press, 1997, 9(2): 275–290.

9. http://www.ourdocuments.gov/doc.php?flash=true&doc=55.

10. Louis A. Perez Jr., *Cuba in the American Imagination*, University of North Carolina Press, Chapel Hill, 2008, p. 119, note 88.

11. http://www.marxists.org/history/cuba/subject/bay-of-pigs/index.htm.

12. The Cuba Company was the largest foreign investment in Cuba in the first two decades of the twentieth century. It was critical in the development of the relationship between American business and national counterparts that formed the new republic's relationship between the two countries under US hegemony. Business History Review, 2000. http://www.jstor.org/pss/3116352.

13. Henry Louis Taylor, Jr., *Inside El Barrio*, Kumarian Press, Virginia, 2009, p. 23.

14. One such example in the early 1900s, in part reads: "Fortunes in Cuba. The Cuban Colonization Company. Owns and holds deeds for two large tracts of the best land in Cuba, situated on the north coast in the Province of Puerto Principe, the most fertile and beautiful portion of the island. This region is being rapidly colonized by enterprising Americans, who own and are developing thousands of plantations in the immediate vicinity of our holdings." Enrique Circules, *Conversacion con el ultimo Norteamericano*, Editorial Letras Cubanas, La Habana, Cuba, 1988.

15. Jane Franklin, *Cuba and the United States*, Ocean Press, Melbourne, 1997.

16. Louis A. Perez Jr., *Cuba under the Platt Amendment 1902–1934*, University of Pittsburg Press, 1986, pp. 71–80.

17. Ibid., p. 159.

18. Ibid., p. 337.

19. Ibid.

20. This theme is covered extensively in the Perez works cited earlier. Credit must be acknowledged for his outstanding efforts on the historical perspective of the relationship between the United States and Cuba.

21. Said to President Roosevelt on October 28, 1901. Leonard Woods papers, Manuscript Division, Library of Congress.

22. Perez Jr., *Cuba in the American Imagination*, p. 247, note 81.

23. Congressional record, March 1, 1901, 56th congress, 2nd session vol. 34 pt 4.

24. Robert H. Ferrell, *America Diplomacy: A History*, New York, 1959, p. 245.

25. From an interview by Tracey Eaton, May 2011: vimeo.com/24078247 703–528–7953.

26. Leslie Bethell, ed., *Cambridge History of Latin America*, Cambridge University Press, vol. VII, New York, 1990, p. 451.

27. The figures cited here come from Marifeli Perez-Stable, *The Cuban Revolution Origins, Course and Legacy*, Oxford University Press, New York, 1999. Based on United Nation and international agency reports.

28. Luis E. Aguliar, *Cuba 1933*, Cornell University Press, Ithaca, 1972, p. 240.

29. Ibid.

30. From author's interview with Carlos Andrés Escalante, 2008.

31. This data was published by the International Labor Organization in Geneva, Switzerland, in 1960. In 1958, Cuba had a labor force of 2,204,000.

32. Manuel Yepe, *Cuba was Neither a Paradise Nor an Exception*, October 6, 2011.

33. Marifeli Pérez-Stable, *The Cuban Revolution*, Oxford University Press, New York, 1999, p. 31.

34. The Americans kept up support till ending arms supply, March 1958. Right to the end they hoped Batista would survive, but finally convinced him to leave less than one month prior to the triumph.

35. During a debate with Richard Nixon. *The Joint Appearances of Senator John F. Kennedy and Vice President Richard M. Nixon and Other 1960 Campaign Presentations*, 87th Congress, 1st Session, 1961, pp. 147–148.

36. US President John F. Kennedy, interview with Jean Daniel, October 24, 1963: http://www.revleft.com/vb/cuba-under-u-t144678/index.html?t=144678.

37. Perez Jr., *Cuba in the American Imagination*, p. 221.

38. Ibid., p. 220.

39. Ibid., p. 240.

40. Lars Schoultz, *That Infernal Little Cuban Republic*, University of North Carolina Press, 2009, p. 87.

41. Interview with author, June 2011.

42. Aviva Chomsky, *A History of the Cuban Revolution*, Wiley-Blackwell, United Kingdom, 2011, p. 72, note 16.

43. Ibid.

44. Marifeli Perez-Stable, *The Cuban Revolution Origins, Course, and Legacy*, Oxford University Press, New York, 1999, pp. 63–65.

45. The regime proposed if the land valued had been underestimated, it could be changed, but back taxes, plus interest, plus a fine had to be paid. In the case of the United States, compensation would originate from the income generated from the sale of Cuban sugar to the United States. From email interview with Nelson Valdes.

46. Andres Zaldivar Diéguez, *Blockade: The Longest Economic Siege in History*, Capitan San Luis, Havana, 2007, p. 38, citing *New York Times*, April 19, 1959.

47. Schoultz, *That Infernal Little Cuban Republic*, p. 119.

48. Michael Miller, *Cuba Owes U.S. $7 Billion For "Forgotten" Property Claims, Lawyers Propose 10% User Fee*, Miami New Times, March 16, 2012.

49. Olga Miranda Bravo, *Cuba/USA Nacionalizacions y Bloqueo*, Editorial de Cienceias Sociales, La Habana, 1996.

50. Noam Chomksy, *Failed States*, Metropolitan Books, New York, 2006.

51. Ibid. See also Diéguez, *Blockade*, p. 25.

52. www.historyofcuba.com.

53. http://paseovedado.blogspot.com/2010/05/what-about-compensation-for-us-property.html.

54. Franklin, *Cuba and the United States*, p. 21.

55. Schoultz, *That Infernal Little Cuban Republic*, p. 122.

56. Diéguez, *Blockade*, p. 66.

57. http://writing.upenn.edu/~afilreis/50s/guatemala.html. See also Tim Weiner, *Legacy of Ashes The History of the CIA*, Anchor Books, New York, 2008, pp. 106–119.

58. Diéguez, *Blockade*, p. 65.

59. Ibid., p. 254.

60. Schoultz, *That Infernal Little Cuban Republic*, p. 109.

61. Anthony F. Kirkpatrick, *In Brothers to the Rescue Shootdown, U.S. Shares the Blame*, Common Dreams, March 1, 2001.

62. Keith Bolender, *Voices From the Other Side: An Oral History of Terrorism Against Cuba*, Pluto Press, London, 2010, p. 162.

63. Ibid.

64. Ibid.

65. Spain's inquisitorial system including pretrial investigations and detentions can be seen as contrary to presumption of innocence. See Isaac Saney, *Cuba A Revolution in Motion*, Fernwood Nova Scotia, 2004, p. 124.

66. Granma reported legal proceeding against the United States, May 31, 1999.

67. Perez Jr., *Cuba in the American Imagination*, p. 224.

68. Ibid., p. 102.

69. Office of the Historian, Bureau Of Public Affairs, US Department Of State; John P. Glennon, et al., eds., *Foreign Relations of the United States, 1958–1960*, vol. VI, Cuba–Washington DC: GPO, 1991, 885. From *Progreso Weekly* article by Saul Landau, January 2010. This also appeared in counterpunch: http://www.counterpunch.org/2011/01/21/the-context-of-cuba-s-crisis/.

70. Schoultz, *That Infernal Little Cuban Republic*, pp. 124–125.

71. Ibid., p. 134.

72. http://historicaltextarchive.com/sections.php?action=read&artid=693#2.

73. Schoultz, *That Infernal Little Cuban Republic*, pp. 106–107.

74. Alan Luxenberg, "Did Eisenhower Push Castro into the Arms of the Soviets?" Journal of InterAmerican Studies and World Affairs, vol. 30, no. 1, Spring 1988.

75. Aleida March, *Remembering Che*, Ocean Press, Melbourne, 2012, p. 90.

76. Simon Reid-Henry, *Fidel and Che*, Walker & Company, New York, 2009, p. 218.

77. George Lambie, *The Cuban Revolution in the 21st Century*, Pluto Press, London, 2010, p. 135.

78. Reid-Henry, *Fidel and Che*, p. 221.

79. Schoultz, *That Infernal Little Cuban Republic*, p. 126.

80. Cuba's involvement in Angola and Africa in general is recognized as a decision made by Fidel without prior knowledge or approval of the Soviets, who reluctantly came on board afterward.

81. Ibid., p. 116.

82. Ibid.

83. Ignacio Ramonet, *My Life Fidel Castro*, Allen Lane, England, 2007, p. 293. Speaking of efforts to topple Trujillo in the Dominica Republic and the training of antirevolutionaries. Castro has maintained his internationalism was always done under accepted laws and not aimed at civilians.

84. Department of State, *Foreign Relations of the United States 1958–1960, Volume VI, Cuba*. 481. Paper Prepared by the 5412 Committee, Washington, March 16, 1960. A program of Covert Action against the Castro Regime RE BAY OF PIGS 1.

85. The strong do what they can, the weak suffer what they must.

86. Perez Jr., *Cuba in the American Imagination*, p. 248.

87. Castro said it during a speech to intellectuals that led to cultural conformity as well as political/social obedience.

88. Perez Jr., *Cuba in the American Imagination*, p. 272.
89. Ramonet, *My Life Fidel Castro*.
90. CDR had as one model the American Defense Leagues of 1917, set up during World War I to keep an eye on neighbors who were displaying support for Germans or antiwar sentiments.
91. Interview with author, 2011.
92. Schoultz, *That Infernal Little Cuban Republic*, p. 172.
93. Aleksandr Fursenko and Timothy Naftali, *One Hell of a Gamble*, WW Norton & Company, New York, 1991, pp. 99–100.
94. Franklin, *Cuba and the United States*, p. 25.
95. Ricardo Alarcón and Miguel Alvarez, *Blockade: The United States Economic War against Cuba*, Editora Politica, La Habana, 2001.
96. Diéguez, *Blockade*, p. 184.
97. Ibid.
98. Louis A. Pérez, Jr., *Cuba, between Reform and Revolution*, third edn, Oxford University Press, New York, 2006, p. 346.
99. Kennedy aide Richard Goodwin came up with the idea of using the act as an economic weapon, since expressing regret for the move. Before the embargo was finalized the President arranged for 1,200 cigars to be brought to him from Cuba.
100. Acting under the authority of the Foreign Assistance Act, President John F. Kennedy suspended all trade with Cuba. Presidential Proclamation 3447, an embargo on all trade with Cuba, prohibiting the "importation into the United States of all goods of Cuban origin and goods imported from or through Cuba" and "all exports from the United States to Cuba."
101. *638 Ways to Kill Castro*, Silver River Productions DVD, 2007. An excellent account of US government involvement in the assassination attempts against Fidel can be found by Weiner, *Legacy of Ashes*. The book describes how, after 1959, Cuba passed to become a central objective of the actions of the agency, part of which was the consideration of "the elimination of Fidel Castro."
102. Chomsky, *A History of the Cuban Revolution*, p. 85.
103. Perez Jr., *Cuba in the American Imagination*, p. 250.
104. Lars Schoultz, *That Infernal Little Cuban Republic*, University of North Carolina Press, 2009, p. 552
105. The Cuba Project ran from 1959 to 1962, Operation Mongoose its most famous program. Details of historical background and the damage it caused can be found in Fabian Escalante, *The Cuba Project*, Ocean Press, Melbourne, 2004 Escalante claims Robert Kennedy was deeply involved in the Operation's daily activities.
106. Bolender, *Voices From the Other Side*, p. 109.
107. Diéguez, *Blockade*, p. 85.
108. Noam Chomsky, *Hegemony or Survival*, Metropolitan Books, New York, 2003, p. 80. Schoultz, *That Infernal Little Cuban Republic*, chapter 7 covering these activities, titled "State-Sponsored Terrorism."
109. http://www.marxists.org/history/cuba/subject/cia/mongoose/c-project.htm.
110. Bolender, *Voices From the Other Side*; Chomsky, *Hegemony or Survival*, p. viii.
111. Chomsky, *Hegemony or Survival*.
112. Ibid., p. 14.
113. Escalante, *The Cuba Project*, p. 100.

114. Weiner, *Legacy of Ashes*.

115. Interview with author, 2008; the name has been changed to protect original source on his request.

116. The money was granted in September 2011, according to Tracey Eaton's report— October 13, 2011. http://cubamoneyproject.org/?m=201110&paged=2 Cuba program. Total: $8,656,177.

117. See chapter four.

118. Michael Dobbs, *One Minute to Midnight*, Knopf, New York, 2008.

119. Schoultz, *That Infernal Little Cuban Republic*, p. 186. Fears of another invasion leading to the missile crisis based on American military maneuvers in the Caribbean involving 40,000 US troops and 79 ships. Cuban intelligence pointed to planning for a full-scale invasion.

120. Aleksandr Fursenko and Timothy Naftali, *One Hell of Gamble*, WW Northon & Company, New York, 1997.

121. These claims were made by Thom Hartmann and Lamar Waldron, *Ultimate Sacrifice*, Carroll & Graff, New York, 2005. The authors also claimed Che Guevara was in on the plot. While evidence for the second invasion is substantial, the claim Che and Almeida were involved in the plan to kill Castro and take over the government under US support is less so.

122. Richard Gott, *Cuba A New History*, Yale University Press, New Haven, 2004, p. 197. Fourteen voted in favor, two against (Cuba and Mexico), and five abstained. The Venezuelan foreign minister resigned in protest.

123. Schoultz, *That Infernal Little Cuban Republic*, p. 175.

124. Diéguez, *Blockade*, p. 21.

125. http://www.treasury.gov/resource-center/sanctions/Programs/pages/cuba.aspx.

126. "It's Not Easy Being Arrested for Illegal Travel to Cuba," July 31, 2009, 5:16 P.M. http://www.moon.com/blogs/cuba-costa-rica/its-not-easy-being-arrested-illegal-travel-cuba.

127. "US Treasury OFAC Has 6 Times More Personnel on Cuba than Bin Laden," *Havana Journal*, May 2004.

128. David Ivanovich, "OFAC More Focused on Cuba than BayOil Case or Terrorism Funding," *Houston Chronicle*, Washington Bureau, February 26, 2006.

129. Schoultz, *That Infernal Little Cuban Republic*, p. 526. Incidents about a 75-year-old retired Wisconsin woman fined for travel to Cuba and a group of scuba divers on a charter boat who were all threatened with thousands of dollars in fines. The 2004 OFAC letter revealed that over $8 million were collected in embargo violation fines since 1994, and over 10,683 "enforcement investigations" opened since 1990. www.history of cuba.com.

130. Under Torricelli and Helms-Burton Acts the requirements tightened, see later.

131. Diéguez, *Blockade*, p. 107.

132. Ibid., p. 108.

133. Franklin, *Cuba and the United States*, p. 67. Canada immediately refuses, the others vacillated but continue to try and appease US demands while maintaining relations with Cuba.

134. Kelly Knaub, "The Cuban Adjustment Act 44 Years Later," *Havana Times*, May 15, 2010.

135. http://cubantriangle.blogspot.com/2010/12/federal-benefits-are-safe-and.html.

136. Interview with author, September 2011.

137. Knaub, "The Cuban Adjustment."

138. Interview with author, September 2011. One of the most famous rafters was Elian Gonzalez.

139. Schoultz, *That Infernal Little Cuban Republic*, p. 471.

140. This incident can be found at http://www.cubasocialista.com/adjust1.htm; anyone interviewing in Havana will easily find similar stories.

141. Interview with author, September, 2011.

142. Smith, *Closest of Enemies*. Speculation from Nelson Valdes is that the CIA took the first boats over to pick up Cubans from Mariel, which prompted the Cuban-Americans to follow suit and precipitated the crisis.

143. Amnesty International, *Annual Report, 1975–1976*, London, p. 54.

144. Schoultz, *That Infernal Little Cuban Republic*, p. 456.

145. Smith, *Closest of Enemies*, p. 243.

146. This included the CIA working with the Mafia on the various attempts to assassinate Castro in the early 1960s, as well as such plans as the Cuba Project and Operation Mongoose, state-sponsored terrorist programs. Described in Lamar Waldron, *Watergate the Hidden History*, Counterpoint, Berkeley, 2012.

147. Interview with author, September 2011.

148. Schoultz, *That Infernal Little Cuban Republic*, p. 437.

149. For total funding, see the NED website and annual reports, beginning in 1984. www.ned.org.

150. Jean-Guy Allard, *Corruption in Radio-TV Marti: Director Pedro Roig Submits his Resignation*, September 9, 2010.

151. Ann Louise Bardach and Larry Rohter, "Key Cuban Foe Claims Exile's Backing," *NY Times*, July 12, 1998, p. 10.

152. Schoultz, *That Infernal Little Cuban Republic*, p. 521.

153. See Jean-Guy Allard, http://machetera.wordpress.com/2009/09/18/meet-pepe-hernandez-canfs-terrorist-president/.

154. Chomsky, *A History of the Cuban Revolution*, p. 58.

155. Described during author interview with film documentarian Marina Ocoha, 2008.

156. Interview with author, February 2011.

157. USAID program aimed at Cuban young, through cell phone texting and other methods; see chapter four.

158. Schoultz, *That Infernal Little Cuban Republic*, pp. 428–429.

159. Ibid., p. 425.

160. Ibid., p. 432.

161. Ibid., p. 461.

162. Ibid., p. 556.

163. Alarcón and Alvarez, *Blockade*, p. 31.

164. Schoultz, *That Infernal Little Cuban Republic*, pp. 451, 464.

165. *Cuba vs Bloqueo*, July 2011 Report by Cuba on resolution 65/6 of the UN General Assembly. "Necessity of ending the economic, commercial and financial blockade imposed by the United States against Cuba" (p. 83). This includes losses due to US cruise ships not being able to visit Cuba.

166. Ann Louise Bardach, *Cuba Confidential*, Vintage, 2003, p. 132.

167. www.progresoweekly.com/index.php?progreso=Jane_F (August 2006). According to historian Jane Franklin, citing a newspaper report by J. Scott Orr (Newark, NJ, *Star-Ledger*, November 24) that Torricelli talked with President

Fidel Castro one night "from 8 p.m. until 2:30 a.m." Orr noted that in "touring Cuba during the trip," Torricelli found living conditions "quite good compared to other Latin American nations." Torricelli said, "Living standards are not high, but the homelessness, hunger and disease that is witnessed in much of Latin America does not appear evident." Torricelli lost his congressional position over corruption charges in 2003.

168. Nestor Nunez, "Economic Blockade Attempts to Turn Cuba into US Colony," *Cuban News Agency*, 2010.

169. Diéguez, *Blockade*, p. 200.

170. http://www.cubatravelusa.com/history_of_cuban_embargo.htm.

171. Canadian nickel mine company Sherritt Gordon President Ian Delany and his family were one of the first affected, prohibited from entering the United States under the regulations.

172. Schoultz, *That Infernal Little Cuban Republic*, p. 484.

173. Ibid. The new law, like the other US measures seeking to change the political situation in Cuba, poses serious questions regarding whether or not Helms-Burton violates basic principles of international law. A fundamental principle of international law is territorial sovereignty, i.e., each nation is sovereign and so has the right to exercise jurisdiction and control over matters within its territory. From its inception, territorial sovereignty has been derived from three broad principles: (1) all states are formally equal; (2) no state may legally interfere in the purely internal affairs of another state; and (3) territory and jurisdiction are coextensive. Walker, *A Manual of Public International Law* (1984). There are two other important concepts related to territorial jurisdiction: (1) territorial integrity, which gives a state the right to demand that other states refrain from committing acts that violate the independence or territorial supremacy of that state; and (2) nonintervention, which requires that a state not interfere with the internal or external affairs of another state. A state may thus make laws that pertain to persons and activities within its territory and with which no other state may interfere (note: "The Cuban Democracy Act: Another Extraterritorial Act That Won't Work," *Brooklyn Journal of International Law*, v. 20 [1994], pp. 397–442). Helms-Burton would appear to violate these principles as well as the United Nations' Declaration on Principles of International Law (Declaration) concerning friendly relations and cooperation among states called for in the charter of the United Nations. The Declaration, which was adopted by the General Assembly in 1970, prohibits a state from using or encouraging the use of economic, political, or any other type of measures to coerce another state in order to obtain from it the subordination of the exercise of its sovereign rights and to secure from it advantages of any kind.

174. Canada instituted the Foreign Extraterritorial Measures Act specifying that any judgment from the measure "shall not be recognized or enforceable in any manner in Canada." It did nothing to prevent subsidiaries of US companies to stop doing business with Cuba. Schoultz, *That Infernal Little Cuban Republic*, p. 493.

175. Peter Dale Scott, *Jose Basulto Leon: Background*, in Lisa Pease's Real History Archives (http://www.webcom.com/~lpease), February 1996.

176. Gott, *Cuba: A New History*, pp. 304–306. Basulto was in another plane, and escaped. The controversy remains where the planes were shot down, but evidence shows they had been over Havana airspace. New evidence from book by Brazilian researcher Fernando Morais, *The Last Soldiers of the Cold War*, suggests testimony that the planes were shot down in international waters was

given from a source linked with CANF: "Evidence against the Cuban Five Found to be Biased," *Prensa Latina*, October 27, 2011.

177. Alarcón and Alvarez, *Blockade*, p. 36.

178. Ibid., p. 37.

179. http://thinkexist.com/quotation/farewell-fidel-that-s-the-message-of-this-bill/589400.html.

180. Eric Bates, *What You Need to Know about Jesse Helms*, Mother Jones, May/June 1995.

181. Steve Clemons, "Rep. Dan Burton to Support End to Cuba Travel Ban," *The Washington Note*, March 22, 2007.

182. Percy Francisco, *Confessions of Fraile*, Capitan San Luis, Havana, 2004.

183. Stephen Kimber's forthcoming book on the Five, *What Lies Across the Water*, asserts the FBI had known the agents for a few years, and the Cuban information did not reveal their identities, only confirmed their activities.

184. http://www.thecuban5.org/wordpress/the-case/: Opinions adopted by the Working Group on Arbitrary Detention, OPINION No. 19/2005, pp. 60–65. http://www.ohchr.org/english/bodies/chr/docs/62chr/E.CN.4.2006.7.Add.1.pdf.

185. Anne Louise Bardach and Larry Rohter, "Key Cuba Foe Claims Exile's Backing," *NY Times*, July 12, 1998, p. 10.

186. http://caselaw.lp.findlaw.com/data/constitution/amendment01/13.html.

187. http://www.counterpunch.org/2010/09/17/the-confessions-of-roger-noriega/.

188. For details of how the commission will deal with all aspects of Cuban society, see http://www.cfr.org/cuba/commission-assistance-free-cuba-report-president/p11093.

189. Perez Jr., *Cuba between Reform and Revolution*, p. 328.

190. Bolivarian Alliance for the Peoples of Our America (ALBA) is Latin America's answer to the European Union. The concept to provide financial, social, and political assistance to the Latin and Caribbean countries as a counterweight to US influence.

191. Patricia Gross, *Cuba Never Asked to Attend Summit of the Americas*, IPS, March 9, 2012.

192. China is investing increasing amounts in Cuba's infrastructure-, tourism-, and energy-based industries, and the regime leaders have expressed serious interest in augmenting its economic contacts.

193. Perez Jr., *Cuba in the American Imagination*, p. 247.

194. Arturo López-Levy, "'Chaos and Instability': Human Rights and U.S. Policy Goals in Cuba," NACLA Report on the Americas September/October 2011, p. 16.

195. Perez Jr., *Cuba in the American Imagination*, p. 247.

196. Ibid., p. 248.

197. Ibid., p. 242.

3   Siege and Society

1. Lars Schoultz, *That Infernal Little Cuban Republic*, University of North Carolina Press, 2009, p. 552.

2. Author interviews with William Soler patients, parents, and staff, September 2011.

3. The State Department lists hospitals denied, but do not offer explanations as to why. No Cuban official spoken to could offer an explanation.

4. http://www.msnbc.msn.com/id/34277833/ns/world_news-americas/t/embargo-genocide-us-cuba-spar-over-it.
5. Randal C. Archibold, "Cuba Takes Lead Role in Haiti's Cholera Fight," *New York Times*, November 7, 2011.
6. http://killinghope.org/bblum6/aer94.html#note-7.
7. *Cuba vs Bloqueo*, 2010 Report by Cuba on Resolution 64/6 of the UN General Assembly, "Necessity of Ending the Economic, Commercial and Financial Embargo Imposed by the United States against Cuba": www.cubavsbloqueo.cu.
8. http://www.lawg.org/action-center/78-end-the-travel-ban-on-cuba/935-un-cuba-vote-happy-20th-anniversary.
9. Mark Lemstra, "Cuba's Health Results Better at Fraction of Cost," *Star Phoenix*, September 29, 2011.
10. José A. De la Osa, "50 Years of Immunization in Cuba," *Granma*, February 10, 2011.
11. http://www.letcubalive.org/CU_Apr11.html.
12. The manipulation of visas continues, with a number of Cuban scholars denied entry into the United States to attend the Latin American Studies Association conference in San Francisco in May 2012.
13. Ecuador agreed to purchase $1-billion worth of products in 2011: http://www.cubastandard.com/2011/08/15/ecuador-buying-up-to-1–5bln-of-cuban-medicine/.
14. "Cuba's Molecular Immunology Center Increases Exports," *Prensa Latina*, Havana, January 16, 2012.
15. "Cuba to Test New AIDS Vaccine on Humans," *Viet Nam News*, AFP, March 6, 2012.
16. *Cuba vs. Bloqueo*, Report by Cuba on Resolution 65/6 of the UN General Assembly, "Necessity of Ending the Economic, Commercial and Financial Embargo Imposed by the United States against Cuba," July 2011, p. 66: www.cubavsbloqueo.cu.
17. Ibid., p. 70.
18. Ibid., p. 72
19. Ricardo Alarcón and Miguel Álvarez, *Blockade: The United States Economic War against Cuba*, Editora Política, La Habana, 2001, pp. 4–6.
20. http://www.penultimosdias.com/wp-content/uploads/2011/06/TWOF-01_WelcomeDrCondoleezzaRice.pdf.
21. There is growing discontent with the aftermath of revolution in Egypt, with complaints of no change, military control, and the same old corruption ("Egypt: A Revolution without Justice," *Toronto Star*, November 20, 2011). One of the complaints in Egypt has been that the new authorities did not act ruthlessly enough against the old regime.
22. Interview with author, February 2011.
23. Ibid.
24. Interview given on condition of anonymity.
25. Ibid.
26. http://www.internationalviewpoint.org/article.php3?id_article=1052.
27. Interview with author, September 2011.
28. Ibid.
29. Declaration of the First National Congress for Education and Culture, 1971.
30. David Craven, *Art and Revolution in Latin America, 1910–1990*, second edn, Yale University Press, London, 2006, p. 75.

31. Ignacio Ramonet, *My Life Fidel Castro*, Allen Lane, England, 2007.
32. Donald G. McNeil, Jr., "Cuba's Fortresses against a Viral Foe," *New York Times*, May 7, 2012.
33. http://en.wikipedia.org/wiki/El_Diario_de_la_MarinaCite reference
34. See Geoffrey R. Stone, *Perilous Times*, W.W. Norton & Company, Inc, New York, 2004, for similar US examples, including the *New York Times*, vilified and threatened with legal action after running extensive excerpts from Wikileaks, many touching on foreign relations matters. Historically the American example occurred when President John Adams shut down a dozen newspapers during the Alien and Sedition Acts of 1798, the legislation giving him near dictatorial powers.
35. Peter Orsi, "Cubans Test Official Limits on Criticism," *Associated Press*, October 24, 2011.
36. Aviva Chomsky, *A History of the Cuban Revolution*, Wiley-Blackwell, United Kingdom, 2011, p. 128, note 45.
37. John McAuliff, "Counterproductive Contradictions Undermine US Policy on Cuba," *Havana Note*, March 22, 2011.
38. http://web.gc.cuny.edu/dept/bildn/publications/documents/Font4_000.pdf. An extensive examination of the Battle of Ideas can be found in the report.
39. Pascal Fletcher, "Singer Pablo Milanés Urges More Freedom in Cuba," *Reuters*, August 14, 2011.
40. http://groups.yahoo.com/group/CubaNews/message/112481.
41. Luis Sexto, "Church Magazine re Freedom of Expression," *Progresso Weekly*, February 10, 2011.
42. Bartolomé Sancho Morey, "Pablo Milanés: Freedom Democracy and Racism," *Rebelión*, September 2011 at: http://www.walterlippmann.com/docs3256.html.
43. www.nationalreview.com/nrd/article/?q=NzdkZTFmMjY4YzQxN2RhOTM0MDgzMWNlYzlkZTQ0NjE=.
44. Orsi, "Cubans Test Official Limits."
45. Havana Note: www.havananote.com, 2011.
46. From *Huffington Post* article "La Alborada," October 26, 2011: http://www.huffingtonpost.com.
47. Salim Lamrani, Conversations with Cuban blogger Yoani Sánchez, April 30, 2010: http://www.rebelion.org/noticia.php?id=104205. Photos of her injuries, which Yoani said she had, were never released.
48. She even appealed to Brazilian President Dilma to assist in getting her permission to leave in order to attend a documentary on Cuba's free press: http://www.cubagreenscreen.com/forum/showthread.php?tid=14903.
49. Ibid.
50. http://ajiacomix.wordpress.com.
51. Margarita Alarcón, "Censorship is a Two Way Street," *Cubadebate*, January 2010.
52. Marjorie Cohn, "Puerto Rican Political Prisoner Carlos Alberto Tores Released Today After 30 Years," *Z Magazine*, November 2010, p. 6.
53. Stone, *Perilous Times*, p. 529.
54. A comprehensive overview can be found in the video documentary: Bernie Dwyer and Roberto Ruiz Rebo, *The Day Diplomacy Died*, Two Island Production 2009.
55. Isaac Saney, *Cuba A Revolution in Motion*, Fernwood Publishing, Nova Scotia, 2004.
56. http://www.cubavsbloqueo.cu/Default.aspx?tabid=330.
57. Schoultz, *That Infernal Little Cuban Republic*, p. 532.
58. One of the rationales for continuing to keep Cuba on terrorist list is that they weren't sufficiently supportive of America's war against terrorism.

59. http://ctp.iccas.miami.edu/JCason.htm. Cason is now mayor of Coral Gabels in Florida and connected with antirevolution organization Cuban Transition Project.
60. http://realcuba.wordpress.com/2012/04/02/illusions-told-as-forecasts/.
61. Saul Landau, *Progresso Weekly*, http://www.zcommunications.org/confessions-of-roger-noriega-muscular-diplomacy-or-law-breaking-by-saul-landau.
62. Dwyer and Ruiz Rebo, *The Day Diplomacy Died*.
63. Ibid.
64. Saul Landau, *Progresso Weekly*, http://www.zcommunications.org/confessions-of-roger-noriega-muscular-diplomacy-or-law-breaking-by-saul-landau (Noriega).
65. Ibid.
66. Dwyer and Ruiz Rebo, *The Day Diplomacy Died*.
67. Wayne S. Smith, *New Cuba Commission Report: Formula for Continued Failure*, Center for International Policy, July 10, 2006.
68. Dwyer and Ruiz Rebo, *The Day Diplomacy Died*.
69. Sec. 321 of the Antiterrorism and Effective Death Penalty Act of 1996, (Pl 104–132, 110 Stat. 1214), June 3, 1996.
70. Schoultz, *That Infernal Little Cuban Republic*, p. 538, note 59.
71. Taken from: Salim Lamrain, *U.S. Diplomacy and Cuban Dissidence*, March 15, 2011: http://www.zcommunications.org/zspace/salimlamrani.
72. Ibid.
73. His death turned into another example of the siege against information as various antirevolutionary elements tried to propose the accident was caused by government agents. A thorough investigation showed it was the result of the driver, a former right-wing politican from Spain, speeding on a broken section of highway. Claims were made that the Spaniard was in Cuba giving financial aid to Paya. "Truth and Reason," *Granma*, July 31, 2012.
74. Schoultz, *That Infernal Little Cuban Republic*, p. 550.
75. Ibid.
76. Interview with author, February 2012.
77. http://www.oswaldopaya.org/es/up/VARELA%20PROJECT.pdf.
78. http://www.thefreelibrary.com/Elizardo+Sanchez.
79. Ladies in White counterpart are the wives of the Cuban Five, who have traveled internationally promoting their cause to have their husbands released from US jail.
80. "Cuba 'Ladies in White' Protest Blocked in Havana," BBC, September 2011.
81. "Disidente cubana teme que pueda ser encarcelada," *El Nuevo Herald*, May 21, 2008. Tracey Eaton, "Factions Spar Over U.S. Aid for Cuba," *The Houston Chronicle*, December 18, 2010.
82. Schoultz, *That Infernal Little Cuban Republic*, p. 536.
83. See note 68.
84. http://www.zcommunications.org/u-s-diplomacy-and-cuban-dissidence-by-salim-lamrani.
85. Jean-Guy Allard, *Cuban "Ladies in White" Suspect Recently Deceased Leader of Embezzling $20,000*, October, 28, 2011.
86. Lorraine Bayard de Volo, "Heroines With Friends in High Places: Cuba's Damas de Blanco," NACLA Report on the Americas September/October 2011, p. 20.
87. Pawns of the Empire documentary; see also http://knightcenter.utexas.edu/blog/cuba-reveals-dissident-journalist-fact-was-government-agent.

88. "A Daughter's grief," *Cuban Triangle*, Thursday, October 20, 2011. Posted at: http://cubantriangle.blogspot.com/.
89. "Fidel Castro Defends Treatment of Dead Dissident," *Latin America Herald Tribune*: http://laht.com/article.asp?CategoryId=14510&ArticleId=353106.
90. "Cuba's Response to Dissident Death," *Granma*, May 10, 2011.
91. Médico asegura que Juan Wilfredo Soto murió por causas naturales y no por una paliza de la Policía cubana: http://www.europapress.es/internacional /noticia-cuba-medico-asegura-juan-wilfredo-soto-murio-causas-naturales-no-paliza-policia-cubana-201105092010.
92. http://cubajournal.blogspot.com/2010/11/real-guillermo-farinas-who-pays-for-his.html from Salim Lamrani article, November 2010.
93. http://www.ddcuba.com/opinion/58-opinion/2108-el-oportunismo-de-la-iglesia.html.
94. http://213.251.145.96/cable/2009/04/09HAVANA221.html. "Jonathan D. Farrar, The U.S. and the Role of the Opposition in Cuba," United States Interests Section, April 9, 2009, cable 09HAVANA221. Jean-Guy Allard wrote: "Dissidents don't have much resonance in Cuba, Despite all the political, economic, media and financial resources dedicated to the Cuban opposition, it has always lacked any popular base."
95. Known as Peterson-Moran bill Representatives Collin Peterson (D-MN) and Jerry Moran (R-KS).
96. Will Weissert, "Cuban Dissidents Cheer Bill to End US Travel Ban," Associated Press, June 11, 2010; Letter from Members of Cuba's Civil Society to the U.S. Congress, June 9, 2011
97. Zoe Valdés, *De la disidencia vendepatria*, June 11, 2010: http://zoevaldes. net/.
98. Cuba Triangle, June 2010: http://cubantriangle.blogspot.com/2010_06_01 _archive.html.
99. http://www.elnuevoherald.com/2010/06/12/740297/carta-de-disidentes -crea-fuerte.html.
100. http://www.bbc.co.uk/blogs/mundo/cartas_desde_cuba/2011/06/la _conspiracion_catolico-comun.html#more.
101. http://www.elnuevoherald.com/2011/05/27/950264/ex-presos-cubanos-protestan-por.html.
102. http://www.europapress.es/latam/cuba/noticia-cuba-denuncian-deten-cion-cuatro-ex-presos-cubanos-protestaban-madrid-ministerio-exteriores-20120523115509.html.
103. Jean-Guy Allard, *Comíamos mejor en Cuba: ex presos cubanos en España protestan y "El País" de repente no ve nada.* http://contrainjerencia.com/index. php/?p=21096, June 27, 2011.
104. Valentina Cifuentes, "Cubans Jailed for Handing Out Flyers?" *Reuters*, May 31, 2011: http://www.ntn24.com/news/news/cubans-jailed-handing -out-flyers.
105. http://www.brainyquote.com/quotes/quotes/d/dwightdei149095.html.
106. Juan Antonio Blanco, with Medea Benjamin, "Cuba: Talking About Revolution," *Ocean Press*, Melbourne, Australia, 1994, p. 65.
107. "The Mex Files: Our Man in Havana," Posted by Cuba Journal at February 7, 2011 http://cubajournal.blogspot.com/2011/02/mex-files-our-man-in-havana .html.
108. http://tinyurl.com/yab3vqc.

109. "Actions Against the Independence and Territorial Integrity of the State." In accordance with Article 91 of the Cuban Penal Code.
110. Leslie Clark, "U.S. Rejects Conviction of Contractor by Cuba, Demands His Release," *Miami Herald*, March 13, 2011: http://www.miamiherald. com/2011/03/12/v-print/2112694/us-rejects-conviction-of-contractor. html#ixzz1GUObbEBa.
111. http://www.usaid.gov/locations/latin_america_caribbean/country/cuba.
112. Fulton Armstrong, "Time to Clean Up U.S. Regime-Change Programs in Cuba," *Miami Herald*, December 25, 2011: www.miamiherald.com/2011/12/25/v-fullstory/2559755/time-to-clean-up-us-regime-change.html#storylink=cpy.
113. Ibid.
114. Tracy Eaton, "Along The Malecón": http://alongthemalecon.blogspot.com/, wrote December 3, 2010: "I Met With a Leader of Cuba's Jewish Community over the Summer and She Knew Nothing of Gross."
115. http://pennyforyourthoughts2.blogspot.com/2011/03/curious-case-of-alan -gross-his-usaid.html.
116. Desmond Butler, *Associated Press*, "USAID Contractor Work in Cuba Detailed," Atlanta Journal Constitution, February 2, 2012.
117. Tom Diemer, "White House Condemns Prosecution of American Alan Gross in Cuba," *Huffington Post*: http://www.politicsdaily.com/2011/02/05 /white-house-condemns-prosecution-of-american-alan-gross-in-cuba.
118. "Ros-Lehtinen Condemns Cuba's Sentencing of Alan Gross, Demands Release of All Wrongly Imprisoned in Cuba," Press Release, House Foreign Affairs Committee, U.S. House of Representatives, Ileana Ros-Lehtinen, Chairman, March 12, 2011: foreignaffairs.house.gov/press_display.asp?id=2115.
119. Debbie Wasserman-Schultz, "Opposing View on Cuba: Don't Reward Atrocities," *USA Today*, September 26, 2010.
120. Philip Peters, "US-Cuba Policy Needs Dose of Common Sense," *Miami Herald*, March 16, 2011.
121. "Cuba Should Finally Release Alan Gross," *Washington Post* Editorial Board, December 31, 2011.
122. Andres Oppenheimer, "Obama Unlikely to Make New Gestures to Cuba without Action from Havana," *Miami Herald*, March 23, 2011.
123. http://archive.constantcontact.com/fs002/1101822053869/archive /1108334620504.html.
124. www.washingtonpost.com/politics/wife-american-contractor-imprisoned-in-cuba-since-2009.
125. Desmond Butler, *Associated Press*, "USAID Contractor Work in Cuba Detailed," Atlanta Journal Constitution, February 2, 2012.
126. MONTGOMERY COUNTY, Md. (WJZ), May 10, 2012.
127. http://www.cubaupdate.org/cuba-update/us-cuba/162-mhphil-peters-us -cuba-policy-needs-dose-of-common-sense.
128. Interview with author, September 2011.
129. Along the Malecon, June 1, 2012. http://along the malecon.blogspot.com.
130. ALBA expels USAID from member countries: http://venezuelanalysis.com /news/7069.
131. "Jailed U.S. Citizen Alan Gross: I Would Return to Cuba if They Let Me Visit My Mother before She Dies," *CNN* The Situation Room with Wolf Blitzer, May 4, 2012.
132. www.cubaheadlines.com/2011/10/10/34163.

133. "Clinton: No Concessions to Free American in Cuba," *Associated Press*, February 29, 2012.

134. Interview with author, January 2012.

135. Kelly Knaub, "The Cuban Adjustment Act 44 Years Later," *Havana Times*, May 15, 2010. Dan Erikson, author of *Cuba Wars*, Bloomsbury Press, New York, 2008.

136. Damien Cave, *Americans and Cubans Still Mired in Distrust*, *The New York Times*, September 15, 2011.

137. Interview with author, 2011.

138. Saney, *Cuba: A Revolution in Motion*, Fernwood, p. 179.

139. http://latinofoxnews.com/latino/news/2012/05/21/cuba-mystery-over-undersea-internet-cable.

140. Andrea Rodriguez, *Cuba High Speed Internet: Mystery Shrouds Fate of Internet Cable*, AP, Jay 21, 2012.

141. http://www.havanatimes.org/?p=48196.

142. Manuel Alberto Ramy, Internet: "Theres no political obstacle," ramymanuel@yahoo.com, February 8, 2011.

143. Linares said there is no ban on direct Internet service to individuals, Gerardo Arreola | The Day | 27/10/2010 www.kaosenlared.net / news / admin-Arreola Havana, October 26.

144. Surfing the Net in Havana La Alborada, August 29 from Wikileaks document http://213.251.145.96/cable/2009/04/09HAVANA221.html. "Jonathan D. Farrar, The U.S. and the Role of the Opposition in Cuba," US Interests Section, April 9, 2009, cable 09HAVANA221.

145. http://alongthemalecon.blogspot.com/2011/10/talking-and-even-screaming-about-text.html;http://articles.latimes.com/2011/oct/24/opinion/la-ed-cuba-20111024.

146. Juan O. Tamayo, "Cyber Commandos Spill Phone Numbers of Top Cuban Officials," *Miami Herald*, November 26, 2011.

147. http://www.miamiherald.com/2011/11/26/v-fullstory/2519901/cyber-comma...phone-numbers.html#ixzz1erTJBJ00.

148. For detailed examination of Internet in Cuba, see http://www.travelblog.org/Central-America-Caribbean/Cuba/Oeste/La-Habana/blog-219325.htm.

149. http://www.ohchr.org/en/udhr/pages/introduction.aspx.

150. Arturo López-Levy, "'Chaos and Instability': Human Rights and U.S. Policy Goals in Cuba," NACLA Report on the Americas September/October 2011, page 16

151. EXTRA, February 2012.

152. Ibid., p. 1.

153. Marc Bossuyt, "The Adverse Consequences of Economic Sanctions on the Enjoyment of Human Rights," Working Paper prepared for the Commission On Human Rights, Sub-Commission on the Promotion and Protection of Human Rights. UN Doc. E/CN.4/Sub.2/2000/33, Geneva: UN Economic and Social Council, June 21, 2000, para 98–100.

154. "Arabs Will Decide Who Governs," *Toronto Star*, November 19, 2011.

155. James Peck, *Ideal Illusions*, Metropolitan Books, New York, 2010, p. 97, note 111.

156. Arnold August, *Democracy in Cuba & the 1997–98 Elections*, Canada Cuba Distribution, 1999.

157. Interview with author, December 2011.

158. Henry Louis Taylor, Jr., Inside El Barrio, Kumarian Press, VA, 2009.
159. Interview with author, December 2011.
160. Chomsky, *History of the Cuban Revolution*, p. 129, note 47.
161. Julia E. Sweig, *CUBA What Everyone Needs to Know*, Oxford University Press, 2009, p. 45.
162. http://www.independent.co.uk/news/world/americas/the-castropedia-fidels-cuba-in-facts-and-figures-432478.html.
163. Hugo Azcuy, "Estado y sociedad civil in Cuba," *Temas* 4, 1995.
164. George Lambie, *The Cuban Revolution in the 21st Century*, Pluto Press, London, 2010, p. 164.
165. Interview with author, 2011.
166. Jesús Arboleya Cervera, *Progreso Weekly*, August 10, 2011.
167. Chomsky, *History of the Cuban Revolution*, p. 126, Blanco talking about the revolution.
168. Ibid., p. 127.
169. Ibid.
170. From International Socialist Review, CUBA: Image and Reality: http://www.isreview.org/issues/51/cuba_image&reality.shtml; http://groups.yahoo.com/group/DemocraticLeft/message/23982. Is there "direct democracy," or any democracy, in Cuba?
171. Jeff Franks, *Raúl Castro Defends One-Party System as Bulwark against U.S. Imperialism*, Havana, January 29, 2012.
172. Prensa Latina, *Single Party System Guarantees Sovereignty, Raúl Castro Says*, January 30, 2012.
173. Bush Jr's still controversial 2000 election, increase in voter identification laws in states such as Wisconsin, South Carolina, Indiana, aimed at poor and black voters critics claim.
174. Susie Madrak, *Change Only Comes When People Organize and Fight from Outside the System*, November 28, 2011. This is from an interview with Bill Moyers on Richard Heffner's PBS show "The Open Mind."

4   The Political Economics of Siege

1. Interview with author, 2011.
2. Michael Miller, "Cuba Owes U.S. $7 Billion for 'Forgotten' Property Claims, Lawyers Propose 10% User Fee," *Miami New Times*, March 16, 2012.
3. Isaac Saney, *Cuba A Revolution in Motion*, Fernwood, Nova Scotia, 2004, p. 160.
4. *Cuba vs. Bloqueo*, Report by Cuba on Resolution 65/6 of the UN General Assembly, "Necessity of Ending the Economic, Commercial and Financial Embargo Imposed by the United States against Cuba," July 2011: www.cubavsbloqueo.cu.
5. Ibid.
6. Ibid.
7. See chapter three in this volume.
8. Jay Weaver and Tere Figueras Negrete, "Castro Victims Awarded $91 Million," *Miami Herald*, November 28, 2006.
9. Robert Sandels, "Cuba, Claims and Confiscations": www.counterpunch.org, October 27, 2007.

10. Juan O. Tamayo, "Cuban Bank Deposits Abroad Plummet from $5.65 to $2.8 Billion," *Miami Herlad*, July 31, 2012.

11. Rafael Lorente and Tamara Lytle, "Cuban Exile Leaders Choose Political Friends," *Florida Sun Sentinel Washington Bureau*, June 18, 2000. The report estimated $1 million in donations in the past 20 years.

12. Jean-Guy Allard, "A 10 000 dólares la mesa, se reúnen los mayores patrocinadores del odio a Cuba," December 19, 2010.

13. http://cubamoneyproject.org/.

14. Interview with author, January 2012.

15. "USAID Shields Freedom House," March 25, 2012. Alongthemaleconblogspot. com.

16. Juan O. Tamayo, "After a Day-Long Bustle, U.S. Funds for Cuba Programs were Partially Freed," *The Miami Herald*, July 29, 2011.

17. "Where Did the $45 Million Dollars for 'Democracy in Cuba' Go?" Cubajournalblogspot.com, April 8, 2010.

18. Ibid.

19. Ibid.

20. Request for Proposals: To Expand Cuban Civic Participation and Leadership in Social Relationships and Independent Civil Society Groups, found at website current as of February 2012: http://www.devex.com/en/projects/request-for-proposals-for-programs-to-support-democracy-human-rights-and-labor-in-cuba.

21. From Tracey Eaton's website, cubamoneyproject.org, October 2011. Nine companies won more than $8.6 million in Cuba grants in September, federal records show.

22. http://www.latimes.com/news/opinion/opinionla/la-ed-cuba-20111024, 0,3770098.story.

23. For complete details, see http://cubamoneyproject.org/?p=1467.

24. Five agents arrested in Florida on conspiracy to spy charges, sentenced to long jail terms, and subject of international movement to free them based on the irregularities of the case.

25. Abby Goodnough, "U.S. Paid 10 journalists for Anti-Castro Reports," September 2006. See also http://www.pslweb.org/reporters-for-hire. "Let's Not Confuse U.S. Propaganda With Journalism," *Miami Herald*, September 13, 2006.

26. Wilfredo Cancio Isla, "Cuba Used Hallucinogens to Train its Spies," *El Nuevo Herald*, June 4, 2001.

27. Salim Lamrani, "Reporters Without Borders' Lies About Cuba," Global Research July 2, 2009: http://www.globalresearch.ca/index.php?context=va&aid=14202.

28. Cubannews/ycr/13:21/map/ amp 14:35 www.cubanews.ain.cu.

29. Interview with author, 2012.

30. Lars Schoultz, *That Infernal Little Cuban Republic*, University of North Carolina Press, 2009, p. 547.

31. "Snowplowing in Havana?" April 7, 2011: http://alongthemalecon.blogspot. ca/2011/04/snowplowing-in-havana.html. D&M Snowplowing, which shows an address of 11 Bowers Street in Massena, New York, has also received government contracts for snow removal.

32. Schoultz, *That Infernal Little Cuban Republic*, p. 547.

33. "More Details on $18 Million in Cuba Grants," October 28, 2011: cubamoneyproject.org/?p=3369.

34. Ibid.

35. See chapter two in this volume. Also: afrocubaweb.com/canf.htm;; http://amy-holguin.blogspot.com/2011/07/corrupt-ex-director-of-radio-tv-marti.html.

36. "More Details on $18 Million in Cuba Grants."

37. www.miamiherald.com/2011/12/17/2551467_us-defends-34m-grant-to-cuba.html#storylink=addthis.

38. Tracey Eaton, "Former Bush Aide Expected to Finish Jail Term This Month," July 9, 2011: http://alongthemalecon.blogspot.ca/2011/07/former-bush-aide-expected-to-finish.html.

39. Lizette Alvarez, "Florida Senator Denies Claim he Gilded His Family History," *St. Petersburg Times*, October 20, 2011.

40. http://www.libreonline.com/home/index.php?option=com_content&view=article&id=18063:dialogo-con-antunez-y-soler-desde-cuba-en-cumbre-de-libertad-el-senador-rubio-da-apoyo-a-los-opositores&catid=19&Itemid=29.

41. Dawn Gable, "Congressman Díaz-Balart Seeks to Punish Cuban-Americans," *Havana Times*, June 24, 2011. The amendment would return to Bush-era restrictions of requiring specific license for family travel, limit travel to every three years, and limit remittances.

42. http://Cubacentral.wordpress.com/2012/06/01/deportations-for-visiting-cuba.

43. See chapter three in this volume.

44. "Who are the Democratic Party's Gang of 66," July 30, 2007: http://cubajournal.blogspot.com/2007/07/who-are-democratic-partys-gang-of-66.html.

45. Ibid.

46. www.democraticunderground.com/discuss/duboard.php?az=view_all&address=389x3035179. Wayne Smith, "The Only Ones Hurt by the Amendment's Defeat are American Farmers," March 2008.

47. "638 Ways to Kill Castro," Chanel 4 documentary directed by Dollan Cannell, 2006.

48. Keith Bolender, *Voices From the Other Side: An Oral History of Terrorism Against Cuba*, Pluto Press, London, 2010.

49. Cuban children's theater directory responds to harsh attack by prominent US Congresswoman, Cuba Debate, October 18, 2011: http://en.cubadebate.cu/news/2011/10/20.

50. http://havanajournal.com/cuban_americans/entry/more-anti-american-behavior-from-ileana-ros-lehtinen-330/.

51. Interview with author, 2011.

52. Barbara Barrett, "Lawmakers Shift on Cuba," *National*, November 16, 2009.

53. Ibid.

54. Ibid.

55. Ibid.

56. Nick Sabloff, "How Cuban American Hard-Liners Influence U.S. Policy With Campaign Donations: Report," *Huffington Post*, March 18, 2010: http://www.huffingtonpost.com/2009/11/16/how-cuban-american-hard.

57. Leslie Clark, "Money Talks: Report Links Donations, Cuba Embargo Support," *McClachy Newspapers*, November 16, 2009.

58. Jim Geraghty, "Torricelli, Menendez Near Top in Donations by Cuban-Americans," *The Record* (New Jersey) Colaboracion Armando F. Mastrapa III, La Nueva Cuba, August 23, 2001; http://www.plenglish.com/index.php?option=com_content&task=view&id=30 . . .

59. "Anti-Cuban Committees Donated More Than $3 Million to Democratic and Republican Party Electoral Campaigns," *Granma International*, July 15, 2011: http://www.granma.cu/ingles/international-i/15julio-Anti-Cuban.html.

60. See this chapter.

61. This was latest in series of legislative attempts to end the travel ban including in 2009 H.R. 874, the "Freedom to Travel to Cuba Act." On February 12, 2009, Senator Byron Dorgan (D-ND) introduced S. 428, entitled the "Freedom to Travel to Cuba Act."

62. http://www.sunshinestatenews.com/story/bid-lift-travel-ban-cuba-stalls-congress.

63. "Nine Corrupt Gang of 66 Democrats Block Tomorrow's Vote on H.R. 4645," *cubajournal*, September 28, 2010 http://cubajournal.blogspot.ca/2010/09/nine-corrupt-gang-of-66-democrats-block.html.

64. William E. Gibson, "Wasserman Schultz Defends Cuba Travel Ban," *Orlando Sentinel*, Washington Bureau, September 27, 2010.

65. Debbie Wasserman-Schultz, "Opposing View on Cuba: Don't Reward Atrocities," *USA Today* editorial, September 26, 2010.

66. Dan Sweeney, "The Wasserman-Schultz Waltz," *Huffinton Post*, June 6, 2008.

67. http://www.miller-mccune.com/politics/cuba-libre-345?article_page=2. Cuba Democracy PAC. In the past two election cycles, Wasserman-Schultz received $22,000 from the committee, and members of the PAC's board of directors gave her another $29,000 in individual contributions, for a total of $51,000. Smith, "The Only Ones Hurt By the Amendment's Defeat": http://www.democraticunderground.com/discuss/duboard.php?az=view_all&address=389x30351.

68. "Wasserman-Schultz Slaps Obama's Cuba Policy," *Florida Sun Sentinel*, February 15, 2011.

69. The 2000 Trade Sanctions Reform and Exportation Enhancement Act. In October 2000 the US Congress passed the Trade Sanctions Reform and Export Enhancement Act (TSRA), which started to relax the enforcement of the economic and trade embargo and allowed the sale of agricultural goods and medicine to Cuba: http://www.treasury.gov/resource-center/sanctions/Programs/Pages/tsra.aspx.

70. Cuba was permitted to buy food from the United States after 2000 when the government started buying after Hurricane Michelle. The largest amount bought was in 2008 at $700 million; it has since diminished by almost 50 percent annually: http://www.cubagreenscreen.com/forum/showthread.php?tid=15227.

71. Wasserman-Schultz Slaps Obama's Cuba Policy.

72. Schoultz, *That Infernal Little Cuban Republic*, p. 510.

73. Winston Galt, "Free Trade with Cuba—The Real Economic Stimulus Plan," March 4, 2009: http://squarewondotorg.wordpress.com/2009/03/04/free-trade-with-cuba-the-real-economic-stimulus-plan/.

74. "After Years of Trying There is Positive Movement on Trade with Cuba," staff report, *Farm Futures*, July 2, 2010: http://farmfutures.com/story.aspx/after-years-of-trying-there-is-positive-movement-on-trade-with-cuba-0-39716.

75. Schoultz, *That Infernal Little Cuban Republic*, p. 510.

76. In a forum early in the 2008 campaign, Senator Obama stated that it was time to end the embargo with Cuba: www.thepoliticalguide.com/Profiles/President/US/Barack_Obama/Views/Cuba/.

77. "US Seeks Additional $4 Million for Cuba Operations," March 1, 2011: cubamoneyproject.org/?p=414.

78. Ibid.
79. Ibid.
80. Interview with author, 2011.
81. Lilliam Riera, "U.S. Blockade Delivers a Blow to Cuban Tourist Industry": www.granma.cu/ingles/cuba-i/21octubre-turisbloqueo.htm.
82. Andrea Rodriguez, "Cuba: Travel Ban Costs US Businesses $1.1B a Year," *Business Week*, December 17, 2009.
83. http://weblogs.sun-sentinel.com/news/politics/dcblog/cuba/.
84. Anya Landau French, "Groundhog Day in Florida: Bill Targets Firms Doing Business with Cuba," *The Havana Note*, March 14, 2012.
85. Doreen Hemlock, "License for Ferry to Cuba Denied," *Florida Sun Sentinel*, March 7, 2012: http://articles.sun-sentinel.com/2012–03–07/news/fl-cuba-ferry-denied-20120307_1_ferry-service-ferries-last-year-communist-led-island.
86. "Direct Maritime Shipments from Miami to Havana Begin," *Havana Note*, July 11, 2012.
87. Lilliam Riera, "U.S. Blockade Delivers a Blow to Cuban Tourist Industry," *Granma*, October 21, 2010.
88. Interview with author, June 2011.
89. http://thehavananote.com/2010/07/dorgan_v_menendez_cuba_travel_1.html.
90. Adam Liptak, "A Wave of the Watch List, and Speech Disappears," *New York Times*, March 4, 2008.
91. Ibid.
92. "Washington Sanctions Cuba Online," *Juventude Rebelde*, March 2011.
93. Julien Neaves, "US Big Stick for Raul," December 6, 2011: http://www.trinidadexpress.com/news/US_BIG_STICK_FOR_RAUL-135145443.html.
94. "Hilton Slammed in Oslo for Cuba Embargo," *Ottawa Recorder*, May 1, 2007 http://www.cubaheadlines.com/hilton_slammed_in_oslo_for_cuba_embargo.html.
95. Andres Zaldívar, *Blockade: The Longest Economic Siege in History*, Capitan San Luis, Havana, 2007, p. 215.
96. "US Fines French Shipping Company for Services to Cuba," *Pensa Latina*, August 2011.
97. "US Seizes UN Health Funds for Cuba," *Prensa Latina*: http://www.cuba-standard.com/2011/03/13/u-s-seizes-un-health-funds-cuba-says/.
98. "Cuba Exposes US Breach of WTO Regulations," *Prensa Latina*, Geneva, January 21, 2012.
99. Zaldívar, *Blockade*, p. 224.
100. Ibid.
101. Marc Frank, "Cuba Struggling to Pay Off Debts . . . Again. Bond Interest Rates at 9%," *Reuters*, June 10, 2009.
102. Duncan Campbell, "Bank Ditches UK Firms Trading With Cuba," *The Guardian*, June 16, 2008.
103. "The Case of Scotia Bank, Dangerous Precedent That Threatens Other Nations," *Granma International*, April 7, 2006: http://www.cubavsbloqueo.cu/Default.aspx?tabid=1258.
104. Abogados de Florida cobran herencias en Cuba, May 14, 2010: http://www.cubaencuentro.com/es/multimedia/videos/abogados-de-florida-cobran-herencias-en-cuba; http://cubantriangle.blogspot.com/2007/10/wills-and-sanctions.html.

105. http://cafefuerte.com/index.php?option=com.

106. "ING Says Could Face Fines Following U.S. Investigation," *Reuters*, July 25, 2011.

107. Andrew Clark, "British Bank Fined for Doing Business With Cuba," Guardian.co.uk, August 16, 2010.

108. Karen Freifeld, "ING to Pay $619 Million over Cuba, Iran Sanctions," *Reuters*, June 12, 2012.

109. Eamon Javers, "JPMorgan to Pay $88 Million for Violating US Sanctions," *CNBC*, August 2011: http://www.cnbc.com/id/44276107.

110. "The U.S. has Confiscated More Than $493 Million in Cuban Funds since 2010," *Prensa Latina*, Havana, April 11, 2012.

111. Zaldívar, *Blockade*, pp. 28–29.

112. Cuba vs. Bloqueo, Report by Cuba on Resolution 65/6 of the United Nations General Assembly, "Necessity of Ending the Economic, Commercial and Financial Embargo Imposed by the United States against Cuba," July 2011: www.cubavsbloqueo.cu.

113. http://www.cubaheadlines.com/2010/10/19/27242/swift_turning_away_cuban_banks.

114. Ibid and through email correspondence with Simon McGuiness, Cuban solidarity group, Ireland, March 2012.

115. Email to author, February 2012.

116. Email to author, March 2012, you tube; By Redaction AHORA / redacc...@ahora.cu / Wednesday, April 27, 2011, 09:07 speech was delivered to a public audience in Liberty Hall, Dublin, on April 2011, on the 50th anniversary of the revolution's triumph over the Bay of Pigs invasion.

117. "German Store Selling Cuban Rum Online Cut Off By PayPal," *ExportLaw*, August 3, 2011: http://www.exportlawblog.com/archives/category/foreign-countermeasurest.

118. http://www.huffingtonpost.com/2009/01/22/wal-marts-entry-into-chil_n_160115.html.

119. Manuel E. Yepe, "How Cuba Could Ease the Oil Crisis": http://www.walterlippmann.com/docs3254.html. Cuba's state oil company Cubapetroleo (Cupet) says the reserves may be four or five times larger.

120. "Cuba's Oil Dreams Take Hit from Failure of First Well, But High-Stakes Gamble Has More Rolls," *Associated Press*, May 27, 2012.

121. http://www.upstreamonline.com/incoming/article1250183.ece.

122. Lawrence Wilkerson, "Oil Drilling in Cuba," the Havana Note, April 2011: http://thehavananote.com/2011/04/hello_washington_anyone_there_.

123. Interview with author, 2012.

124. Leslie Clark, "US Pressures Others Not to Drill for Oil in Cuba," *Miami Herald*, February 3, 2011. Ros-Lehtinen has previously been a strong supporter of drilling for oil in the Gulf, and expressed no concerns for BP's operation prior to the spill.

125. "Cuba Readies to Dive into Offshore Oil Exploration," *Reuters*, July 31, 2010. Why Ros-Lehtinen wants to sabotage Cuba's access to oil reserves, contrainjerencia.com, May 3, 2011.

126. Lesley Clark, "Oil Drilling off Cuba Coast Draws U.S. Foes," *Miami Herald*, February 4, 2011.

127. "Senator Nelson's Better Idea," May 3, 2011: http://cubantriangle.blogspot.ca/2011/05/senator-nelsons-better-idea.html.

128. http://thomas.loc.gov/cgi-bin/query/z?c112:S.405.
129. Tim Padgett, "The Oil Off Cuba: Washington and Havana Dance at Arms Length Over Spill Prevention," *TIME*, January 27, 2012.
130. David Goodhue, "Oil Rig to Drill South of Keys by September," *Miami Herald*, May 20, 2011.
131. Ibid.
132. Clark, "US Pressures Others Not to Drill."
133. Robert Sandels, "An Oil-Rich Cuba?," *Monthly Review*, September 2011: http://monthlyreview.org/2011/09/01/an-oil-rich-cuba.

5   A Changing Cuba—A Stagnant Siege

1. "UN Member States Condemn US Embargo of Cuba for 20th Consecutive Year," *Associated Press*, October 25, 2011.
2. Marce Cameron: cubasocialistrenewal.blogspot.ca/.
3. Cuban officials use this term more than "reform."
4. Cubasocialistrenewal.blogspot.ca/March 1, 2012.
5. José Alejandro Rodríguez, "Cuba's Changes Go Deep," *Progreso Weekly*, August 20, 2011.
6. Chavez told this on Venezuelan television, saying Castro told him in an informal talk. Jeff Franks, "Raul Castro Turns 79 With Eyes on Future," June 4, 2010.
7. Interview by Manual Alberto Ramy, Radio Progreso Alternativa, April 27, 2011.
8. Marc Frank, "Cuban Government to Contract With Private Sector," *Reuters*, November 28, 2011.
9. Shasta Darlington, "Cuba Studying Ways to Allow Residents to Travel Abroad," *CNN*, May 9, 2011.
10. Portia Siegelbaum, "Raul Castro Says Cuban Economy Will Be Tweaked but Remain Socialist," *CBS*, Havana August 1, 2010.
11. http://cubantriangle.blogspot.ca/2011/12/tax-relief-for-entrepreneurs-and-other.html.
12. http://www.lexingtoninstitute.org/library/resources/documents/Cuba/ResearchProducts.
13. http://www.trabajadores.cu/sin_pausa.
14. Damien Cave, "Cubans Can Buy and Sell Property, Government Says," November 3, 2011. Arturo López-Levy, "Houses, Used Cars and Markets: Change Cubans Can Believe In," November 9, 2011. The article explained, "For decades, rigid communist regulation of real estate and car sales created major resentment in Cuba... After a brief interregnum from 1984 to 1988, when Cubans could sell their houses, Fidel Castro cancelled this right arguing that it was fomenting inequalities, creating a class of intermediaries who were capitalizing on transactions, and rewarding the nouveau riche. His characteristic aversion to market mechanisms also exerted a virtual veto against the sale of automobiles acquired after 1959."
15. The permuta allows the buying and selling of homes, a swap accompanied by a payment to compensate who gives up the higher value property. Lawyers ensure all have clear title. A chain of swaps also can result among many buyers and sellers. "In Cuba Houses Never Sale, Just Swap," *Tampa Bay News*, June 2008: http://www.tampabay.com/news/world/article606065.ece.

16. Jeff Franks, "Cuba to Offer Loans to Self-Employed in Latest Reform," *Reuters*, November 2011.

17. Yenia Silva Correa, "Subsidies for Home Construction and Repair to benefit low-income families," *Granma*, January 2012.

18. Ibid.

19. Jose Pertierra report, March 2012.

20. Ibid.

21. Interview with author, September 2011; he declined to give his last name.

22. Richard Feinberg, "Reaching Out: Cuba's New Economy and the International Response," November 2011: http://www.brookings.edu/topics/cuba.aspx. For most Cubans this is their first experience with taxes and filling out income tax forms. Entrepreneurs who hire employees will have to pay a 25 percent payroll tax on their salaries, and all Cubans who are self-employed must allot 25 percent of their income into a social security system from which they will eventually draw a pension.

23. Se extiende a otras actividades modalidad de arrendamiento para trabajadores por cuenta propia: http://www.granma.cubaweb.cu/2011/12/26/nacional/artic10.html.

24. Marc Frank, "In Cuba, Peso Makes a Comeback, Pleasing Customers," *Reuters*, February 1, 2010.

25. "Cuba: Securing the Revolution": http://realcuba.wordpress.com/, March 17, 2012.

26. Andrea Rodriguez, "Cuba Has Given Private Farmers Nearly 2.5M Acres," *Associated Press*, June 25, 2010.

27. Ibid.

28. Elsa Claro, "Agriculture: The Key to the Reform," *Granma*, Wednesday, May 25, 2011.

29. Andrea Rodriguez, "Cuba Authorizes 1,100 Stores Selling Agricultural Inputs," *Associated Press*, October 2010.

30. Yaima Puig Meneses, "Autorizan venta directa de los productores agrícolas a las entidades turísticas," *Granma*, November 21, 2011.

31. http://cubantriangle.blogspot.ca/2012/04/new-pilot-project-cooperatives.html.

32. John O. Tamayo, "Cuba Announces Changes in Health System," *Miami Herald*, June 2, 2011.

33. //www.elnuevoherald.com/2010/10/29/828125.

34. Marc Frank, "Cuba Cracks Down on 'Guayabera' Crime," *Reuters*, May 20, 2011.

35. Ibid.

36. Ibid.

37. Ibid.

38. http://estebanmoralesdominguez.blogspot.ca/.

39. Esteban Morales, "Corruption: The True Counter-Revolution?" April 2010, From the UNEAC website.

40. Interview with author, March 2012.

41. Marce Cameron, "Cuba's Socialist Renewal: Changes under Raul Castro," Direct action.

42. Paul Haven, "Cuba Says Travel Restrictions to Remain in Place," *Associated Press*, December 23, 2011.

43. http://www.cubagreenscreen.com/forum/showthread.php?tid=1338.

44. Haven, "Cuba Says Travel Restrictions to Remain in Place."
45. http://www.cubagreenscreen.com/forum/showthread.php?tid=1338.
46. Haven, "Cuba Says Travel Restrictions to Remain in Place."
47. "Truth about Cuban right to Travel," Communication popular blog, October 2010. The truth is that under Cuban law there is no impediment to leave the country temporarily or permanently. Those interested in leaving the country must apply for their passport at the Immigration and Nationality Directorate and then apply for an exit visa. Given the acute shortage of currency caused by the blockade (which generates a constant trade deficit settled only by the inflow of foreign exchange from tourism), permission for temporary leave is granted to those who really need it for work or other reasons that are really a priority.
48. "Alarcon Announced Immigration Reform Ensures That Will Be Radical and Profound in the Coming Months," *Agence France Presse*, April 14, 2012.
49. http://realcuba.wordpress.com/2012/04/05/cuba-meets-the-challenges-of...
50. "Alarcon Announced Immigration Reform." Just prior to publication of this book the Cuban government announced the ending of the tarjeta blanca and letter of invitation. The only requirement for Cubans to travel now is a valid passport and visa issued by the country of destination. Cubans can also stay outside the country for two years without losing property or rights. Restrictions still apply for doctors and members of the military, top athletes and certain other groups Cuba does not want to lose for national security reasons. The new regulations will take affect January 2013. Jeff Franks, "Cuba lifting travel restrictions", *Reuters*, October 16, 2012.
51. Jaime Suchlicki, "Is Cuba Planning a Legal Mariel?," Cuba Transition Project Institute for Cuban and Cuban-American Studies, University of Miami, Issue 164, May 3, 2012.
52. http://thecubaneconomy.com/.
53. Omar Everleny Pérez, "These Reforms Will Update the Cuban Model and Spur Economic Growth": http://www.americasquarterly.org/node/2450.
54. Elsa Claro, "Nevertheless, It Moves," *Progress Weekly*, 2011.
55. Lecture to CCFA meeting, Toronto, April 2011.
56. Ibid.
57. José Antonio Ocampo, "The Reforms Do Not Go Far Enough to Jump-Start the Economy and Protect the Vulnerable," *Americas Quarterly*, Spring 2011.
58. http://www.trabajadores.cu/news/20120429/259252-fiesta-por-conquistas-irrenunciables.
59. Marc Frank, "Exclusive: Cuban Government Set for Broad Reorganization," *Reuters*, September 30, 2011.
60. "What Would You People Have Done With Frank Pais?," August 2, 2011: http://cubantriangle.blogspot.ca/2011/08/what-would-you-people-have-done-with.html.
61. Ibid.
62. Gerardo Arreola, "Application of Market Rules Reveals Black Holes in Cuban Economy," *La Journada*, June 18, 2012, p. 28.
63. Gerardo Arreola, "Act in Favor of Economic Reform, As Agreed in the Last National Conference," *La Jornada*, February 6, 2012, p. 23.
64. Andrea Rodriguez, "Cuba's Economic Czar Heads New Generation of Leaders," *Associated Press*, July 4, 2011.
65. www.csmonitor.com/World/Americas/2011/0420/Castro-hails-new-generation-of-Cuba-leaders-but-appoints-old-guard.

66. Ricardo Alarcón, President of Cuba's parliament, interviewed by Manuel Alberto Ramy, Radio Progreso Alternativa, April 27, 2011.
67. Carlos Fuenes, "El socialismo cubano se ha estancado," *Publico*, December 29, 2008.
68. Interview with author, June 2011.
69. The Cuban government however continues to refuse entry on many returning Cuban-Americans who left the country during the *balsero* (rafter) crises of 1994. Alvaro F. Fernandez, "Lying is Not a Solution to the Balsero Dilemma," *Progresso Weekly*, March 28, 2012.
70. "Reaching Out to the Cuban People," Office of the Press Secretary, the White House. For Immediate release, January 14, 2011.
71. There are many sources, including Elizabeth Newhouse, *The United States Should Take Immediate Steps to Improve Relations With Cuba*, February 14, 2011. Center for International Policy.
72. President Obama in first meeting with Hispanic journalists, September 12, 2011: http://www.thehavananote.com/archive/201111.
73. President Obama in second meeting with Hispanic journalists, September 28, 2011: http://www.thehavananote.com/archive/201111.
74. "Cuba Issue Deals Blow to US Stature at 'Summit of the Americas,'" msnbc.com and news services, April 15, 2012.
75. "A no recibe respuesta a una agenda de diálogo que presentó a EEUU," *Europa Press*, Madrid, May 21, 2009.
76. Interview with author, March 2012.
77. Andres Oppenheimer, "Obama Unlikely to Make New Gestures to Cuba without Action from Havana," *Miami Herald*, March 23, 2011.
78. http://www.capitolhillcubans.com/2011/02/valenzuelas-defense-of-castros-trickle.html.
79. Feinberg, "Reaching Out."
80. Albor Ruiz, "In Spite of Changes, Washington Remains Dead Set in Old Cuba Policy," *New York Daily News*, April 27, 2011.
81. http://www.csmonitor.com/World/Americas/Latin-America-Monitor/2012/0302/Obama-administration-gets-real-on-Cuba.
82. Feinberg, "Reaching Out."
83. Interview with author, March 2012.
84. Ibid.
85. http://www.cnn.com/video/#/video/bestoftv/2012/05/10/tsr-vidal-full-intv.cnn.
86. See chapter one in this volume.
87. Interview with author, March 2012; the person asked for anonymity.
88. http://www.lonelyplanet.com/thorntree/thread.jspa?threadID=2035142.
89. Interview with author, April 2012.
90. http://www.theatlantic.com/past/docs/issues/91mar/shut.htm.
91. "U.S. Lifts Trade Embargo against Vietnam," President Bill Clinton's speech, Transcript US Department of State Dispatch, February 14, 1994.
92. http://www.usvtc.org/info/crs/CRS-BTA-Dec01.pdf.
93. Binh P. Le, "Doi Moi, a Selected Bibliography of Vietnam's Economic Transformation 1986–2000," The Pennsylvania State University.
94. Feinberg, "Reaching Out."
95. Pavel Vidal Alejandro, "Monetary and Exchange Rate Reform in Cuba: Lessons From Vietnam," Institute of developing economics, Japan external trade organization.

96. "Cuba and Viet Nam Sign Cooperation Agreement on Pharmaceutical Sector," acn Havana, December 2011.

97. "Cuba and Viet Nam Implement Program to Boost Rice Production," acn, Pinar Del Rio.

98. Gerardo Arreola, "Cuba, en la etapa más difícil: el cambio de mentalidad, señala líder vietnamita," *La Journada*, April 16, 2012.

99. Peter Kornbluh, "Jimmy Carter: Lift Trade Embargo against Cuba," *The Nation*, March 30, 2011.

100. Hillary Rodham Clinton, Celebrating the 15th anniversary of United States-Vietnam relations, US Department of State, Hanoi, July 22, 2010: www.state.gov/secretary/rm/2010/07/145064.htm.

6   THE FUTURE OF SIEGE

1. http://www.altiusdirectory.com/Society/fidel-castro-biography.html.

2. Moisés Nami, "The Havana Obsession," *Newsweek*, June 22, 2009.

3. Lars Schoultz, *That Infernal Little Cuban Republic*, University of North Carolina Press, 2009, p. 499, note 123.

4. Humberto Fontova, "Jimmy Carter Does Havana," *Washington Times*, April 6, 2011.

5. "Biden Says U.S. Does Not Plan to Lift Cuba Embargo," *Reuters*, March 28, 2009.

6. Daniel Bruno Sanz, "Cuba at a Crossroads, The New American Strategy," *Booksurge*, 2009.

7. www.brainyquote.com/quotes/quotes/a/alberteins133991.html.

8. George C. Herring, *From Colony to Superpower*, Oxford University Press, New York, 2008, p. 786.

9. Manuel E. Yepe, "Illusions Told as Forecasts," April 2, 2012: http://realcuba.wordpress.com/2012/04/02/illusions-told-as-forecasts/.

10. Louis A. Perez Jr., *Cuba in the American Imagination*, the University of North Carolina Press Chapel Hill, 2008, p. 247.

11. Harvey MacKay, "Sanctions on Cuba are Hitting a Different Target," *Star Tribune*, April 12, 2012: http://www.startribune.com/business/147367625.html.

12. http://www.thefreemanonline.org/columns/potomac-principles-washingtons-inadvertent-support-for-cuban-communism/.

13. James Bamford, "The NSA is Building the Country's Biggest Spy Center," *Wired*, March 15, 2012.

14. See chapter four in this volume.

15. *Agence France Presse*, April 14, 2012.

16. Juan O. Tamayo, "Cuban Diplomats in Washington Will Host Émigrés for Talks on U.S. Policy toward the Island," *Miami Herald*, April 25, 2012.

17. Interview with author, May 2012.

18. http://www.cubastudygroup.org/index.cfm/our-opinions?Content Record_id=b99d0d50-d598-4e22-a378-9dd473965507.

19. Cindy Boren, "Ozzie Guillén Says He'll Apologize in Miami for Fidel Castro Comment," *Washington Post*, April 9, 2012.

20. http://espn.go.com/espn/otl/story/_/id/7821105/ozzie-guillen-contro versial-comments-fidel-castro-reveal-depths-change-play-miami.

21. ainnews@ain.cu.
22. Michael Miller, "Travel Agency Destroyed, Owner Suspects it was Firebombed for Booking Trips to Cuba," *Miami Herald*, April 27, 2012.
23. Interview with author, April 2012.
24. Jackie Calmes and William Neuman, "Americas Meeting Ends with Discord over Cuba," *New York Times*, April 15, 2012.
25. "Influential U.S. Senator Says Washington's Cuba Policy is 'Out of Step,'" *acn, Havana*, April 17, 2012.
26. "Obama 'Open to a New Relationship With Cuba,'" *ABC News* (blog) September 28, 2011.
27. One of the most thorough examinations of the legalities the President has to ease embargo regulations, from: Memorandum produced by Michael Krinsky, *U.S. Economic Measures Against Cuba: Presidential Authority*, Rabinowitz, Boudin, Standard, Krinsky & Lieberman, P.C., Attorneys at Law, New York, December 2, 2008.
28. Ibid.
29. John McAuliff, "One Year On: The Semi-opening of Cuba Travel," January 20, 2012.
30. http://www.state.gov/j/inl/rls/nrcrpt/2012/vol1/184099.htm#Cuba. 2012 INCSR: Country Reports—Croatia through Haiti Bureau of International Narcotics and Law Enforcement Affairs, March 7, 2012.
31. Ramón Muñoz and Miguel Jiménez, "Washington Pressures Spain's Telefónica over Cuban Affiliates," *El Pais*, March 21, 2012.
32. Richard Read, "Feds Investigate Portland's Esco Corp. for Violating U.S. Embargo against Cuba," *The Oregonian*, March 16, 2012.
33. BBC interview, March 2010.
34. Edmund Burke, *Reflections on the Revolution in France*, 1790, Penguin Classics, 1982.
35. John Sayles, *Los Gusanos*, Nation Books, New York, 1991, p. 420.

BIBLIOGRAPHY

Alarcón de Quesada, Ricardo, and Miguel Álvarez Sánchez. *Blockade: The United States Economic War against Cuba*, Edítora Política, Havana, 2001

Allard, Jean-Guy, and Eva Golinger. *La agresión permanente Usaid, NED y CIA*, Colección alfredo maneiro Serie Testimonios, Caracas 2010

Benjamin, Jules R. *The United States and the Origins of the Cuban Revolution An Empire of Liberty in an Age of National Liberation*, Princeton University Press, Princeton, 1990

Bohning, Don. *The Castro Obsession U.S. Covert Operations Against Cuba 1959– 1965*, Potomac Books, Washington, 2005

Bolender, Keith. *Voices From the Other Side: An Oral History of Terrorism Against Cuba*, Pluto Press, London, 2010

Bravo, Olga Miranda. *Cuba/USA Nacionalizaciones y Bloqueo*, Editorial de Ciencias Sociales, Havana, 1996

Castro Espin, Alejandro. *The Price of Power*, Capitan San Luis, Havana, 2009

Chomsky, Aviva. *A History of the Cuban Revolution*, Wiley-Blackwell, United Kingdom, 2011

Chomsky, Noam. *Failed States: The Abuse of Power and the Assault on Democracy*, Metropolitan Books, New York, 2006

Cluster, Dick, and Hernandez, Rafael. *The History of Havana*, Palgrave Macmillan, New York, 2006

Davis, Paul K. *Besieged 100 Great Sieges From Jericho to Sarajevo*, Oxford University Press, New York, 2003

Demanda Del Pueblo Cubano Contra El Gobierno De Estados Unidos Por Los Daños Económicos Ocasionados A Cuba, Editora Politica, La Habana, 2000

Erikson, Daniel P. *The Cuba Wars Fidel Castro, the United States and the Next Revolution*, Bloomsbury Press, New York, 2008

Escalante, Fabian. *The Cuba Project CIA Covert Operations 1959–62*, Ocean Press, Melbourne, 1995

Franklin, Jane. *Cuba and the United States: A Chronological History*, Ocean Press, Melbourne, 1997

Gott, Richard. *Cuba: A New History*, Yale University Press, London, 2004

Haney, Patrick J., and Vanderbush, Walt. *The Cuban Embargo: The Domestic Politics of an American Foreign Policy*, University of Pittsburgh Press, Pittsburgh, 2005

Hnuong, Bui Huy. *FDI Disbursement in Vietnam*, The Gioi Publishers, 2010

Kapcia, Antoni. *Cuba in Revolution: A History Since the Fifties*, Reaktion Books, London, 2008

Lambie, George. *The Cuban Revolution in the 21st Century*, Pluto Press, London, 2010

Peck, James. *Ideal Illusions How the U.S. Government Co-opted Human Rights*, Metropolitan Books, New York, 2010

Pérez, Louis A. Jr. *Cuba between Reform and Revolution*, Oxford University Press, New York, 2006

———. *Cuba in the American Imagination Metaphor and the Imperial Ethos*, The University of North Carolina Press, Chapel Hill, 2008

———. *Cuba under the Platt Amendment 1902–1934*, University of Pittsburgh Press, Pittsburgh, 1986

———. *The War of 1898: The United States & Cuba in History & Historiography*, The University of North Carolina Press, Chapel Hill, 1998

Pérez-Stable, Marifeli. *The Cuban Revolution Origins, Course, and Legacy*, Oxford University Press, New York, 1999

Ramonet, Ignacio. *My Life Fidel Castro*, Allen Lane, London, 2007

Reid-Henry, Simon. *Fidel and Che: A Revolutionary Friendship*, Walker & Company, New York, 2009

Roman, Peter. *People's Power Cuba's Experience with Representative Government*, Rowman & Littlefield, Lanham, 2003

Saney, Issac. *Cuba: A Revolution in Motion*, Fernwood Publishing, Nova Scotia, 2004

Schoultz, Lars. *That Infernal Little Cuban Republic*, The University of North Carolina Press, Chapel Hill, 2009

Schwab, Peter. *Cuba Confronting the U.S. Embargo*, St. Martin's Griffin, New York, 1999

Smith, Wayne S. *The Closest of Enemies: A Personal and Diplomatic Account of U.S.-Cuban Relations Since 1957*, W.W. Norton & Company, New York, 1987

Spadoni, Paolo. *Failed Sanctions: Why the U.S. Embargo against Cuba Could Never Work*, University Press of Florida, Gainesville, 2010

Stone, Geoffrey R. *Perilous Times Free Speech in Wartime from the Sedition Act of 1798 to the War on Terrorism*, W.W. Norton and Company, New York, 2004

Sweig, Julia A. *Cuba: What Everyone Needs to Know*, Oxford University Press, New York, 2009

Taylor, Henry Louis Jr. *Inside El Barrio: A Bottom Up View of Neighborhood Life in Castro's Cuba*, Kumarian Press, Sterling, 2009

Weiner, Tim. *Legacy of Ashes: The History of the CIA*, Anchor Books, New York, 2007

Wylie, Lana. *Perceptions of Cuba; Canadian and American Policies in Comparative Perspective*, University of Toronto Press, Toronto, 2010

Zaldívar Diéguez, Andrés. *Blockade: The Longest Economic Siege in History*, Capitan San Luis Publishing House, Havana, 2007

INDEX